Medical Research for Hire

De Jane Kinsey
November 2012

Critical Issues in Health and Medicine

Edited by Rima D. Apple, University of Wisconsin–Madison,
and Janet Golden, Rutgers University, Camden

Growing criticism of the U.S. health care system is coming from consumers, politicians, the media, activists, and health care professionals. Critical Issues in Health and Medicine is a collection of books that explores these contemporary dilemmas from a variety of perspectives, among them political, legal, historical, sociological, and comparative, and with attention to crucial dimensions such as race, gender, ethnicity, sexuality, and culture.

Medical Research for Hire

The Political Economy of Pharmaceutical Clinical Trials

Jill A. Fisher

Rutgers University Press

New Brunswick, New Jersey, and London

Library of Congress Cataloging-in-Publication Data

Fisher, Jill A., 1976–
    Medical research for hire : the political economy of pharmaceutical clinical trials / Jill
A. Fisher.
        p. ; cm.—(Critical issues in health and medicine)
    Includes bibliographical references and index.
    ISBN 978–0-8135–4409–0 (hardcover : alk. paper)—ISBN 978–0-8135–4410–6 (pbk. : alk.
paper)
    1. Drugs—Testing—Economic aspects—United States.   2. Clinical trials—Economic
aspects—United States.   3. Drugs—Testing—Moral and ethical aspects—United States.
4. Clinical trials—Moral and ethical aspects—United States.   5. Contracting out—United
States. I. Title. II. Series.
    [DNLM: 1. Drug Industry—ethics.   2. Clinical Trials as Topic—ethics   3. Research
Subjects. QV 736 F534m 2009]
    RM301.27.F57 2009
    362.17'82—dc22   2008007760

A British Cataloging-in-Publication record for this book is available from the British
Library

Visit our Web site: http://rutgerspress.rutgers.edu

Manufactured in the United States of America

This book is dedicated to Nelly K. Murstein,
who inspired a freshman to become a scholar . . .

Contents

Acknowledgments

This book is the product of years of dialogue with colleagues, mentors, and friends about the politics of medicine and human subjects research. I have been fortunate to be embedded in networks of talented and generous scholars who have helped make this work better in many different ways. Several colleagues read the manuscript in its entirety at various stages of preparing it for publication; I am especially grateful to David Hess, Sharra Vostral, Sal Restivo, Nancy Campbell, Sharon Anderson-Gold, Torin Monahan, Lorna Ronald, and Rose Weitz for their invaluable insights. Other colleagues read parts of the book in manuscript form. I owe many thanks to Steven Epstein, Joseph Dumit, Raymond DeVries, Virginia Eubanks, Ann Koblitz, Cynthia Schairer, and Jameson Wetmore for reading draft chapters and providing critical and encouraging feedback on the material. In addition, many colleagues have provided stimulating conversation about the clinical trials industry and about scholarship more generally. These colleagues include James Sorenson, Sergio Sismondo, Kristin Peterson, Jeanette Simmonds, Nate Greenslit, Kathryn Milun, Michael Montoya, Natasha Lettis, Jason Patton, Jean-François Blanchette, Hector Postigo, Dorothy Roberts, Charles Bosk, Howard Brody, Kenneth Richman, Paul Appelbaum, Leigh Turner, Kaushik Sunder Rajan, Melinda Cooper, Chloe Silverman, Andrew Munro, Alesha Durfee, Yasmina Katsulis, Mary Margaret Fonow, Karen Leong, Clark Miller, and Dan Sarewitz.

The research for this project was supported by the National Institutes of Health under a Ruth L. Kirschstein National Research Service Award 5F31MH070222 from the National Institute of Mental Health. I was only able to complete this project, however, because of the generosity of many individuals in the clinical trials industry who agreed to be interviewed and who allowed me to conduct participant observation at their investigative sites. Arizona State University, particularly the Women and Gender Studies Program, supported the preparation of the manuscript through the provision of a junior sabbatical that provided time to complete revisions. I also owe many thanks to Doreen Valentine for her enthusiastic support and the entire editorial team at Rutgers University Press for the publication of this book being a transparent process. I also thank the following journals for permitting the use of previously published chapters or chapter sections: *Harvard Health Policy Review, Science and Public Policy,* and *Sociology of Health and Illness.*

Thanks are also due to my family and to friends outside of academia. I have received support from my family throughout my education and in my career. I am forever grateful to my parents and grandparents for providing me the opportunities that enabled the pursuit of this profession and way of life. I am particularly pleased that my mother Carol Fisher and brother John Fisher have read much of the book as it was being developed. It is wonderful to be able to share this work with them, particularly because it has consumed so much of my time, energy, and thoughts for the past several years and, in many ways, represents who I am. In addition, Ken and Diane Monahan have become a second family to me. They always express interest in my work and celebrate my accomplishments with me.

All of my friends outside of academia have provided support in various ways at various times over the years that I worked on this project. Elise Giroudon has been a good friend since she saved me on my first day of school in a foreign land, and I appreciate her continued interest in the content of my work as well as the process for giving it an audience. I must particularly acknowledge Noelle Robertson and her partner Scott Reid whom I can always depend upon for the most stimulating, thought-provoking conversations about the medical profession. I would also like to thank Rebecca Lord for her warm friendship and her technical skills.

The person to whom I have the most profound gratitude is my favorite colleague and my life partner: Torin Monahan. It has been through our conversations over meals and the work ethic of our home that I have come to understand my research in the way that I do. Most of the valuable insights I have had about my data have come because of forcing articulations about my work for Torin. I cannot even begin to express my gratitude to him for establishing with me this exchange of ideas and for encouraging each other to think better and harder about not only our research but also about the world.

Finally, I must not forget to express my gratitude to Paris who ensures my continued sanity through our nightly outings that force me to stop and smell the cactus flowers . . .

Medical Research for Hire

Chapter 1

Clinical Trials

Coming Soon to a Physician Near You

A woman and her son wait for the doctor to see them. The doctor, however, is no longer a clinician. Instead, the white male neurologist has transitioned from treating patients to conducting clinical trials for the pharmaceutical industry. To do so, he has converted his private practice into a research center. Running studies in diverse therapeutic areas, including Alzheimer's disease, arthritis, diabetes, gastrointestinal disorders, and psychiatric illnesses, the doctor recruits and enrolls human subjects in drug studies through mass media advertisements. This physician is not alone. Pharmaceutical companies are increasingly contracting with private-sector physicians to conduct their studies. Clinical research responds to U.S. federal regulations mandating that pharmaceutical products be tested on human subjects to ensure safety and effectiveness before they are made available on the market. This physician, like many others, has successfully established a company to profit from drug development.

On this particular day in December 2003, I am shadowing the doctor as part of an extended interview regarding his involvement with pharmaceutical clinical trials. He has invited me to observe his interactions with human subjects and their families so that I will have a better sense of his role. One of these interactions is with the woman and her son. The human subject in this case is the son, a ten-year-old boy who is enrolled in a pediatric study to test the efficacy of a treatment for attention deficit hyperactivity disorder (ADHD). Because the purpose of this visit is to assess how well the investigational treatment is working to alleviate the symptoms of ADHD, the doctor asks a series of questions that are primarily directed to the mother. She explains that, from her perspective, her son seems to be noticeably more "mellow," but she has concerns about the drug because the boy's teacher is still complaining about his disruptive behavior in the classroom.

Although the teacher's impressions of the boy's behavior could be construed as anecdotal or incidental to the clinical trial, they are of primary concern to the woman. This working-class family has no health insurance, so standard medical care is not an option for the woman to address her son's disruptive behavior in the classroom. Under pressure from her son's teacher, the woman has turned to a clinical trial as a means both to provide some sort of treatment for her son and to prove to the teacher her own commitment to addressing the problem.

The situation of neither the physician nor the woman and her son is unique. In the past two decades, the pharmaceutical industry has reorganized the clinical testing of its products. Currently, about three-quarters of studies in the United States are conducted in the private sector by nonacademic physicians who recruit their own patients or local community members into drug studies.[1] Over 60,000 of these studies take place in the United States each year, accounting for 75 percent of the 80,000 clinical trials conducted worldwide; to execute these studies, more than 50,000 U.S. physicians registered with the Food and Drug Administration (FDA) as principal investigators on one or more clinical trials in 2001.[2] As for the human subjects, 3.62 million Americans participated in pharmaceutical clinical trials in 2003 alone.[3]

What explains such staggering numbers of Americans engaged in the business of screening new drugs? The expansion of pharmaceutical clinical trials in the private sector can be seen as addressing two problems in U.S. health care: decreasing revenue for physicians and decreasing access to treatment for patients. Physicians report diminishing income due to restrictive relationships with insurers and government agencies, ever-increasing malpractice insurance premiums, and inflated overhead costs to operate private practices. As a result, many physicians are attracted to pharmaceutical *contract research* because it is perceived as a lucrative field. These physicians are hired as investigators to conduct predefined study protocols that have been developed by scientists and project managers at pharmaceutical companies.[4] As contract investigators, they have no input on study design, inclusion-exclusion criteria dictating which human subjects can enroll in the study, or interpretation of the study results. The participation of physicians instead involves following the instructions of the pharmaceutical companies in administering the investigational product, collecting the required data, and monitoring the safety of human subjects. More importantly, participating physicians have the right combination of financial motivations and access to patients to make contract research an excellent arrangement for themselves *and* for the pharmaceutical industry. Thus, clinical research can no longer be said to be the domain of elite academic physicians but rather an activity in which many private-practice physicians routinely engage.

Pharmaceutical clinical trials also serve to fill the health care gap in the United States by providing limited medical access to individuals who have no or inadequate health insurance. They are frequently marketed to the general public as a way to obtain "free" doctors' visits, diagnostic tests, and medications. Not only do clinical trials promise access to the medical establishment, they also commonly offer stipends to encourage human subjects' participation. On one hand, pharmaceutical clinical trials can be seen as a service for individuals who have health problems but no other means of getting treatment or for individuals who desire to supplement their incomes. On the other, they can be seen as exacerbating and profiting from existing social and economic inequalities. The United States, with its growing number of uninsured citizens and individuals and families living in poverty, offers fertile ground for recruitment of subjects into drug studies. Although clinical trials provide them with temporary access to medical treatments that they might need, these groups disproportionately bear the burden of risk associated with clinical testing of investigational products, and they are the least likely to benefit long-term from advances in pharmaceutical medicine.

Individuals working in the pharmaceutical and clinical trials industries are well aware of the trend to recruit and enroll uninsured and impoverished Americans in clinical trials. Outside of these industries, it is a phenomenon rarely discussed.[5] Perhaps this is because no federal agency currently requires that data be collected about the insurance status of subjects participating in clinical trials. Even without the mandate, one research team did collect data on the insurance status of their participants and found that uninsured individuals were seven times more likely than those with insurance to enroll in their cardiac drug studies.[6] Other research teams have strategically recruited uninsured populations to fill studies. For example, a group found that through the process of direct solicitation, 96 percent of recruited Latino immigrants—a segment of the U.S. population that tends to have the least access to health care—agreed to participate in their cancer control studies.[7]

Another factor contributing to low levels of awareness regarding the participation of uninsured Americans in clinical trials could be that such individuals tend to participate in clinical trials that attract little public attention. The bulk of popular press coverage of medical research focuses on two illness categories: cancer and HIV/AIDS. Both types of disease are often seen as more life-threatening or as having few effective treatments. Cancer studies, in particular, attract a different demographic of participants than do clinical trials for other illnesses that are not fatal or those that already have drugs available on the market. In fact, some evidence suggests that because cancer studies are likely to share costs with insurance companies, Americans without insurance may actually be *excluded* from participating in those clinical trials.[8] If more public attention turned to clinical trials for chronic—yet, by and large, treatable—conditions such as insomnia, depression, allergies, and obesity, a different portrait of human subjects would emerge. In other words, what is invisible to most Americans is that the clinical testing of prescription drugs is conducted on uninsured individuals who then lose access to those treatments when they are made available on the market.

Confronted with these trends, I ask two questions. How did pharmaceutical clinical trials become an industry alternative to standard medical care both for physicians and patients? And what are the implications for doctor-patient relationships when physicians recruit their own patients into drug studies? These questions provide both a social and ethical perspective on contemporary human subjects research and drug development.[9] Drawing upon fieldwork in the Southwest,[10] I focus on local clinics conducting pharmaceutical research and their connection to the broader political and economic contexts of health care in the United States. Within these clinics, the needs and goals of the pharmaceutical industry mediate relationships among physicians, research staff, and human subjects. Similarly, the experiences of patients and subjects, as well as the practices of clinicians, reflect national economic imperatives and inequalities, especially neoliberal policies, which fuel the health care sector and catalyze the clinical trials industry.

The Clinical Trials Industry

Pharmaceutical research has become a complex, lucrative industry during the last twenty years. Before 1990, over 80 percent of all pharmaceutical research was conducted in academic medical centers. By 2005, only about 25 percent was conducted in those settings.[11] Academic sites have been replaced by numerous types of support companies to conduct and manage clinical

trials—private practices, dedicated research centers, site management organizations (SMOs), contract research organizations (CROs), for-profit, commercial institutional review boards (IRBs), central patient recruitment
companies, and clinical trials advertising agencies. The proliferation of
auxiliary companies used for pharmaceutical companies' research is part
of larger corporate trends that emphasize outsourcing, cutting production
costs, and maximizing profits. These changes in managerial culture have
been described as characteristics of globalization, neoliberalism, and post-
Fordism. In particular, the emergence of these companies as part of a "clinical trials industry" represents the key to quick and cheap drug development
for pharmaceutical companies.

The Pharmaceutical Industry's R&D "Problems"

In 2004, pharmaceutical companies spent a record-high $49 billion on
research and development (R&D) of new products, which is a reported 19
percent of industry sales from the same year. Approximately $15 billion of
that budget was used for clinical trials.[12] The total amount of clinical research
sponsored by pharmaceutical companies was three times the amount funded
by the National Institutes of Health (NIH), which in turn equals about 75 percent of all government-funded clinical research projects.[13] It may not be surprising that pharmaceutical companies invest so much in R&D because this
process is necessary for maintaining their lines of patent-protected products
that are crucial for the profitability of those companies into the future.

The intersection of clinical trials and future profit derived from pharmaceutical R&D hinges on the patent.[14] Patent protection and the profitable
life of new drugs begin at the start of clinical research, not at FDA approval
to market those products. Therefore, saving time on clinical development
is seen as critical for maximizing profits on pharmaceutical drugs and
devices. Within the clinical trials industry, an often-repeated statement is
that each day a drug's arrival on the market is delayed by logistical factors,
like slow recruitment of human subjects, the pharmaceutical company loses
one million dollars in unrealized sales of that product. To compensate for
such a loss, pharmaceutical companies strive to earn an additional $90 mil-
lion per product by outsourcing the problems of recruitment so as to enroll
patients into clinical trials three months faster than academic medical centers might.[15] Outsourcing clinical trials to for-profit clinical trial companies
has become one of the pharmaceutical industry's answers to speeding up
drug development.[16]

The relocation of clinical trials from academic medical centers to small private clinics is based on the premise of "ready-to-recruit" patient populations.[17] In other words, clinical trials are taken to the patient populations that are required for the studies, rather than waiting for those patients to appear at university hospitals. Patient recruitment and subsequent enrollment have been targeted for outsourcing because these components of research studies have been identified as the most significant and common delay to clinical trials. Currently, most research protocols allot about a quarter of their clinical development time to recruitment, and 80 percent of clinical trials must extend their timelines because of slow enrollment.[18]

The problem of human subject recruitment is made poignant when the industry compares the number of patients responding to recruitment campaigns to the eligible populations that it would like to capture. By industry estimates, only 10 percent of eligible populations enroll in studies. In contrast, pediatric oncology models what is possible within the industry because it captures a much higher proportion of eligible subjects. Specifically, 50 percent of all children with cancer participate in clinical trials.[19] Delays in recruitment and enrollment have led to the widespread use of advertising ranging from print to radio and television campaigns to promote either specific clinical trials or specific companies conducting pharmaceutical studies.

On a basic level, the pharmaceutical industry has reorganized drug development because executives fear that clinical trials will fail on *logistical* grounds. The most common logistical problem during clinical development is recruiting the number of human subjects required by the research protocol. If a study cannot enroll the target number of volunteers, it cannot move forward. A similar logistical problem is the retention of volunteers; not only must individuals enroll in studies, but a certain number must remain in them until the protocol is completed. If too many volunteers drop out, the protocol will need to be recommenced with a new group of volunteers, costing pharmaceutical companies more time and money. A final logistical problem concerns the regulatory aspects of clinical research. All human subjects' case reports must strictly follow the research protocols, be prepared according to FDA specifications, and be monitored for accuracy.

As part of their rhetoric of "risk-sharing partnerships," pharmaceutical companies outsource clinical trials to companies that promise to assume the logistical risks as part of their own corporate bottom lines. These auxiliary companies are hired to take care of the logistical details of clinical trials from selecting where the clinical trials will be conducted, monitoring the data, recruiting human subjects, and preparing FDA applications for the products under development. The industry view is that logistical failures of clinical trials can be circumvented by putting into place the right organizational infrastructure.

But logistics are not the only source of failure. Importantly, pharmaceutical companies risk the *clinical* failure of the investigational drugs or devices as well. The pharmaceutical industry recognizes that the probability of successfully completing clinical development is only 25 to 30 percent, a major concern for companies. After the investment of millions of dollars and years of laboratory work, a drug might not prove to be both safe and efficacious and, as a result, never reach the market.[20] The low rate of successful R&D is quickly understandable when examining the production pipeline. The clinical development cycle divides the process into three primary "phases" through which an investigational new drug must pass successfully in order to be considered for approval by the FDA (see table 1).

After successful experimentation on laboratory animals, an investigational drug is used in *phase I* studies on humans. The primary purpose of phase I studies is to test the safety of a new substance. This testing normally involves the use of twenty to eighty healthy individuals and can have a duration of a few days to a year. Currently, investigational drugs are tested in an average of twenty-one clinical trials before completing the phase I stage of development.[21] Seventy percent of new drugs warrant *phase II* studies, which

Table 1 **Phases of Clinical Development**

Study phase	Primary purpose	Duration	Number of human subjects	Success rate
Phase I	Safety	Up to 1 year	20–80 healthy subjects	70%
Phase II	Safety, efficacy	Up to 2 years	100–300 diseased subjects	50%
Phase III	Efficacy	2–4 years	1,000–3,000 diseased subjects	80%
FDA approval		25–30% of all products		
Phase IV	Cost benefits	2–10 years	Several thousand diseased subjects	n/a

Sources: U.S. Food & Drug Administration, *An Introduction to Clinical Trials,* http://clinicaltrials .gov/ct/info/whatis#whatis, accessed 27 May 2007; CenterWatch, *An Industry in Evolution* (Boston: Thomson CenterWatch, 2003).

require up to several hundred volunteers with the targeted disease, take one to two years to complete, and provide preliminary information about efficacy and further information about safety and tolerability (because the substance is now used by ill individuals). Each investigational drug is tested in an average of six phase II trials.[22] Only 50 percent of products tested in phase II studies continue development.[23]

Those drugs that make it to *phase III* enter the clinical testing most commonly associated with popular understandings of medical research. These studies require several thousand volunteers with the targeted disease, usually involve the random placement of subjects into experimental and placebo arms of the study, and take from two to four years to complete. These studies measure the efficacy of the product and sometimes a comparative benefit. In other words, phase III studies not only ask whether a drug works in the treatment of *x,* but also whether a drug works in the treatment of *x* better than a placebo or better than the standard medical treatment. The average investigational product is tested in ten phase III trials during clinical development.[24] Although a full 80 percent of the drugs that begin phase III testing are successful, that corresponds to only 25 to 30 percent of investigational drugs that started clinical development.[25] It should also be noted that there is a *phase IV* in the clinical development cycle, known as "post-marketing" research. Generally, phase IV clinical trials take anywhere from two to ten years to complete, enroll thousands of patients, and compare multiple approved products. The purpose of such studies is to measure short- and long-term efficacy as well as the cost benefits of different treatments.

The Clinical Trials Industry's R&D "Solutions"

The proliferation of auxiliary agents in the clinical trials industry attests to the salience of their promise to mitigate pharmaceutical companies' losses from R&D investments. Whether new products eventually fail or succeed in getting to the market, auxiliary companies market themselves on the speed with which they are able to perform tasks that the pharmaceutical giants are slower at completing. By offering highly specialized or diversified services, clinical trials companies replace (or in some cases invent new) functions that have historically been done by pharmaceutical companies or have been outsourced to university researchers. The new system has created not only an organizationally complex industry but a "commodity business" out of the pharmaceutical research process itself, generating $13.6 billion in revenue in 2003.[26] By industry estimates, there are 129,000 individuals involved in administering clinical trials, from physician-investigators to clerical staff employed by auxiliary companies, compared with 78,000 employees of pharmaceutical companies.[27]

What are these new companies, and what services do they offer to pharmaceutical companies to—ostensibly—speed up and simplify the clinical trials process? Figure 1 illustrates a rough schematic of the organization of clinical trials as a full-fledged auxiliary industry. The most basic level organization is called an *investigative site*. These are companies or clinics that conduct studies through contracts with pharmaceutical companies. Investigative sites are any setting in which clinical trials are being conducted, from large university hospitals to small private practices. Increasingly, the majority of investigative sites are small, operating within private practices and using existing staff to manage clinical trials. Physicians working as contract researchers are given the title "principal investigator," and their staff members are called "clinical research coordinators."[28] A traditional gendered division of labor is reproduced in contract research based on the organization of medicine more generally; physician-investigators are predominantly men, and research coordinators and other site staff are predominantly women.

As physicians conducting pharmaceutical studies find that they can make more money in clinical trials than they can in their practices, many decide to create "dedicated" investigative sites that only conduct research and have no private patients associated with them. Some of these sites generate high profiles and high profits, but most tend to remain small, with only one or two locations within their communities. The larger sites are often more corporate in structure with a much higher volume of studies conducted and significantly more division of labor among research staff. In particular, larger companies frequently employ "site administrators" who oversee both the financial and clinical operations of the sites.

The higher organizational form of investigative sites is the *site management organization* (SMO) that provides a centralized structure for oversight and management of multiple investigative sites. The idea behind SMOs is to cut down on costs to participating sites by sharing resources like recruitment, regulatory affairs, and contract negotiation and by staffing sites with appropriate numbers of individuals performing specialized jobs. SMOs seemed to be the wave of the future in the mid-1990s, peaking at forty-nine companies in the United States in 1998.[29] An advantage of SMOs for pharmaceutical companies is to streamline the process of identifying and negotiating contracts with investigative sites by including as many as fifty different sites from one

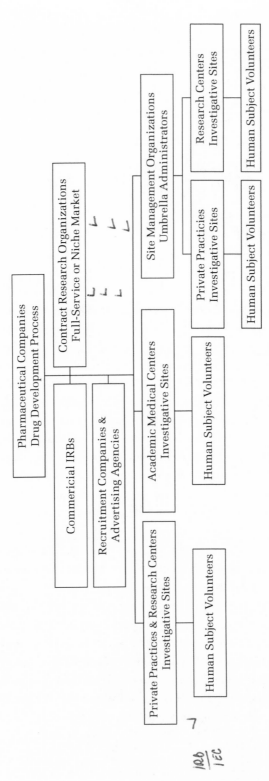

Figure 1 Current Organization of Clinical Research

7

106
121

SMO in a single contract. Many SMOs failed, however, because they could not achieve consistent quality across all of their sites or the cost effectiveness they desired. Presently, there are only four SMOs operating in the United States, but they captured $235 million (6 percent) of the contract research market in 2002, indicating that those that are established have become major players in the industry.[30]

Contract research organizations (CROs) are the most commonly used type of auxiliary company. CROs act as intermediaries for pharmaceutical companies and serve two primary functions. First, they identify prospective investigative sites and negotiate contracts on pharmaceutical companies' behalf. Second, they monitor the data that are produced by sending clinical research associates, known as *monitors,* to each site to ensure that data are reported correctly and to detect any fraud that might occur. CROs can take on a variety of other functions as well, including study conduct, patient recruitment, data management and analysis, protocol design, and/or medical writing. In 2003, there were 270 CROs operating in North America and 466 CROs operating in Europe.[31] Industry reports estimate that in 2003 and 2004, CROs played a role in 64 percent of all clinical trials worldwide and generated a combined $11.8 billion in business from pharmaceutical companies.[32]

Other types of auxiliary companies in the clinical trials industry that are not considered CROs are for-profit institutional review boards, study brokers, clinical trials advertising agencies, and central patient recruitment companies. There are over 40 for-profit *institutional review boards* (IRBs) in the United States that collected almost $60 million in fees in 2002, with the Washington-based Western IRB holding about 50 percent of the market share.[33] These companies are hired to complete centralized ethical and scientific reviews of research protocols for investigative sites participating in clinical trials before a study can by conducted. For-profit IRBs market themselves on the speed of review that they offer. For instance, it is not unusual to see advertisements in industry publications that promise same-day or next-day review of clinical protocols.

Study brokers—sometimes referred to as *trial management organizations*—are companies that act as intermediaries in matching investigative sites with pharmaceutical contracts. They are sometimes seen as informal SMOs because they provide similar infrastructural assistance to individual sites, but there are no exclusivity agreements binding sites to study brokers. Sites pay study brokers a commission as a percentage of contracts awarded. Physicians and research staff often criticize study brokers because they are trying to make a profit at the sites' expense rather than from the pharmaceutical companies. A physician I interviewed called these companies "pond scum," and some sites and SMOs explicitly state in their marketing materials that they will not work with study brokers. In fact, only 11 percent of sites use study brokers to find contracts; the majority rely instead on personal contacts, industry publications, and cold calls.[34]

Clinical trials advertising agencies specialize in creating advertisements that will meet regulation (for example, ads must clearly state that the therapies offered are experimental, and they cannot use the word "new" in describing the drug, therapy, or device), pass IRB review, and be effective. Advertising agencies are often hired not only for their ability to design a good campaign but also for appropriate expertise regarding where to place ads to reach target audiences effectively. These companies recommend types of radio stations, times of the day, and so on for reaching the specific demographics required for studies.

Central patient recruitment companies have a similar function to advertising agencies within the clinical trials industry. Although recruitment companies often provide the same services as advertising agencies, many of them specialize in what are called "ready-to-recruit"—or directly solicitable—populations. In most cases, this service consists of databases of individuals' names and contact information that are cross-referenced by disease state, geographic location, sex, age, and other variables. The recruitment companies can build these databases from scratch, or they create them by cobbling together preexisting databases. One example of the latter is a single database compiled from data on health insurance claims, U.S. census demographics, and marketing data on media exposure. The compilation of such information is designed to answer questions such as "What television programs are favored by middle-class asthmatics in New England?" The answer to this type of question is valuable to companies searching for an effective way of recruiting potential subject volunteers. Another simple function that central patient recruitment companies serve is to offer centralized call centers to complete the prescreening of individuals. This service removes from investigative sites the burden and expense of talking with individuals who are not eligible for given protocols.

With so many companies and services propagating within the industry, one would expect that they demonstrate considerable efficacy in speeding up the pace of clinical trials. Indeed, new drugs were approved on an average of sixteen months faster in 1999–2001 (about 5.92 years) than in the period

1994–1998 (about 7.25 years). In part this shift can be attributed to the reorganization of the industry, but changes made at the FDA played an important role as well. Specifically, pharmaceutical companies were *filing* applications to the FDA for new products six months faster: in 4.9 years (from 1999–2001) instead of 5.4 years (1994–1998).[35] The more dramatic change has been in the speed of the FDA's review of new drug applications.

Initiated in 1992, the FDA created a system of application fees, mandated by the Prescription Drug User Fee Act (PDUFA). In order to supplement the federal budget designated to the FDA, PDUFA requires that companies pay applications fees to subsidize the FDA clerks employed to review pharmaceutical companies' data and make a determination on the marketability of their products.[36] For fiscal year 2008, fees were set at $1,178,000 for each new drug application requiring clinical data.[37] The hiring of additional staff has shortened the FDA's drug approval decisions by an average of twelve months. If pharmaceutical companies' products are approved, the application fee is more than compensated for by the expected $120–550 million in additional sales during a patent life that is extended by bringing products to market more quickly.

Political and Economic Context of Clinical Trials in the United States

The clinical trials industry in the United States is successful because the current context of health care is ripe for what contract research can offer both to patients and physicians. The most profitable companies—from the pharmaceutical companies themselves to the auxiliary companies—are those that have most effectively marketed clinical trials to underserved patient populations and private-sector physicians. The current medical climate in the United States is characterized by increasing health care costs and underinsurance as a result of the decline in the overall economy and the decrease in jobs offering benefits to employees. In this national context, pharmaceutical clinical trials become an option for patients who would not receive medical attention otherwise.

In addition to the constraints placed on patients for the rising costs of medical care, physicians themselves are facing increasing pressure from insurance companies and from the threat of malpractice suits. Over the past two decades, physicians have reported a steady decrease in revenue and an increase in constraints on their ability to care for patients. In this context, clinical trials serve to not only cut the cost of drug development for pharmaceutical companies but provide an alternative means for physicians to earn revenue and for patients to have access, albeit limited, to the health care system. In short, the United States is well suited to pharmaceutical clinical trials because health care in this country is characterized by *medical neoliberalism*.[38]

The term neoliberalism has been used to describe late-twentieth- and early-twenty-first-century governance emphasizing free markets and free trade.[39] Although the focus of neoliberal economic policies tends to be international in scope, neoliberalism affects domestic policies just as dramatically. Neoliberal policies on the national level are manifested in state cutbacks in social goods through the privatization of those functions and the ongoing deregulation of the private sector. An interesting aspect of neoliberalism is that as the state transfers responsibility to its citizens to provide for themselves, it simultaneously increases the amount of monitoring of citizens' actions.[40]

In the United States, evidence of neoliberalism can be found in policies surrounding welfare, health care, education, and social security.[41] More subtle examples of the influence of neoliberal ideologies can be seen in the decline in unions and the antiunion rulings of the National Labor Relations Board, in military and defense expenditures, and even in recent proposals for immigration reform. Regardless of the domain of public life, however, political spin reframes neoliberal policies to claim that this form of governance is in the best interests of the citizenry.[42] For example, the rhetoric of neoliberalism extols the benefits that will come both to the recipients and the providers of privatized services, stressing the increased efficiency for beneficiaries and the profitability of these systems for private companies.

The resulting cultural logic of neoliberalism is articulated in a variety of ways with the same message at its core: what is good for industry must be good for America. What counts as "America," however, is rarely unpacked. The rhetoric obscures the social burdens placed on citizens and others by focusing on an economy over which average citizens can make few or no claims. In other words, neoliberalism ought to be examined on the level of the state and its policymaking but also on the level of its differential effects on citizens depending on their social locations.

Neoliberalism extends into and has particular effects on health care in the United States. To understand how the clinical testing of pharmaceutical products fits into this ideology and mode of governance, attention must be given to medical neoliberalism not only as part of broader national trends toward privatized social services but as a cultural sensibility toward the commodification of health and wellness.[43] Neoliberalism extends the commodification of health so that consumption is not only a right but an obligation if one wants health care at all.[44]

Within this expanded frame, medical neoliberalism has several striking features. First, on the policy level, neoliberal ideologies infuse interpretations of the limitations of the current U.S. health care system. Rather than the "problem" being defined as the system itself, the problem is instead understood in terms of opportunities for "choice." True to its roots in economic liberalism, U.S. health care is defined individually, according to who is willing to pay and for what kind of care. The focus on individuals within neoliberalism, however, does not mean that individuals themselves are privileged within its rubric; neoliberalism offers a *discourse* of the individual and choice while foreclosing options in the name of rationality and efficiency. Moreover, the focus on individual choice serves to obscure the ways in which health care inequalities are generated by the system itself. In other words, medical neoliberalism leads to a prioritization of "choice" over equity and access.

Second, on the institutional level, medical neoliberalism is characterized by a commodification of health that transforms individuals from patients to consumers.[45] The difference in terms is not merely semantic. This new orientation toward medicine not only emphasizes autonomy but also accountability for both patients and health care providers.[46] Unlike patients, *consumers* seeking health care bear the responsibility for the choices they make—or fail to make—regarding their health. Because they are positioned as having the "right" to make choices about health care, consumers also have the obligation to use whatever products and services are available to ensure health or to treat illness and disease. This is not to say that medical professionals are not liable for malpractice claims. If anything, assessing the appropriateness of care is another burden on consumers, and malpractice suits serve as a means to make claims that the products and services they sought were not delivered as promised.

Finally, on the cultural level, through the process of making health care a commodity, medical neoliberalism also commodifies the body itself. Medical neoliberalism fragments the body by homing in on specific problem areas with or within the body to the detriment of holistic analysis.[47] The implication of this fragmentation is that body parts are seen in terms of the products designed to maintain, cure, or enhance them. Potential dangers of this consumerist fragmentation are new perceptions of disability and the rise of "technoluxe" and transhumanist models of medicine in which the focus is no longer on health but on enhancement of the body.[48]

In practice, medical neoliberalism is most easily identified in two changes in health care since the 1970s: managed care and direct-to-consumer advertising. U.S. president Ronald Reagan significantly advanced neoliberalism in the 1980s by crafting federal policy in accordance with these political and economic ideologies. For example, in response to the rising cost of medicine and the interpretation of the federal Medicare system as being in crisis, Reagan ushered in the economically rational strategy of managed care to reduce government spending on health care. After its implementation, the Medicare model quickly became the dominant form of health insurance in the private sector as well.[49]

The widespread move to reduce the costs of health care was crafted as economic policy. However, changing the structure of payment for medical services had profound effects on the authority of physicians, who under managed care must adhere to rules of medical diagnostics and treatments set by insurance providers. Thus, managed care contributed to reshaping the interactions between physicians and their patients.[50] Ultimately, managed care played a key role in the commodification of health care. By assigning values and standards to clinical practice, medicine became less a social good and more a set of commodities to which individual patients have differential degrees of access.[51]

In addition to managed care, another key federal policy contributing to medical neoliberalism was the reinterpretation of U.S. regulations governing the pharmaceutical industry's right to advertise to prospective patients. In 1997, the FDA ruled that pharmaceutical companies could market their products to patients through "direct-to-consumer" advertising. In large part, discourses about patient empowerment and the creation of informed consumers persuaded the FDA to allow mass media marketing campaigns.[52]

The influences of the media and direct-to-consumer advertising have also shifted the doctor-patient relationship.[53] For example, patients' perceptions of their health are shaped by targeted messages from the manufacturers of health care products.[54] These changes in U.S. health care have succeeded in recentralizing power toward pharmaceutical companies and insurance providers and away from physicians. By creating new structures within which medical decision making occurs, physicians' authority is shared or at times overshadowed by these industries.[55] Nowhere is the extent of neoliberalized medicine more apparent than in current models of treatment for psychiatric illness. In this realm, depression, anxiety, and other disorders are decreasingly located in the contextual lives of individuals with these conditions. Instead, these illnesses are frequently said to inhabit the brain and can thus be treated solely by changing the brain's chemistry rather than finding any psychosocial roots of those conditions.[56]

Patients as consumers have embraced the neoliberal logics of health care so that they too see illness in reductionist terms and seek pharmaceuticals as targeted magic bullets. This orientation toward health and medicine has been referred to as the pharmaceuticalization of health care, in which the conditions of health and illness are ever more cast in terms of products that can be purchased by health-engaged consumers.[57] A medical system that revolves around pharmaceuticals contributes to a culture of medical neoliberalism. It ties together the commodification of health care with the fragmentation of the body where illness is treated in terms of discrete systems for which there are tailored products.

Within the political, economic, and cultural contexts of neoliberalism, the offering of pharmaceutical clinical trials is positioned as adding another option for health care consumers. Because the majority of these pharmaceutical studies are located in familiar contexts, such as private practices, the process of research is normalized, meaning that clinical trials become a routine part of the clinic. Equally important, drug testing further fragments the body by positioning illness as an attribute that can be used for testing pharmaceutical products. Clinical research becomes the "responsible choice" for individuals who do not otherwise have access to—but require—medical intervention. Or, put another way, participation in clinical trials becomes almost a duty for those who have no other access to health care *because* it is available as a "choice."

By privileging the individual and choice, a health care system mediated by neoliberal policies and cultural sensibilities tends to obscure the inequalities to which those who participate in clinical trials tend to be subject. Within this frame, the systematic use of uninsured or economically disenfranchised people as human subjects in pharmaceutical studies is not seen as being exploitative but is instead positioned as an opportunity for members of those groups.[58] This discursive maneuver diminishes both the individual risks of participating in drug studies and the broader inequities of the health care and economic systems in the United States. Clinical trials may indeed address two major shortcomings in American health care—decreasing amounts of revenue for physicians and decreasing access to medicine for patients—but they also exacerbate existing social inequalities.

The mother and son introduced at the beginning of this chapter illustrate the complex social and ethical implications of including uninsured individuals in clinical trials. The opportunity that pharmaceutical studies provide for the boy and many others should not be disregarded. The woman is able to leverage this particular study to help minimize her son's problems in the classroom. Yet it must not be forgotten that clinical trial participation is not equivalent to medical care. The extent to which the physician running the study can provide medical intervention is constrained by the study protocol. The investigational product, its dose, and even the administration of a placebo are not chosen by the physician for a patient but by the pharmaceutical company to generate study results. Moreover, clinical trials are finite. The woman will have to find another ADHD clinical trial in which to enroll the boy or, more likely, end treatment for him at the conclusion of the current study. If and when the product he is taking is available on the market, the cost of the new medication will preclude his access to it. Because of these issues regarding treatment and access that are symptoms of medical neoliberalism, pharmaceutical clinical trials cannot be said to provide sufficient health care at all. In what follows, I explore the contours of medical neoliberalism by examining the regulatory context for and current clinical practices associated with the testing of pharmaceutical products on human subjects in the United States.

Chapter 2

Governing Human Subjects Research

At root and by definition, the clinical trials industry would not be possible without the participation of human subjects. Although it is a highly regulated industry, the research terrain has changed significantly since the United States enacted laws in the 1970s to protect human subjects. To date, there has been little explicit examination of how the development of a for-profit clinical trials industry might influence research practices and ethics and what regulation might be necessary under these new conditions of medical research.[1] By examining the organization of pharmaceutical clinical trials, the limitations of and problems with current federal policies governing human subjects research become evident. In spite of regulation, ethical misconduct can and does occur in the process of pharmaceutical drug development. Unfortunately, the misuse, if not abuse, of human subjects is not simply a problem of the past; rather, the historical legacy of exploitation has been carried forward into the current political and economic landscape.

Historically, scientific research has led to the abuse of human subjects. During the past sixty years, the U.S. government has been aware of the need to create and revise federal policies to protect the health and safety of those who are subjects in research. Worldwide attention to this issue emerged after World War II during the Nuremberg trials when an American military tribunal adjudicated cases against physicians in the Nazi party accused of inhumane and unnecessary medical experimentation on humans.[2] The medical malfeasance that occurred in Nazi Germany was perceived as a symptom of the national depravity of the German people. American science, in contrast, was viewed—and continues to be viewed to a large degree—as immune from such immorality. This was due to the popular belief that American physicians and researchers would never allow or participate in the unethical research practices in which the Nazis had engaged.[3] As a result, the United States did not adopt comprehensive federal regulations governing human subjects research until the 1980s, after decades of ethically problematic research had already been conducted in this country.[4]

Despite much discourse about the ethicality of American science and the presence of regulation, the treatment of human subjects in medical research is a persistent problem. Moreover, the exploitation of disenfranchised groups and the reproduction of social inequalities are deeply entrenched in the research enterprise. Protecting human subjects has been and continues to be insufficient because most approaches, historically and currently, prioritize (neo)liberal, individualized responses to structural problems. Both the scientific community and regulatory apparatus largely conceptualize the ethics of human subjects research in individualistic terms. Scientists' claims to self-regulation focus on individual researchers' adherence to professional norms dictating ethical behavior. U.S. regulation focuses on individual human subjects as autonomous agents and aims to protect their rights *to participate* in research. What is not acknowledged in these liberal approaches is that the worst cases of abuses to human subjects occurred not because of the treatment of *individuals* but because of the treatment of *groups*.

U.S. Medical Research: A History of Bodies as Property

Although U.S. researchers and policymakers conscientiously present a front of responsible medical research and treatment of humans, they have not always been so concerned. Most public attention to research abuses has focused on the human atrocities committed by the Nazis and only peripherally on ethically problematic U.S. medical research like the Tuskegee syphilis study. Prior to World War II, human subjects used in medical research were treated and represented as though their bodies were the property of the state, of science, and of "humanity." Slaves, rural African Americans, Native Americans, institutionalized psychiatric patients, and prisoners were deliberately subjected to medical experiments that offered them little or no therapeutic value.

The bodies of members of certain marginalized groups have historically been used to serve the needs of "science" and the state; current regulation of human subjects research has not altogether eliminated this historical legacy.

What is incredible about U.S. medical research is not that it has had high-profile cases of abuse of human subjects but rather that, in spite of its history of systematically exploiting disenfranchised groups for the benefit of "progress," scientific and policymaking communities have treated these as isolated events. These cases were not the result of a few "bad" researchers; instead, social inequalities and prejudices have catalyzed abuse of these groups.

The historical use of African Americans in biomedical research illustrates hypocrisies that are deeply rooted in American racism.[5] Until the civil rights movement in the 1960s, black bodies were spoken of, in political rhetoric, as biologically different than white bodies.[6] For example, the blood of black individuals was described as distinct from that of whites, justifying separate supplies of blood for soldiers during wartime.[7] In spite of this rhetoric, when it was time to find bodies to autopsy and bodies on which to experiment, the medical establishment had no qualms about assuming that the information gleaned from the bodies of black Americans could be applied to whites.[8] Most notably, in the antebellum period, it was not uncommon for slaves to be purchased for the sole purpose of being used in medical experimentation.[9] At this time, southern medical schools boasted "that their cities' large black population provided ample supplies of clinical and anatomical material."[10] Even free blacks and slaves owned by others were used indiscriminately in medical studies because they were thought of as available bodies on which to experiment rather than as individuals with free will.

The most well-known example of mistreatment of African Americans in medical research is the Tuskegee syphilis study.[11] Funded by the U.S. Public Health Service (PHS), the Tuskegee research was designed to observe the effects of untreated syphilis in African American men in a rural community in Alabama. A prior study had been done in Norway to document the effects of untreated syphilis in the early 1920s, and the PHS decided to compare the course of the untreated disease in black Americans. At the outset of the research in 1932, there were variably effective treatments for syphilis but no cure. The 399 men recruited were told that they had "bad blood," were not informed that they were part of a research study, and were given placebos as "treatment" for the illness.[12] In exchange for their participation, the men were promised free meals, free medical examinations, and burial insurance. Even after penicillin was discovered to cure syphilis and was made widely available in the early 1940s, the men were not treated, nor were they told about the existence of an effective cure. Recent evidence indicates the men were not treated because their infected blood samples contributed to the development of a diagnostic test for syphilis.[13] The PHS research continued until 1972, when the study received national media coverage and was terminated.

Native Americans and Latinos also have been targeted for medical experimentation. Native Americans have been referred to as "the Nation's first guinea pigs" because of the exploitative practices of the federal government toward many native tribes.[14] One well-documented example occurred during the 1940s and 1950s when Navajos were employed to mine uranium that would be used in military research for bombs. The U.S. government, particularly the PHS, knew that uranium was highly toxic, but the miners were not provided with any protective clothing or equipment to minimize exposure.[15] The PHS then initiated a ten-year study to document how quickly miners died after their exposure to uranium dust. Profound prejudice likewise has made Latinos targets of scientific research. For example, medical researchers in the 1950s sought Latinas for risky studies during the development of female contraceptives.[16] U.S. researchers even established a base of operations in Puerto Rico to conduct large-scale clinical trials on oral contraceptives, justified by racist views about "overpopulation" and Puerto Rican women's sexuality.[17]

State institutions, such as mental institutions, orphanages, and prisons, have also been a locus of medical inquiry because researchers saw their occupants as convenient, captive populations. In the case of mental institutions, the belief in the biomedical community during the first half of the twentieth century was that if a person was unable to give true consent, that person could be used in research without even being asked.[18] This assumption implied that if individuals were not able to function "normally" in society, their bodies were rendered property of the state, mental institution, and/or medical research facilities.[19]

The best-known case of medical experimentation in psychiatric facilities occurred during the 1960s at the Willowbrook State School for Retarded Children in New York, where the effectiveness of gamma globulin in treating hepatitis was tested.[20] Although hepatitis was extremely prevalent in public institutions at that time, the investigators decided to infect children deliberately with the disease under allegedly carefully controlled research conditions rather than studying children who were already infected with hepatitis. Interestingly, the biggest fallout from public attention to Willowbrook had less to do with research ethics than with the prevalence of hepatitis and the squalid conditions in state institutions. Rather than leading to any sort of regulation of medical research, the Willowbrook controversy resulted in widespread reforms in the sanitary conditions of psychiatric institutions.[21]

Similarly, prisoners were often thought of as a sanctioned group for experimentation because research was seen as a way in which prisoners could repay their debt to society.[22] By the 1960s, medical experimentation was deeply integrated into the penitentiary system, such as military research on LSD, radiation studies, and diverse pharmaceutical trials. Unlike the cases of patients in mental institutions, prisoners were often paid for their participation or were offered a reduction in their prison sentence; wardens and parole boards viewed prisoners' participation in research favorably. In general, recruitment of prisoners was not viewed as "cruel and unusual punishment" because participation was technically voluntary and because prisoners received monetary compensation in exchange for their involvement. Moreover, prisoners often received secondary gains, such as better living conditions and better food. Because of these benefits, prisoners often viewed medical research as a positive means by which to earn some money while serving their sentences. Not unlike Willowbrook, questions about the conditions of prisons and prisoners' need for money resulted in broad reform of the penitentiary system in the 1970s.[23]

With media coverage of the Tuskegee syphilis study and the publication of an exposé on the use of prisoners in research, the early 1970s were marked by public alarm about the conduct of U.S. researchers.[24] Policymakers could no longer ignore the need for regulating human subjects research. To begin assessing the extent of the problem, Congress held hearings on human experimentation beginning in 1973 to investigate the research enterprise. The hearings challenged both researchers' "right" to use institutionalized persons and the specific institutional contexts that enabled such research practices in the first place. Ultimately, the congressional hearings led to the passage of the National Research Act of 1974 and the enactment of regulation in 1981. At the time, however, the issue on the table was if the ethical abuses were indicative of a general depravity within the research community or simply cases of a few immoral researchers whose unethical practices were dominating the headlines.

American Ethics and Scientific Self-Regulation

There are two common explanations offered by historians, ethicists, and policymakers for how and why incidents involving abuses of human subjects happened in the decades leading up to the 1970s. First, abuses occurred because there was no system of normative ethics guiding research on human subjects.[25] Second, abuses occurred because a few unethical researchers did not follow their communities' scientific norms.[26] Both explanations imply, in part, that researchers were not regulating themselves. However, when examining the research practices of scientific and medical communities in the decades preceding World War II, there is ample evidence that there were, in fact, codes of conduct outlining how both humans and animals should be treated as subjects of experiments and that practical problems—such as ambiguities in measuring risk, interpreting results, and determining "lesser harm"—influenced how well researchers followed these codes of conduct.[27]

There have been mitigating norms in science guiding human subjects research since the nineteenth century. From that time to the 1970s, four conditions governed experimentation on humans: (1) prior experimentation on animals, (2) willingness to self-experiment or to use the new drug/procedure on one's own family, (3) therapeutic benefit or at least the absence of injury, and (4) consent or at least noncoercion of the subjects involved.[28] While these guidelines for conducting research were not often enforced by any organization or body per se, the American Medical Association as well as other groups tacitly endorsed these criteria for research on humans.[29]

Because there was some anxiety in the early twentieth century surrounding "medical heroism" and experimental medicine, the revelations of the atrocities committed by Nazi doctors played into the American public's fears that research harmed individuals.[30] In response, the U.S. scientific community articulated distinctions between American and Nazi science and research. Bolstered by early work in the sociology of science, good, legitimate scientific research was framed as both free from politics and national interests.[31] The strength of this position is witnessed in its longevity; even in the contemporary United States, "good" science continues to be defined as autonomous and apolitical.[32]

The ability of scientists to self-regulate was especially subject to debate in the postwar period. Beginning in the 1960s, the medical community began to experience internal conflict surrounding human subjects research. For example, in 1966 an American physician named Henry Beecher sparked controversy by publishing a whistle-blowing article about the abuses of human subjects in the United States.[33] The critique was particularly cutting because Beecher drew from medical journal publications and the information authors provided about human subjects. He argued that extremely prevalent unethical practices were encouraged due to the medical community's complacency in regards to regulating itself concerning the treatment of human subjects. Beecher further accused the medical journals of condoning unethical behavior by publishing the findings from these studies. For Beecher, however, it was still an issue of self-regulation; the problem for him was that the medical community was being lax in its responsibility and thereby encouraging investigators to behave irresponsibly toward their subjects.

The controversy that Beecher instigated with his 1966 article and later publications did have policy effects on the national level.[34] Beecher's article made many waves and generated discussion within the PHS and the National Institutes of Health (NIH). In response, these organizations decided that some regulation was necessary, particularly because they had directly funded many studies that had exploited human subjects. The directors at NIH worried that the public would lose its trust in the medical establishment and wanted to prevent negative public opinion from having an effect on the NIH budget.[35] At the same time, PHS and NIH were afraid of making policies that would discourage research. During the late 1960s and early 1970s, they began to establish systems for institutional review of the ethics of research protocols based on the system of scientific peer review in place at NIH at the time. The changes underway at the federal level did not, however, begin to get teeth until catalyzed by congressional intervention several years later.

The American Policy and Regulatory Environments

The impetus for regulation in the United States did not come until publicity surrounding the Tuskegee syphilis study and exposure of prison experimentation drew public attention. At that point, there was widespread public concern about whether the medical community was able to regulate itself.[36] In response to media and public pressure, Congress passed the National Research Act of 1974, thereby creating the National Commission for the Protection of Human Subjects of Biomedical and Behavioral Research ("National Commission"). This group directly shaped federal regulation through their recommendations.[37]

Identifying Ethical Principles

The National Commission was charged with identifying ethical principles to govern human subjects research. In its deliberations, it drew upon two documents from similar international bodies that had preceded it: the Nuremberg Code and the Declaration of Helsinki. In its prosecution of Nazi doctors, the U.S. military tribunal used a set of criteria for defining permissible and legitimate conduct in human experimentation to assess the guilt or innocence of the physicians who were on trial.[38] These criteria came to embody what is now known as the "Nuremberg Code."[39] The Declaration of Helsinki was developed by the World Medical Association in 1964 as a code of ethics to be followed by physicians in research settings.[40] The hope was that the declaration would prevent research atrocities from happening in the future through a system of accountability.[41] It has since served as a model for regulation by many countries as they have struggled to create rules for human subjects research.[42]

The Nuremberg Code and Declaration of Helsinki provided the National Commission with the initial delineation of how research subjects should be treated, including voluntary and informed participation, and how the risks of research should be balanced against the benefits to society.[43] The National Commission, however, crafted a document, the Belmont Report (1979), that deviated significantly in form and structure from these predecessors. Rather than listing criteria, the National Commission instead adopted a more philosophical approach from which policymakers were to base subsequent regulation. Specifically, it developed three ethical principles that should be the basis of all human subjects regulation: respect for persons, beneficence, and justice. It outlined a complex definition of *research* to indicate what needed to be regulated and proposed three applications to match the respective ethical components: informed consent, risk/benefit assessment, and selection of research subjects.[44]

In the Belmont Report, the National Commission described the ethical principles and their applications in detail and gave them specific meanings and purposes. Defining "respect for persons" as the recognition that individuals are autonomous agents, it asserted that informed consent procedures would maintain and reinforce individuals' autonomy through the three ingredients of information, comprehension, and voluntariness. In other words, providing information about risks and benefits, institutionalizing a procedure to assess whether the information was understood, and recruiting research subjects in a noncoercive way would guarantee respect for persons in the research process. The second ethical principle of beneficence is described in two parts: "Do no harm" and maximize possible benefits while minimizing possible harms. Through risk/benefit analysis, the National Commission stressed the importance of measuring the risk of the research to the individual compared to the benefit of the research to the individual and, more broadly, to society.[45] Finally, the third ethical principle of justice is defined as "fairness of distribution." Concerned with the distribution of the benefits and the burdens of medical research, the report discussed the need for fairness (although not equity). In this view of justice, participation in research is taken as a right and should, therefore, be available to anyone who would benefit.[46]

A major problem with the Belmont Report and the approach taken by the National Commission is that their attention to abstract ethical principles decontextualized the human research enterprise. Whereas the congressional hearings preceding the National Research Act of 1974 attended to the institutional problems that catalyzed abuses of human subjects, the National Commission was more concerned with identifying "universal" principles that could apply to human subjects research regardless of its context. This is not to criticize the desire to have a set of universal principles to guide research but to underscore that they are not enough in practice. The focus on abstract universal principles in the Belmont Report—however mitigated by their concrete applications—resulted in only nominal attention to the historical contingencies and structural conditions leading to their charge.[47] Specifically, the problems at institutions like prisons and state sanitariums were not with the practices of researchers per se, but the conditions that made those institutions ideal places for researchers to conduct their studies. Of course, the only institutional reform under the purview of the National Commission concerned the research enterprise itself, *not* the institutions hosting that research.

Federal Regulation

The task of transforming the National Commission's recommendations from the Belmont Report into federal regulation fell to the PHS—the same agency that funded the Tuskegee syphilis study.[48] First, the PHS defined the scope of the regulation: federal regulation would only apply to research projects that are performed or funded by federal money. Private research is not required to follow the federal requirements. Next, the PHS mandated the creation of local institutional review boards (IRBs) to ensure that researchers follow a procedure of voluntary informed consent with their research subjects. Finally, the regulation discussed "vulnerable populations" and created additional explicit safeguards for research involving "fetuses, pregnant women, and human in vitro fertilization," prisoners, and children.[49] These additional measures resulted in a dramatic decrease in research involving individuals from these groups—particularly prisoners—labeled as vulnerable populations.[50]

Even though groups such as ethnic minorities, the poor, and the terminally ill were identified as potentially vulnerable groups in the Belmont Report, the PHS made no special provisions in the federal regulation to provide additional protections to these groups. By ignoring other types of vulnerability to research abuses, the regulation effectively cast all other human subjects as equally "autonomous" and able to protect themselves through the informed consent process. Thus, in spite of a "vulnerable populations" category, in practice, research ethics are highly individualized, focusing predominantly on human subjects' consent. As a result, those who have important structural reasons for participating, such as poverty, lack of health insurance, and/or illness, must protect themselves individually through the informed consent process. Evidence suggests, however, that because of their personal situations, individuals from these groups are unlikely to have interest in the details of consent forms, enabling a valence toward participation in research studies.[51]

In 1981, the Department of Health, Education, and Welfare (HEW)[52] enacted the federal regulation for human subjects protection (U.S. 45-CFR-46). At that time, the regulation applied only to research activities sponsored by HEW, and the government did not enforce this or any other regulations for human subjects research conducted by or funded through other U.S. departments and agencies for another full decade. In 1991, in response to inquiries into the research practices of the Department of Defense and other agencies, the government expanded the jurisdiction of the regulation to all government bodies engaging in or funding research on human subjects. The HEW regulation became known as the "Common Rule" because it was adopted as the standard for all federal agencies rather than crafting new guidelines or rules specific to each agency.[53]

Yet, even with its increased reach, the regulation does not apply to all research conducted by U.S. researchers. For example, it does not directly regulate human subjects research that is conducted in the private sector. Additionally, research that is done overseas by U.S. federally funded researchers is subject to some but not all of the regulation compared with those projects completed within the physical territory of the United States.[54] Although the FDA has its own regulations for human subjects research (for protocols seeking approval as part of the drug development and approval process), it only governs research directly leading to the marketing of products.[55]

The distinction between public and private-sector research sends an important message: the U.S. government does not want to be implicated in any way for unethical practices concerning human subjects in research settings.[56] Because the same regulations do not apply to private-sector research, this suggests that the government is more concerned about protecting itself than it is with protecting individuals who volunteer for research studies.[57] Moreover, it is clear that while the regulation imposes some constraints on federally funded researchers, it also allows them much autonomy in their research practices.[58]

Regulation and Innovation

At the core of the policy environment is the fear that regulation of human subjects research will discourage or inhibit research, and hence progress.[59] Indeed, policymakers have relied heavily on recommendations from the medical and scientific communities to formulate policy in order to ensure that research and medical innovation would not be stifled by regulation.[60] Physicians, researchers, pharmaceutical companies, and their public and private organizations and lobbying groups have played key roles in the development of regulation.[61] Part of their framing of research and development is the assumption that human subjects are required to undertake risks for the sake of medical progress, and policymakers have not challenged this assumption in their consideration of regulating research activities.[62]

Resulting from their involvement in the policymaking process from congressional testimony, public comments on draft recommendations, and appointments to federal commissions, physicians and researchers have contributed a number of key distinctions that serve to define what needs to be regulated and what does not. One such distinction concerns the definition of research itself. Most physicians and researchers distinguish between *research* and *innovation*. Research is defined as "a systematic investigation designed to develop or contribute to generalizable knowledge."[63] Innovation, on the other hand, is considered different from research because it is "spontaneous," "non-routine," "non-systematic," and not meant to be generalizable. For example, surgeons innovate by tying new surgical knots in their sutures.[64] Because these novel techniques are "spontaneous," rather than premeditated, and are used as "treatments," rather than for the purpose of knowledge, they are considered innovations that fall outside of research and oversight; they circumvent the procedural constraints (that is, IRBs) of the Common Rule since they fall outside of federal jurisdiction. Obviously, the distinction between innovation and research is not always clear-cut, but its supporters have effectively kept "innovation" out of the realm of regulation.

Another important distinction structuring the regulation of research is the categorization of "risk" versus "minimal risk."[65] This distinction is based on the idea that most research involving humans involves little risk to the subjects, so researchers should not be burdened by the same amount of bureaucracy as high-risk research.[66] The dichotomization often explicitly mobilizes the assumption that Americans are ethical and do not need much federal oversight of research. For example, Bernard Lo, a high-profile ethicist who was a member of the National Bioethics Advisory Board in the 1990s, has stated in defense of the distinction between risk and minimal-risk research, "This is not Nazi Germany. We know what is awful. If it is not scientifically sound, no risks are acceptable . . . and the research will not be performed."[67] Importantly, embedded in the perceived need to distinguish between levels of risk to human subjects is frustration with how federal regulation becomes translated into layers of bureaucracy.[68]

Protecting Human Subjects

What have been the effects of the Common Rule on protecting human subjects? Federal regulation has been effective at minimizing particular types of abuses. As a result of the U.S. history of human experimentation, the system is specifically designed to eliminate deception and coercion.[69] The solution to these unethical practices has been an emphasis on informed consent.[70] While informed consent has radically transformed the ways in which researchers interact with human subjects, it does not automatically protect human subjects from harm or exploitation.[71] The reliance on informed consent obscures the inherent risks of research participation and ignores the structural reasons that compel some groups to participate more than others.[72] The translation of the Belmont principles into practice has emphasized the autonomy of individuals involved (that is, both researchers and human subjects) at the expense of the larger structure of scientific research. Thus, the impact of science on *groups* of human subjects is obscured.

Because the approach to formulating U.S. regulations was influenced by philosophical thought, policymaking was seen by government officials as a finite process to solve human subject abuses through the application of universal ethical principles. As a result, the attitude toward regulation during the past twenty-five years has generally been that any problems associated with human subjects research have already been solved and there is little need for further regulation. Within this regulatory environment, policymakers—and frequently bioethicists as well—do not identify or anticipate more systematic abuses that can and do occur.[73]

Contemporary Research and Policy Climates

The U.S. research landscape has shifted significantly since the regulation to protect human subjects was enacted in 1981 and extended in 1991 by the

Common Rule. In response to the regulations, particularly the restrictions placed on experimentation using prison populations, researchers needed to seek out new populations to recruit into clinical studies.[74] The pharmaceutical industry, in particular, slowly began to privatize and globalize its clinical research.[75] The pace of outsourcing to private-sector clinics accelerated as the pharmaceutical industry recognized that academic medical centers could not provide human subjects to enroll in clinical trials as quickly as the industry would like.

In addition to the changes catalyzed by the pharmaceutical industry, advocacy groups have also effected significant changes to research practices and federal policy. The women's movement impressed upon NIH the necessity of including women—as well as minority groups—in clinical trials, and their lobbying resulted in policies requiring research to include women or justify their absence from all clinical studies.[76] The federal mandates regarding the inclusion of women and minorities offer both challenges to recruitment of human subjects and opportunities for researchers. Inclusion of women and minorities can be challenging when researchers are required to meet quotas set by federal grants dictating the inclusion of different groups.[77] On the other hand, the inclusion of women in clinical trials means that the base of human subjects who can be recruited into studies is greatly expanded.

The neoliberal economic policies favored by the Reagan administration have enabled the pharmaceutical industry to conduct thousands of studies each year using U.S. populations.[78] With the profound changes in employment patterns, welfare, and health care delivery, many Americans find themselves without access to health care or in dire financial situations.[79] Clinical trials have increasingly been marketed to these individuals as a way of addressing their needs. As a result, pharmaceutical studies in the United States are overwhelmingly conducted on uninsured and impoverished citizens. Because of the limited definition of who is vulnerable in the context of human subjects research, nothing in the current regulations proscribe or restrict human subjects research on economically disenfranchised groups; the uninsured are not understood to be a vulnerable population.

Although the Common Rule has been updated and revised since the original regulations were issued in 1981, little has changed in terms of the protection it affords human subjects.[80] To assess whether change is needed, during the last decade, policymakers in the executive and legislative branches of government have appointed ad hoc committees and have created agencies within the Department of Health and Human Services to investigate the ethics of current human subjects research and to provide recommendations for new policy and regulation. These committees and agencies have been successful in effecting change in federal guidance regarding subjects' privacy, financial conflicts of interest for researchers and institutions, and centralized reporting of clinical trial results.[81]

Nonetheless, there are profound limitations and problems with current federal policies governing human subjects research. In spite of formal discussions in Washington about better protecting human subjects, there has been little explicit examination of how the pharmaceutical industry takes advantage of political and economic conditions that disenfranchise people living in the United States. In the context of current modes of pharmaceutical drug development, the existing regulations are impotent to prevent new and different forms of misuses, if not abuses, of human subjects. This is in part because of the regulation's liberal philosophical approach to protecting human subjects. Rather than tracking the groups being targeted to take part in human subjects research, an individualistic orientation focuses on whether informed consent from individuals can be documented. If informed consent is given, the research is perceived as ethical.[82] Reform to the current regulation is necessary, as the following chapters will show, because the current system enables the continued unequal use of certain segments of the population to serve the needs of science. The poor and uninsured have become the groups whose disenfranchised bodies are used in the name of medical progress and pharmaceutical profit.

Chapter 3

Pursuing Contract Research

On my first visit to a large practice, I interviewed Richard,[1] a white male physician in his mid-forties who was actively involved in pharmaceutical contract research and had conducted roughly 250 studies since the early 1990s. That day, there were nearly forty studies operating out of his private practice with a dedicated research staff to oversee them. In addition to his impressive experience with drug studies, Richard had a range of organizational and business experiences in the clinical trials industry: he had worked on clinical trials in an academic setting as part of his residency training, in his private practice operating as an independent site, and most recently in his private practice operating as part of a site management organization (SMO).

Richard's involvement with pharmaceutical studies began when he and his partner were seeking ways to augment the revenue generated by their private practice. They had begun to see their incomes diminish as payments from managed care organizations and Medicare dipped, malpractice insurance premiums swelled, and overhead costs for maintaining their office tripled. Initially, both physicians became involved with extracurricular promotional activities for the pharmaceutical industry, including consultant work and paid speaking engagements.[2] Soon, several pharmaceutical companies began offering them contracts to conduct clinical trials out of their practice. Because he had worked on studies during his residency,[3] Richard felt that adding pharmaceutical studies to their practice would be a natural progression of his training and clinical experience.

In spite of his preparation, conducting clinical trials was not as easy a source of income as the pharmaceutical companies had promised. In the beginning, before he and his partner had enough experience to know what kind of infrastructure was necessary to make the studies profitable, they debated the wisdom of accepting more studies simply because they were offered. They were not prepared for the amount of management and business skills necessary to run clinical trials compared to their regular practice. After almost two years of persisting, they came to the decision to split the pharmaceutical studies from their practice by forming a separate company (yet still located within the physical space of the practice) with separate staff to manage the business and conduct the studies. This did not prove to be the solution they had been hoping for either, so when several years later, an SMO offered to buy the clinical trials company and hire them as salaried investigators, both physicians jumped at the deal. The transaction meant that they could continue to "be their own bosses" in the private practice and augment their total income with the salaries they were bringing in as "corporate" investigators for the SMO.

Through navigation of different organizational structures, Richard began to see himself as an entrepreneur in medicine. While this identity at first hinged on the economic aspects of conducting pharmaceutical studies, it morphed to include other, often less tangible, benefits. As his experience with studies grew, he said that his participation in clinical trials gave him the opportunity to have firsthand experience with new drugs before they became available on the market. He argued that he could then apply his direct knowledge of the products to treatment decisions for his private-practice patients rather than relying on the information provided by pharmaceutical companies and their sales force.

Richard's interest in and commitment to clinical trials work was atypical for physicians conducting pharmaceutical studies. While Richard took an incredibly active role in the quotidian operation of the studies he was overseeing, his partner was the epitome of what the industry calls "phantom investigators"; although his partner was quite willing to sign on to trials, he seemed equally unwilling to invest much time in study-related activities. In fact, after their company was acquired by the SMO and both physicians were put on salary, Richard's partner became increasingly absent from the clinic, from seeing both patients in their private practice and subjects for clinical trials.

While his partner is an easy target for criticism due to his lack of active participation in the pharmaceutical studies for which he is responsible, Richard's enthusiasm for conducting clinical trials may not capture the full picture of the work he himself described. He discussed during the interview the incredible constraints placed upon investigators that might encourage physicians to disconnect from the research process. Specifically, physicians have little influence over what types of studies are done, what questions are asked, what procedures are required, and which patients can qualify for clinical trials. At the same time, in spite of the limits to their authority as investigators, physicians are contractually obligated not only to the pharmaceutical companies hiring them but also to the FDA to complete the study protocols as written. Another problem for physicians conducting clinical trials is that they experience an acute conflict between research and care by occupying dual roles of investigators and health care providers. The conflict can be particularly intense for private-practice physicians because they are expected to recruit their own patients for the drug studies. These constraints do not justify physicians' low levels of involvement in clinical trials, but acknowledging them reveals some drawbacks of this mode of clinical entrepreneurialism.

Richard's story highlights several themes that cut across the diverse experiences of many physicians in similar situations: their motivation to conduct pharmaceutical studies, the organizational forms that participation takes, and the constraints that are part of contract research. Unfortunately, what makes Richard unique in the clinical trials industry may be his very active engagement in the studies he conducts. Data indicate that his partner is more likely the norm.[4] However, Richard's story shares with those of many investigators a specific process of identity construction that accompanies physicians' participation in pharmaceutical clinical trials.

Physicians play dual roles in the clinical trials industry as contract researchers for pharmaceutical companies. First, physician-investigators actively construct an identity for themselves, an identity I call *entrepreneurial agent*: physicians must be entrepreneurial to establish successful research businesses and navigate through the competition that has arisen in the industry. At the same time, however, they experience a second role imposed as part of structural constraints that prescribe *how* they conduct drug research and interact with subjects. Cast in the role of *pharmaceutical emissaries,* physicians relinquish their authority over health care decisions so that they often become inadvertent advocates of pharmaceutical products, both those under investigation and other marketed products of the companies for whom they are working.

What conditions within U.S. health care lead physicians to forge relationships with pharmaceutical companies as contract researchers? Economic factors are clearly significant, but so are physicians' experiences of diminishing autonomy and status due to changes in the delivery of health care over the past three decades. While these motivations explain why physicians decide to conduct pharmaceutical studies, they also become critical elements to how physicians see themselves and their role within health care and pharmaceutical drug development. But the gains that physicians can experience from contract research come with a price: they must navigate the tension between their dual roles of entrepreneurial agents and pharmaceutical emissaries.

The Political Economies of Medical Practice and Contract Research

The practice of medicine has changed dramatically over the last three decades. The escalation of the cost of medical care in the latter half of the twentieth century led to the perception that U.S. health care was in "crisis" in the 1970s.[5] While there is some debate about the degree to which the nation's health care expenditure at that time was actually a threat to the overall economy, the rhetorical frame of a crisis allowed conservatives to usher in neoliberal economic policies to reform how federal funds could be spent on health care and who had authority over health care delivery.[6] Because physicians and a fee-for-service payment system were perceived as the sources of the rising cost of health care, much of the regulation in the public provision of care—and subsequently in the structure of private-sector "managed" care—aimed to reduce physicians' autonomy in making decisions about individual patients' care.[7]

Physicians were said to be guilty of excesses in health care spending before the reforms of the 1970s and 1980s because it was in their economic interest to prescribe tests and procedures of dubious necessity.[8] According to this view, physicians enthusiastically embraced the burgeoning number of new diagnostic tools and medical technologies not because they significantly improved most patients' care but because they increased the cost of that care.[9] The perception was that physicians had an inherent conflict of interest when making decisions about their patients' care and that third parties would be able to make better decisions about what type of medical care and treatments were necessary for patients.[10] Thus, the solution to the rising cost of health care was to set limits on physicians' professional autonomy.

Managed care profoundly changed the nature of medical practice in the United States.[11] Whether physicians really could not regulate themselves became moot under third-party-provider systems that determined the conditions under which patients could receive access to specialists, tests, and procedures. Physicians increasingly found themselves in the role of gatekeepers, rather than providers, of medical care.[12] In addition to undercutting physicians' authority in health care delivery, the public's trust in physicians declined as patients were allotted less time with their physicians and began to question whether or not they were receiving adequate treatment for their conditions.[13]

In addition to challenging the nature of the doctor-patient relationship, managed care is said to have diminished physicians' incomes, increased practice overhead costs and malpractice liability premiums, and altered the size and scope of private practices.[14] The extent to which physicians' income has actually declined is subject to debate. According to the Center for Studying Health System Change (HSC), a policy research organization that collects data on the health care delivery system, physicians' net income was reduced by 7 percent over the period from 1995 to 2003 after adjusting for inflation.[15] Although physicians' income has indeed declined, they continue to be some of the highest paid professionals. The HSC, for instance, reports that the average physician net income in 2003 was $203,000.[16] Physicians' frustration, however, may have less to do with their income not keeping up with inflation than with cuts made to their reimbursement rates for services. Specifically, the fees paid by private insurance companies, Medicare, and Medicaid have declined in real terms while the labor associated with collecting those fees has increased.

In addition to collecting smaller fees, physicians have experienced major increases in the overhead or operating costs of running private practices. In the 1970s, the average U.S. practice had to budget $108,000 for operating expenses.[17] Today, the average practice has to budget $329,395, which generally reflects 50 to 60 percent of total practice revenue.[18] Part of the increased expense is that managed care, Medicare, and Medicaid add significant labor burdens to ensure appropriate reimbursement for any medical services provided. As a result, many physicians have hired office staff dedicated to processing reimbursement requests and handling patients' billing inquiries. In addition to staff salaries, operating costs have risen due to a host of other expenses: rent for office space and utility rates have increased faster than practice revenue; the demands for medical equipment purchasing are high because physicians want—and many patients expect—new technologies; and offices must comply with unfunded federal mandates, such as privacy rules resulting from the Health Insurance Portability and Accountability Act (HIPAA).[19]

Another considerable portion of operating costs is allotted to malpractice liability premiums. Given the litigious culture of the United States, malpractice is not seen as a risk but as a threat, and liability insurance providers charge accordingly. During the 1990s, increases in malpractice premiums were said to have reached a "crisis" point that would force physicians out of private practice or, in some cases, out of states with higher liability ratings.[20] In light of media attention to the strain of malpractice insurance on physicians, Congress introduced more than two dozen bills to address the problem, proposing solutions from tort reform to tax credit for insurance premiums.[21] Although these premiums are high, a recent study reports that physicians, the American Medical Association, and the media have exaggerated the increases relative to physicians' total practice expenses: for example, insurance premiums accounted for 6 percent of total office expenses in 1970, 11 percent in 1986, and only 7 percent in 2000.[22] In other words, malpractice insurance premiums have indeed gone up, but relative to all the other operating expenses associated with running medical practices, this expense remains in similar proportion to practice budgets in 1970. Whether or not malpractice liability is currently a "crisis," total operating costs absorb much of the revenue earned by practices, resulting in physicians being paid less for their time.

Costs are not the only changes to medical practice since the 1970s. Physicians have altered the scale and scope of their practices. Specifically, as a response to the increasing costs of running private practices and the constraints of third-party-payment systems, many physicians have moved from their own or small practices to large group practices and specialty clinics.[23] This change is meant to consolidate administrative and overhead costs among more physicians to keep these costs lower per physician. In addition, physicians have created for-profit ventures by starting their own ancillary services, including laboratories, imaging units, and ambulatory surgical centers to which they refer their patients.[24] These companies capture business that would often otherwise go to hospitals or other larger-scale entities.

By responding to the financial constraints of the current health care system, physicians can be seen as entrepreneurs in reshaping and revaluing medicine through business decisions rather than attention to patient care.[25] Examples of new services that physicians offer to patients include cosmetic surgery, Botox® treatments, acupuncture, nutraceuticals and other nutritional supplements, and elite "concierge" or "boutique" care.[26] These services are often criticized within medicine because they cater to affluent clientele and the therapeutic value of many of these products is unknown.[27] While there is little data and much anecdotal evidence to indicate the extent to which physicians offer these services to patients, one study showed that the physicians who were most likely to embrace these types of entrepreneurial activities were those practicing in U.S. markets that experienced the greatest decline in income at the end of the 1990s (that is, Indianapolis, Syracuse, and Phoenix).[28]

Clinical trials provide one more alternative source of income for physicians. The pharmaceutical industry began seeking to outsource studies to community physicians rather than to academic researchers beginning in the early 1990s, and private-practice physicians have proven receptive to the business relationship.[29] In less than one decade, from 1990 to 1997, the number of private-sector physicians involved in pharmaceutical studies tripled from less than 4,000 to nearly 12,000.[30] Although there are no current data on the actual number of physicians participating in clinical trials, estimates can be made from other sources. For example, the number of total investigators conducting at least one study rose from 14,100 in 1996 to 50,000 in 2002.[31] Given that the percentage of studies being conducted in the private sector increased from 50 percent to 80 percent of all studies over roughly the same time period, it would be safe to estimate that at least 35,000 of all physician-investigators are located in the private sector.[32] The number is likely much higher.[33] According to a 2004 Harris survey, 13 percent of practicing physicians are involved in clinical research, and another 33 percent of practicing physicians have conducted pharmaceutical research at some point during their careers.[34]

The amount of compensation that physicians can gain from conducting pharmaceutical studies depends on a host of factors including the complexity, length, and risks of each study. In spite of this variability, part-time physician-investigators—those conducting four or five clinical trials each year—earn an average of $5,500 per subject enrolled, $60,000 per study, and $300,000 in additional income.[35] Full-time dedicated sites earned an average of $1.6 million in revenue in 2000.[36] In other words, there is significant money to be made in clinical trials for physicians seeking to supplement their incomes, particularly when they can work "full-time" simultaneously in both private practice and pharmaceutical research.

The profession of medicine has undergone profound changes since the 1970s. Physicians can no longer earn the wages they desire from simply practicing medicine in their communities. The constraints of managed care, Medicare, and Medicaid as well as escalating practice operating expenses have propelled physicians to look elsewhere for revenue. The political economies of health care in the United States and of pharmaceutical drug development have intersected to make contract research an attractive activity for growing numbers of physicians. While the economic motivations for this activity are an important backdrop for physicians' decisions to conduct clinical trials,

they provide only a partial perspective. More broadly, these financial decisions shape physicians' experiences of clinical trials work as well as their
identities as clinicians and researchers.

Physicians' Identities as Contract Researchers

In many respects, private-practice physicians' attraction to pharmaceutical
contract research can be seen as an attempt to reclaim some autonomy that
has been undermined by the constraints of practicing medicine within a system of managed care. The pursuit of alternative ways to earn income—and
greater income at that—is indicative of the resourcefulness of physicians to
adapt their professional identities from the roles into which they were social-
ized during their medical education and training. This is not to say, however,
that the transformation does not come with its own set of limits. In fact, physicians have far less authority to make individualized decisions regarding
human subjects' treatment and care than they do for patients receiving standard medical care. Within clinical trials, physicians only have the choice to
enroll or not enroll patient-subjects in specific studies.

The professional identities of physicians conducting contract research
can be seen as dual and conflicting. First, physicians actively construct the
identity of what I call an *entrepreneurial agent.* This identity highlights the
business and organizational accomplishments that physicians reap through
their relationships with the pharmaceutical industry. The second identity is
imposed on physicians by the process of conducting clinical trials. This other
identity, what I call the *pharmaceutical emissary,* highlights physicians'
diminished role as healers in exchange for the role of provider of pharmaceutical products. Physicians' two identities as contract researchers can best
be understood within the context of their struggle to gain more professional
autonomy in the current medical landscape.

Entrepreneurial Agents

When asked how and why they become involved in clinical trials, the physicians I interviewed answered in similar ways.[37] They described their entry
into clinical trials as an unexpected part of their careers, but they framed the
new trajectory in terms of a deliberate decision they made about the direction
of their professional lives in response to their diminishing incomes and their
frustration with insurance companies and government programs. Physicians
often turn to contract research as a way of exerting professional autonomy
within a system of health care that limits how they can practice medicine.

Physician informants often told me that the practice of medicine isn't what it used to be. When they described their interest in the clinical trials industry, they explicitly referred to the changes that medicine has undergone in past decades. For example, many physicians told me that they are getting paid less, have a higher risk of malpractice lawsuits, and have less time to treat patients or to educate them about their illnesses. One physician explained,

> As doctors, we're continuously being crunched by Washington and insurance companies. We're paid less and less for the work that we do. In fact, we're paid about 50 percent of what we made twenty years ago. It's pretty, pretty abhorrent. So if you look at any simple graph, the cost of running an office is going up, and revenues are going down. It's not a good trend. So one of the ways that we have to try to offset that is to find an alternative source of revenue; getting into [pharmaceutical contract] research was a way to do that.

Physicians perceive the problem with private-practice revenue stemming from reimbursement for services—from either federal sources like Medicare or private insurance companies—that are becoming simultaneously more restrictive and less lucrative. When physicians look to raise the income in their practices, there are a variety of services they may think about adding to their practices, of which contract research is one. According to a physician who had engaged in many types of additional services,

> With the amount of HMO patients, most physicians *cannot* make money off seeing patients, so they have to find ways with higher profit margins. Most of them offer nutraceuticals. Most of them do facial peels. They do cosmetic Botox® injections. They do all that stuff. So a lot of physicians instead of doing that, instead of hiring an aesthetician to come in as their next provider, they would ask one of the partners to become a clinical researcher.

There are few sources of data, other than anecdotal evidence, about the prevalence of cosmetic procedures and supplement sales, but this doctor's perception was that they are widespread, particularly in the Southwest. As an alternative to increasing physicians' patient loads or catering to wealthy clients who pay medical costs out of pocket, physicians are often attracted to the concept of accepting research contracts from pharmaceutical companies, particularly for studies that have easy protocols and low risk.

While there are many routes to becoming contract researchers, many physicians report that their initial foray into the work is catalyzed by colleagues who are already conducting studies. While this introduction to clinical trials tends to emphasize the profitability of contract research, it also gives physicians a fairly complete picture of what to expect from pursuing this work. For instance, one physician told me that when he was contemplating ways to increase his practice revenue, "A friend of mine . . . called me and said, 'I hear you're looking for something to do,' and kind of introduced me to the field of research. He brought me over to his office, kind of showed me what it was all about, and talked to me about research." Having insider knowledge from other physicians is valuable to new investigators because colleagues can pass on tips about finding and running studies successfully.[38] One physician even told me that his colleague had "given" him a research coordinator to help him get familiar with clinical trials. That physician confessed that he had become successful in research in large measure because of the informal training both his colleague and the coordinator had provided him. Using their own networks of experienced colleagues enables physicians new to pharmaceutical research to learn more quickly the specialized language used in the industry and the process of negotiating complex budgets and contracts.

Another common point of entry into the industry that physicians report is direct contact with companies in the clinical trials industry itself. The pharmaceutical industry as well as ancillary clinical trials companies commonly market drug studies directly to private practices by emphasizing the ease with which drug studies can be incorporated into those practices and the money to be gained from doing so. It is common for SMOs to contact physicians, come to their practice, and invite them to join their organization. As the pitch goes, by working with an SMO, all physicians have to do in order to add clinical trials to their practices is to designate someone in their staff—such as a nurse or technician—as a research coordinator to run the studies. Moreover, they claim that because physicians will be conducting studies only in their therapeutic area of expertise, the basic medical procedures required for data collection will not depart much from regular activities at their practices. SMOs suggest that physicians try a study to see how easy and lucrative contracts with pharmaceutical companies can be.

SMOs and pharmaceutical companies may not be as concerned as physicians' colleagues would be about fully disclosing all of the details of conducting studies. SMOs and pharmaceutical companies grossly misrepresent the amount of work associated with conducting clinical trials.[39] In particular, the amount of staff time that needs to be dedicated to drug studies is frequently underestimated to practices. One coordinator working for an SMO recalled one of these information meetings,

> Our office was approached by a site management organization. . . . They came in, and did a little spiel, said, "Research is lucrative to your practice." . . . [The SMO] said that it only required between six to twelve hours of nurse work a week and that we really didn't even need a full-time person doing it. That was just not true. . . . Actually, we've grown to where I work forty-plus hours a week.

However, from the perspective of the physicians who are interested in becoming investigators, the reality of the workload may not depart that significantly from the sales pitch. Physicians may be surprised by the need to spend more resources on personnel in order to conduct the studies, but their own time spent on the trials can be fully integrated into their practice schedule and few new activities are added to their clinical load.

According to corporate contacts and some seasoned investigators, the secret to being a successful clinical investigator is to learn how to delegate responsibility for clinical trials through effective division of labor. For physicians who want to add clinical trials to their practice but who do not want to cut back on patient care, the ability to delegate most aspects of studies is what makes the work so attractive. An administrator in charge of finding physicians to participate in her SMO explained,

> It's a profitable industry. Doctors want to do the research because it's profitable. They don't want to spend the time to do it, and right now, the way the industry's set up, they can do that. They can hire a nurse and a couple coordinators to essentially run 98 percent of the study for them, make them a lot of money, and they do minimal work.

Having minimal labor required of physicians as part of their participation in clinical trials means that they can either continue seeing the same volume of patients in their private practices (and therefore truly supplement without sacrificing any of that income) or greatly increase the number of studies that they take on at one time. As long as the number of staff corresponds to the demands of the number of studies, investigators can run their clinical trials like a full-fledged business. A physician who continued working full-time in his private practice and who was part of an SMO boasted,

I now am the sole principal investigator heading all these trials. How many trials are we doing? We're doing a lot: forty, fifty trials at a time, not all of them enrolling subjects at one time, but a lot. But I have the infrastructure to do it, and that's the whole key about this. We have the proper number of coordinators, regulatory people, quality assurance people, lab tech, secretary, and an on-site site director to do this.

The message that investigators should delegate the work has become a double-edged sword for the industry. Specifically, the drawback of this delegation for clinical research is that frequently physician-investigators are not really present for the conduct of clinical trials. One study monitor described a typical scenario: "Usually [PIs] will come in on a daily basis, on most days, and they'll sign off on all the things that they need to sign off on, see any patients that they need to see, and they're gone. Usually not more than an hour or two hours at the site." Some coordinators and monitors speculate about what physicians are doing with their time. A running joke they tell is that clinical trials enable physicians to improve their golf games. A coordinator said, "We all need to . . . make sure that the investigator's involved, so that he knows what's going on, even if he's out on the golf course." The industry has dubbed this the problem of contracting with "phantom investigators."[40] Although continuing the message that drug studies do not require significant work from investigators, pharmaceutical companies are now also looking for ways to increase physician-investigators' involvement in studies in minor ways, like requiring more investigator signatures on paperwork. Overall, however, it seems that the industry is more concerned about increasing the number of contracts with private-sector physicians than it is with increasing those investigators' involvement in the studies themselves.

The reasons that physicians have for getting involved with the clinical trials industry are both straightforward and complex. They are straightforward because, as will be no surprise, the physicians I interviewed cited money as the primary motivation. Money too can be why physicians decide *not* to continue conducting studies when the contracts do not prove as profitable as physicians expect. The reasons for physician involvement are also complex because as physicians gain experience as investigators they also describe as motivating factors an increase in professional status and service to their communities. These latter two reasons smack of rationalization rather than motivation, but physicians nonetheless experience them as important benefits of participating in clinical trials.

Conducting clinical trials is remunerative. Physicians are often impressed by the difference in revenue between seeing their patients and seeing subjects in a study. The difference is highlighted for physicians because of the way the financial contracts for studies are negotiated and written. Contracts for studies are awarded on a per procedure basis, so that physicians charge the pharmaceutical companies for each step in the screening process and the study protocol.[41] For instance, contracts designate a specific dollar amount per patient for medical histories taken, physical examinations conducted, informed consents administered, blood drawn, and so on.

The attraction for most physicians is that they can see that for each line item, the pharmaceutical companies are paying at least twice as much (and even up to five times as much) as an insurance company or government agency would for the same services. Each office visit, even for patients who do not end up qualifying for or enrolling in particular studies, generates two to three times the revenue as does seeing patients as part of standard medical visits. This is a significant difference to many physicians, particularly when they are not breaking from routine activities as part of drug studies. On this system of payment, a physician remarked, "So for me, it works out well because this way I don't have to charge anybody anything and I just have the drug companies pay. . . . It's just instead of having the government or the [insurance companies] paying, those pharmaceutical companies are paying."

Although conducting clinical trials is often seen as easy money, obtaining the profits promised by the work is complicated to figure out without guidance. In fact, without any assistance, many physicians do not last long in the industry. To explain high rates of investigator attrition, one physician said, "A lot of what happens is people do a project or two and decide it's too much trouble, it's not worth it, and they get out of it." Although exact rates of physicians not continuing to conduct studies are unknown, they are likely high given the FDA statistic that 63 percent of investigators on clinical trials have one year or less experience as investigators.[42]

Part of the trouble for many physicians is that studies may not prove as profitable as they appeared before overhead costs, especially coordinators' salaries, were figured in. To make matters worse, pharmaceutical companies are notoriously slow at paying physicians for their services, and the burden of paying intermediary companies for laboratory services, imaging, and even shipping generally falls on the investigative site. A site administrator reported:

We get paid by many sponsors [that is, pharmaceutical companies] net 120 days or 360 days. We don't get paid for the work that we do many times until *long* after the work is completed. There's very little up front money paid by sponsors for studies. It puts a significant strain on the industry, particularly smaller groups, especially for the physician who's trying to do the study out of his office and doesn't have the overhead or the available capital. Right now, the profit margins are very, *very* narrow for most studies.

Problems with the payment system are, according to those who have been in the industry over ten years, relatively new. One physician recalled being given one third of the budget up front when he began doing clinical trials over twenty years ago. He emphasized that it was this money that helped him establish the research arm of his practice, enabling him to lease additional office space and hire experienced coordinators to work on the studies. Other established physicians bemoan the fact that they have to take on more studies now to make the same profits that they did a decade ago. A physician articulated the problem in this way, "So clearly what has happened in the last ten years is that the screws are on, the vices are tightening up, the budgets are getting more difficult, and it's harder and harder to do things and financially be able to do it well." The prospect of robust profits attracts a large number of new physicians into the clinical trials industry each year, but due to the difficulty of managing studies and making the promised profits, many do not go on to conduct future studies.

Physicians who do continue to conduct pharmaceutical studies report that they are motivated by the professional prestige or symbolic capital that they believe the work bestows on private-practice physicians. Within their professional organizations, physician-investigators find that they have more status in their areas of specialty than do private-practice physicians who do not conduct clinical trials. The importance physicians attach to professional prestige is especially apparent when they discuss their membership in medical societies and the conferences that they regularly attend. For example, they comment that they experience their change in rank firsthand when attending annual society meetings and other professional events because of the way they are treated by academic physicians. One physician told me,

The [specialty professional society] is made up of mainly academic types. There are few people like me, and largely academic types who are the leaders. To me, part of the nice part of doing this stuff [clinical trials] is I interact with the best people. I enjoy the interaction because

I have some ideas that they haven't thought of, and they have some different ones that I don't know. We get to exchange ideas.

Although they experience an elevation in their professional status, private-
sector physicians still recognize that pharmaceutical studies do not put them
on par with academic physicians.

The additional status, however, seems to be limited to their professional
organizations and interactions with other physicians. As far as the general public is concerned, private-practice physician-investigators are aware that their
patients do not see them as having an elevated status compared to other practicing physicians. Those physicians maintaining a private practice know that
their patients do not see them as being better or smarter for doing clinical trials.
In their view, this is because patients do not sufficiently understand or appreciate the hierarchies and politics associated with medicine as a profession.

Even without recognition from their patients and the lay community, physicians also say they are motivated to conduct clinical trials because of the
service pharmaceutical studies often provide for patients and the community.
The physicians I interviewed who framed their work as a service to the community discussed this in both direct and indirect terms. Several physician-
investigators and their staff stressed the importance of giving out free medical
attention and drug samples to help patients who have limited access to medications, even when those patients do not want to participate in a research study.
They can do this because the pharmaceutical companies will pay for potential
subjects to be screened for studies, and physicians can then give away any free
samples they have received from drug reps. A physician explained the direct
benefit clinical trials have for the community in which he practices:

> What we do here is I can give out free blood pressure, diabetes, and
> lipid medication as well as free blood pressure, diabetes, and lipid *care*
> to the community in between research studies. . . . A lot of my patients
> come from a lower socioeconomic background, and so it's very nice
> because I sort of had the ideal when I went into medicine that I wanted
> to do that, but somehow you get taken away from that as years go by,
> and you have to make a buck to support a family.

Many physicians feel that clinical trials provide a tremendous opportunity for people in the community who do not have health insurance or do
not have adequate coverage. A pediatrician who had given up her practice
to do clinical trials full-time told me, "I thought it was a good opportunity

for kids who had no insurance to participate and get good health care and medications for free." Given the crisis of health care coverage in the United States, many physician-investigators feel proud that they can offer assistance to people who would not see a physician without the pharmaceutical studies. It is important to note, however, that the physicians above said "medication" not "experimental drugs" when discussing the service they provide to the community by offering clinical trials. Like many other physicians and others in the clinical trials industry, when highlighting the benefits of clinical trials to disenfranchised patient-subjects, the research element drops out. They never mention that a percentage of patient-subjects receive placebos and that physicians cannot dictate—or often know—which subjects receive them.

In addition to services that investigators can render to patient-subjects who would otherwise not get any medical attention, some physicians argue that the quality of the care they provide is better in clinical trials than it is in their private practices. Whether it is the physicians themselves or their coordinators, the interaction with patients is much lengthier in the context of clinical trials than it is in standard medical care. One physician who had recently transitioned out of private practice to conducting studies full time explained the mutual benefit of a clinical trials setting for patients and himself:

> The patient contact is different [in contract research], and it's on a smaller scale. It's more intense, and it gives me my chance to teach again, which I enjoyed and [it] worked great for the first three or four years of private practice. But the last five or six years when I was seeing 3,000 patients in a practice? You can't teach; you can prescribe and diagnose and try and not make a mistake, but you really can't teach. . . . What *I* get that their [personal] physicians don't get is I get an hour with them to talk. I get to teach them about diabetes and draw them diagrams. I get to explain why they have IBS [irritable bowel syndrome] that someone else told them they had and what that means.

Of course, not all physician-investigators are equally involved in the research enterprise, but they—or site administrators—still often set an educational agenda for the investigational site. For example, one physician emphasized the role of coordinators in improving the quality of interactions:

> People [subjects] recognize that there is that benefit to doing studies with us, you know. My [coordinators] do a lot of psychosocial interactions with people. We're staffed so that people can drop in if they need to talk, and so we do a lot of counseling and handholding. My

coordinators even help people move, a lot of things that are kind of side benefits [to the subjects] from being here.

The increase in status and the service to the community that clinical trials can provide extend physicians' sense of entrepreneurialism beyond the important monetary success they can gain through contract research. In fact, the combination of their motivations to be involved in drug research contributes to the formation of a new professional identity.

Not all physicians are cut out to be contract researchers even if they are all technically qualified to assume the role. Physicians who have been successful in the transition to investigators share an identity in which they emphasize their control and dominance over the practice of medicine and the clinical trials industry. Through the construction of this identity, they frame themselves as physicians who autonomously forge their own way into a new specialty of medicine and in so doing establish the meaning and purview of the role of "principal investigators" in the private sector. This identity, what I call "entrepreneurial agent," is particularly marked in those physicians who retire from private practice in order to conduct pharmaceutical studies full time.

Private-sector physician-investigators struggle in their attempts to define who is qualified to conduct clinical trials. On one hand, they feel that someone with a medical degree is generally overqualified to run drug studies. This perception is cultivated by the competence that their coordinators display in managing the day-to-day operations of clinical trials. And yet at the same time, most physicians willingly admit that their experiences in private practice did not prepare them to conduct studies. Some indicate that they think of clinical trials as an emergent specialty not taught in medical school:

> There's a lot of business in the industry. And medical training is certainly important because there's, of course, a lot of medicine in there; but that's not enough, it's not sufficient. Clinical trials is a specialty unto itself, both the business of clinical trials as well as the ethics of clinical trials, dealing with IRBs, dealing with pharmaceutical companies, dealing with a whole bunch of things, as well as how to manage a large center. For instance, I have about thirty-five employees here. So there are certainly a lot of things lacking in a medical education that didn't prepare me for that.

For this physician, the information that makes physicians perceive clinical trials as a specialty is the organization and process of drug development, not medical knowledge.

Successful physician-investigators often share a very sophisticated understanding of the clinical trials industry. Their entrepreneurialism is expressed through their ability to navigate through the channels of obtaining business, negotiating contracts, and recruiting subjects. They have been able to make their participation in drug studies profitable for themselves, and they have been flexible enough to change their practices as the industry and regulations changed. Perhaps it is not surprising that most of those physician-investigators who really fit the identity of entrepreneurial agent have been in the industry for some time, usually more than ten years. Many of those physicians began conducting clinical trials long before it became common to do so in the private sector, and this early entry helps to explain why entrepreneurialism is central to their identities.

Many experienced investigators acknowledge that they had it much easier when they started doing studies than do those physicians who are trying to break into the industry now. The advantage these early entrants had was that they were able to adapt gradually to the procedures and regulations put in place over the course of that time. One physician spelled out this advantage:

> I mean, there are always new things coming out all the time. That's why I can't understand how a person could get into the field of clinical trials now. *We* can tweak our procedures a little bit when we find out there are new rules and regulations and new laws here and there. We just change things a little bit. But how could someone new *ever, possibly* begin? There are so many procedures and laws it's mind-boggling!

According to established investigators, knowledge of the industry is key to being able to maneuver through it and to get the most from it. These physicians are not surprised when they hear about physicians who decide to try to conduct clinical trials only to find that they cannot make studies work within the context of their practices.

Thus, many private-sector physicians define investigator competency in terms of knowledge and savviness about the clinical trials industry, not of the research process per se. For physicians who embody the role of entrepreneurial agent, the expertise that private-sector physicians offer to the pharmaceutical industry is their ability to execute studies. Although they are quick to acknowledge that academic physicians have more professional prestige than they do, private-sector physicians have developed keen criticisms of their academic counterparts, seeing themselves as better skilled, better paid, and better equipped to make a contribution to their communities. For example, one physician asserted,

> What do we bring that the academic medical centers don't? We bring a
> *techne*—it's an old Greek work—as opposed to a science. Pharmaceuti-
> cal companies can hire the scientists, but at some point the end has to
> be executed, so that's what we bring to the table: our capability, inter-
> est and motivation, drive. Because that's it for most of us (not all but
> most of us) in the private sector, it is a priority for us to succeed, fun or
> not. . . . So I think at this point, what [we] offer is an execution.

To some extent, physician-investigators' opinions about academic medical centers reflect the pharmaceutical industry's perspective. Physician-investigators in the private sector are seen as bringing speed to drug development. Some of the physicians I interviewed claimed that if it were not for academic physicians' prestige, the private-sector investigators would have made them obsolete. As one physician articulated,

> The academic centers still do these studies, but they usually do them
> miserably slow. And the only reason they're brought on is for the inves-
> tigator's name, so the great academician has his name on the study.
> When it goes to press, he can have his name on there to give the study
> some legitimacy and authority. And it's okay, but in fact, a lot of these
> people in many cases are not directly involved in the research, and a
> lot of times, they don't recruit but one or two people into the study.

Generally speaking, pharmaceutical studies can move at a faster pace in the private sector because those investigators are not at the mercy of slow-moving university IRBs. Moreover, private-sector physicians already have the patient population from which to recruit whereas academic medical centers generally must wait until potential human subjects contact them. As one private-sector physician stated, "We're better, we're closer to the patients. That's why academic medical centers in general are failures at clinical research, and that's why sponsors [pharmaceutical companies] come looking for guys like me because they can't get what they want at academic medical centers."[43]

There is an explicit distinction here that, unlike academic physicians, private-sector physicians are not scientists. From their perspective, conducting pharmaceutical contract research requires clinical skills, not scientific knowledge. As one physician explained,

I do not do original research; I do *contract* research. I read the neurology literature; I do not read the psychiatry literature; I don't read the obesity literature. You know for certain things, I'm pretty smart. And in other things, I don't even pretend that I'm smart about those. But I'm *very* good at running clinical trials, so in a sense. . . . I'm a highly *skilled practitioner* of clinical trials who has an appreciation for the science, plus the scientific need, plus the fact that they rely on the data that we give them to be scientifically valid because there are lives at stake in that data. But I'm *not* a scientist.

In comparison, private-sector physicians think of academic physicians as scientists because they pursue "original" research through grants from federal agencies.[44]

Because the identity of contract researchers is not constructed in relation to science, private-sector physician-investigators are all the more quick to embrace the entrepreneurial and business aspects of their professional positions. This manifests in their choices about which continuing medical education (CME) courses to take. In particular, physicians told me that they increasingly tend to eschew courses on medical practice and pharmaceutical science and instead seek out courses about the business aspects of medicine. As a physician explained,

I go religiously to the [annual meeting] strictly for business development purposes . . . That doesn't mean that I don't like and appreciate the science. . . . I try to understand the direction each pharmaceutical company goes when they're using this compound in this indication, which is targeting blah blah blah whatever it is.

Private-sector physician-investigators' focus on business courses at medical meetings also distinguishes them from their academic counterparts, who (my interviewees claim) are rarely in attendance at the same CME courses.

Physicians who have the identity of entrepreneurial agent make judgments about who is competent to run studies, what counts as expertise in contract research, and what specific skills private-sector physicians have that academic physicians do not. Thus, the entrepreneurial identity is not simply about making money off of clinical trials; rather, these physician-investigators see themselves as forging the field of private-sector, for-profit drug research, and setting the standards to which other physicians will—or at least, should—be held. This identity, however, is in tension with another one that accompanies the constraints of contract research.

Pharmaceutical Emissaries

When celebrating their successes in the clinical trials industry, many physician-investigators are loath to admit the structural constraints of pharmaceutical drug development that limit their autonomy as entrepreneurial agents. Nonetheless, investigators are very much constrained in conducting clinical trials by the types of studies available, the details of the protocols, and the eligibility criteria for patients to participate. At the same time that physicians have few mechanisms for input into the types of clinical trials that can be done, they must accept full responsibility for the studies not only with the pharmaceutical companies paying them but also with the FDA. By becoming contract researchers, physicians' power and authority become subordinated to the pharmaceutical industry through the role of "pharmaceutical emissaries," or providers of pharmaceutical products instead of health care.

Pharmaceutical companies offer clinical trials to physicians without negotiation on the specific details of the studies. One physician described the process of evaluating a study offered:

> In general, no, the investigators don't have that much input into the protocol design. So the idea is that when you're signing this [contract] you really agree that you will participate in this project, given your understanding of what the protocol design is. [Agreeing to the study means that] it's okay as far as you're concerned: it's ethical, it's safe, it's not too dangerous, and this kind of thing.

Physicians' choices, therefore, are to take it or leave it; the pharmaceutical companies supply the details of a study and give physicians a few days, or sometimes only a few hours, to decide whether they are interested. One physician offered an example of a typical conversation with pharmaceutical companies: "[The companies] just say, 'Here's a project, do you want it or not? I mean, let me know by Monday because I've got to move on.'" The only details that are negotiable are those related to the contract itself, most often focusing on the budget.

The lack of investigators' input into the design of studies or even the types of studies that can be conducted reveals the nature of the arrangement the pharmaceutical industry is seeking with private-sector physicians.[45] Drug companies are not looking for scientists to conduct their clinical trials; they are looking for practitioners to execute them. In the context of this relationship between the pharmaceutical industry and investigators, private-sector physicians' identity as practitioners then can be seen to serve as a justification for their limited authority over study protocols.

The degree to which physician-investigators have insights into the science of clinical trials structures the operation of power in their relationship with the pharmaceutical industry. When physicians claim no understanding of protocol design or the mechanism by which an investigational drug works, they must trust that the pharmaceutical companies with which they are working are making scientifically sound and ethical decisions in their research and development. In my sample of physicians, every investigator declared that he or she did not understand the science behind clinical trials and, therefore, could claim little insight into the products under investigation. For instance, one physician explained,

> You know, we really don't have a lot of leeway in the scientific department. I mean if somebody says we have this really great drug that works for blood pressure, I have no idea how this damn thing works! But I'm still going to go down the hall and do physicals and check blood pressures and sign off adverse events and stuff like that. . . . I have no idea about science! Whether that's good or bad or indifferent. That's why we're doing the research, and I figure someone's putting several million dollars, or $20 million into doing this study, so they must believe in what they're doing.

In this physician's case, because he could not judge the safety of investigational drugs and the protocols themselves, he placed his trust in the pharmaceutical industry based on the amount of money they invest in the products. From his perspective, the investment needed for drug development alone ensures that pharmaceutical companies create trustworthy products and safe clinical protocols.

In spite of physicians' trust that the clinical trials they are conducting are safe for their patients, many recounted examples of studies that had been stopped because of problems with the experimental drug. The tension between investigators' continuing trust in the pharmaceutical companies and their personal experiences with unsafe clinical trials was a recurring motif in my interviews. Yet instead of these examples making them question the science or safety of clinical trials, many physician-investigators felt that these cases were the exceptions that proved that studies are ultimately safe for patient-subjects. Because pharmaceutical companies were quick to respond to problems (even if their response served primarily to protect their investments), physicians assumed that any future problems would be dealt with swiftly. The following is a physician's description of one such failed drug study:

> Part of the preclinical studies are the long-term toxicity studies [on animals] and when you get the results of those, *then* you move into human studies: phase I, phase II, phase III, and then you get FDA approval. Well, *now* they start the human studies *before* they get the results of the long-term tox studies. So we just had a big study, actually we had *nine* studies going on because we had been doing a lot of work for this one company, where all of a sudden, they had long-term tox studies that showed the drug was bad. It caused tumors in mice. So as soon as they found out, they stopped development, but of course, we were well on the way, we had a *huge* number of patients involved. . . . They really try to get [their products] quickly to market, but boy are they quick to respond [when findings are negative]!

Even physician-investigators working primarily on phase I, first-in-human trials argue that their studies are designed so tightly and are so routine in their protocols that problems with investigational drugs will be caught very quickly and human subjects will be well safeguarded.

Physicians' trust in pharmaceutical companies and their clinical trials permeates into their view of safety and risk to patients. In those cases in which physicians do feel that clinical trials are unsafe, they argue it is then their *own* responsibility to decline those studies. Experiencing it as a conflict between the interests of their relationship with their patients and their relationship with pharmaceutical companies, the decision to accept or reject a study is premised on a personal decision. Physicians justify their decisions to decline conducting particular clinical trials in terms of their own tolerance for risk. If studies seem like they might be too much risk for their patients, physicians then decide *as individuals* not to conduct those studies. For instance, one physician explained,

> My concern as an investigator is, is it safe for the patient? If it's not safe or if I don't like the fact that they're going to put an actively psychotic schizophrenic patient on a placebo, then I'm just not going to do it, or a seizure patient on an inadequate dose of the medication. Sorry, I've got plenty of other business down here without having to lose sleep at night.

The issue of whether it is good *science* to put those patient-subjects on placebos or inadequate medications is not debated; it becomes simply a matter
of physicians' personal "comfort" with the studies. In other words, the overall appropriateness of particular clinical trials is never addressed because
physician-investigators do not critique the "science" behind drug studies.

The norm then in private-sector clinical trials is that physicians individually weigh whether or not they would like to accept a contract for particular
studies. They are asked to read through the study protocol—after signing a
confidentiality and nondisclosure agreement from the pharmaceutical company—and come to a decision about whether they would like to negotiate a
contract. Thus, the pharmaceutical industry strips away some of physicians'
autonomy and professional authority by reducing clinical trial participation
to a simple take-it-or-leave-it decision.

Not only is physicians' clinical decision-making authority diminished
as contract researchers, but their responsibility or liability is increased.
This dynamic is another component of the structural constraints imposed
on physician-investigators. An interesting aspect of the liability associated
with conducting pharmaceutical studies is that physicians often see it as a
trade-off wherein they exchange one type of clinical liability (malpractice
risk) for another (federal oversight). By engaging in contract research, physicians accept professional responsibilities to the FDA as part of the federal
regulation of drug development.

In contrast to medical malpractice liability with private practice, physician-investigators are indemnified by the pharmaceutical companies that hire
them.[46] As long as physicians follow the study protocols, the risk of malpractice is passed on to the pharmaceutical company.[47] The reason for this shift in
liability is clear: physicians' role in contract research has little clinical ambiguity because any decisions regarding human subjects' participation are set
by the pharmaceutical companies, not the physicians conducting the studies.
Unlike with patient care, physicians rely on the study protocols to define the
exact parameters for which subjects should be included in or excluded from
studies, instructions on how to randomize subjects into the experimental or
placebo arms of the clinical trial, and guidance on when to remove subjects
from studies to minimize potential harm. A physician explained the reduced
liability in contract research and his preference for it:

> [Contract] research . . . is less stressful on the physician in terms of
> most of the time you're not dealing with managing illness. . . . I think
> with *research* our expectations are a lot clearer because as long as we

pay attention to the safety of the participants, informing them of everything we know about that is pertinent to the study that they should
know, following the protocol which has been reviewed by the client
[pharmaceutical company] and an institutional review board. As long
as we focus on those things and we do well, we [physicians] probably
will be okay. Not that we *can't* get sued or have problems with our
medical board, but our expectations are at least clear.

Thus, because clinical trials remove much of the decision making from physicians by providing study protocols that detail precisely what physicians
must do to fulfill their clinical responsibility to subjects, many physicians
find that conducting studies affords them protection from malpractice suits.[48]
The responsibility—and therefore liability—for decision making in contract
research rests with pharmaceutical companies. One physician saw this as an
important reason to begin conducting clinical trials:

Some people may find that with today's medical climate . . . [with] a
high potency and vigilance of legal issues like lawsuits—they may find
that research can help them think less about those kinds of worries
that all physicians have to think about every day. Until the climate
improves for the *practice* of medicine, those kinds of people may find
a haven in research.

Reduced malpractice liability is very attractive to many physicians, but
what new liabilities do they assume in exchange? As physician-investigators'
liability in regards to human subjects is diminished, their liability to the
FDA is increased. All investigators—regardless of the sector in which they
work—are required to submit to the FDA a 1572 form, which is technically a
contract. The explicit purpose of the form is (1) to provide proof to the FDA
that the investigators contracted by the pharmaceutical companies are qualified to do clinical research (as proven by investigators' curriculum vitae) and
(2) to obtain a formal commitment from investigators to conduct clinical trials according to the protocols designed by pharmaceutical companies and
approved by the FDA.

Admittedly, on one level the 1572 form sounds banal in its bureaucratic
purpose; however, in practice, physicians' commitment to the FDA as codified by the form places the full responsibility of conducting clinical trials
on the investigators. This commitment feels ominous to many private-sector
physician-investigators because it means that investigators are obliged to conduct the studies according to protocols even if the pharmaceutical companies

fail to meet *their* part of the contract. Moreover, any deviation from study protocols or from federal regulation is, according to the 1572 agreement, the ultimate responsibility of the physician-investigators, regardless of who makes the error within the organization. One physician in particular whom I interviewed had strong opinions about the responsibilities engendered by the 1572 form. Because the SMO in which he worked went through a very rough period, he worried what the implications would be for him if the SMO failed and he was unable to complete the studies. He stressed the precariousness of his situation to me at length:

> [I am] promising to the FDA, the *Food and Drug Administration*, that I will perform that protocol according to the rules of the protocol and will not deviate from those rules, and that it is *my* responsibility. . . . If [SMO] goes under, *when [SMO] was going to go under,* there was a huge question: what happens to the studies, what happens to the subjects, whose responsibility is it? Who's going to get the work done according to the windows set by a protocol? You have to see a subject at this point in time one or two days; you have to get this measurement done; you have to get that test done, etc. Who's going to do that? And who's responsible for it? Who's going to *pay* for it? etc., etc. Well, the 1572 makes it very clear, you know, the *investigator* does. So that liability is fairly ominous. And particularly if you're in a situation where there's a potential for your structure where you're doing these protocols to dissolve or fall apart, it creates for some sleepless nights.

In short, through a neoliberal policy, the FDA removes from pharmaceutical companies the liability for executing clinical drug protocols and places it on the individual physicians who agree to be investigators on a study. Thus, the pharmaceutical industry can delegate some of the risks of drug development to investigators even though the profits gained from the clinical development of their products are not similarly shared with investigators.[49]

The sense of threat that many physician-investigators describe from their contract with the FDA may not be far-fetched. The number of complaints to the FDA against investigators has significantly increased from around fifteen per year before 1998 to consistently over a hundred each year since 1999 and peaking at nearly two hundred in 2003.[50] Complaints against investigators are largely anonymous (about 35 percent), but known complaints come from pharmaceutical companies (about 20 percent), employees at the investigative sites such as coordinators (30 percent), and IRBs (12 percent).[51] In response to complaints, the FDA completes inspections of study sites and of investigators.[52] FDA audits have three goals: to ensure (1) the site is compliant with all federal regulation and guidelines, (2) the data produced from studies is valid, and (3) the rights of human subjects have been protected by the investigators and sites.

More than 60 percent of FDA audits result in some action against the investigator.[53] The consequences to physician-investigators of an FDA action depend on the severity of the offense.[54] The most common action by the FDA is to require sites to change their practices and prove compliance. Other consequences include the elimination of the all data produced by the investigator, disqualification or restriction from conducting future studies, and in rare cases fines and imprisonment.[55] There is liability associated with investigators' relationship with the FDA, but provided that physicians follow the study protocol and federal regulation, they are not at risk of official action.

Many physicians are bothered by their liability to the FDA because they feel that the regulatory environment is out of synch with actual investigative site practices. The clinical trials industry is predicated on delegation of responsibility from the pharmaceutical companies to CROs to physicians to coordinators. A physician said,

> When you think about it, that's an amazing amount of responsibility in a situation where the reality is—*and everybody knows the reality*—that there are numerous people and even in the smallest of practices one or two people, you know a nurse and/or secretary, who will have some delegation of authority and responsibilities for helping to get that protocol done. . . . But the contract is between the *investigator* and the FDA.

As a result, investigators feel that they are being unfairly targeted by the FDA. A physician declared,

> When [the FDA] jumps on you, you feel so hassled. You really do, you feel so put upon. And the [pharmaceutical] companies are doing things, such stupid things, "Well, we're worried about the FDA coming in and inspecting us, so we want you to do it thus and such a way, we want you to do this thus and such a way." You know, everybody's so afraid of the FDA, FDA, FDA! . . . The industry's so regulated, so much more legal. I mean you can't blow your nose without some lawyer jumping up somewhere and getting involved. It's really, really something.

In sum, physician-investigators are exchanging the risk and liability normally associated with their private practices for the risk and liability that are structured into the clinical trials industry through the FDA 1572 form. Yet it is not a simple exchange for most physicians. The shift in liability also represents to physicians that their responsibility is no longer explicitly toward their patients but to the pharmaceutical companies and the FDA. This is a change that becomes especially difficult for them to reconcile within the researcher-subject relationship.

Although many physicians have been able to integrate drug studies easily into their practices, clinical trials are at root a very different form of medicine than standard medical care. This creates both a role and ethical conflict for many physicians because they must not think about patient-subjects in terms of the administration of individualized care but in terms of whether a patient should be enrolled in a study.[56] In fact, a desire for sameness between research and care or the failure of investigators to see differences between the two modes of interaction often make physicians very poor investigators. In an attempt to explicate why this happens, the CEO of a community-based SMO that recruits local physicians to take part in clinical trials framed what she has observed as the problem that physicians may experience in the role of investigator:

> In their clinical practice, they treat patients. They take an illness, diagnose it, and attempt to make it better. In clinical research, that is *not* our primary objective. We take somebody who has a diagnosis, and we put them in a clinical study, and we watch them as our primary goal. We collect data about how well a possible treatment is working, but we also have patients that are on placebo. So our *primary* objective in clinical research is to *safeguard* the patients while collecting data.

The administrator remarked that many physicians feel conflicted that the clinical goal vis-à-vis their patients shifts from treating illness to collecting data on whether specific products eliminate, alleviate, or even exacerbate their symptoms. She continued,

> Many physicians just can't jump out of the clinical arena. There may be times when a patient may be on a clinical study, and you can see that they're probably not improving, and you may guess that they're on placebo or that they're having a side effect from the medication. In a clinical practice, you might discontinue them and switch them to something else. If your objective was to continue to see how this plays out for a clinical study, you would safeguard the patient's well-being, make sure that they were being cared for, and *continue* them in the study even though their condition was not improving. Sometimes physicians can't

make that switch mentally, and then they're not suited to be involved
in clinical research.

This articulation shows that care can be antithetical to research. When physicians cannot make the mental switch to research, the CEO of this SMO does
not invite those physicians to continue conducting studies for her company.

What is difficult for many physician-investigators is that the focus of the
doctor-patient—or more aptly researcher-subject—interaction in clinical trials
centers around a pharmaceutical product. As such, investigators are required
to limit their involvement with patients to a specific illness and even more
specific treatment. Investigators must not be overly concerned with the *general*
health of their patient-subjects. Instead they must think of their relationship
with patient-subjects in terms of a temporary and narrowly focused involvement. The physician who earlier in this chapter described himself in the role
of investigator as a teacher rather than a provider of health care explained his
view on this interaction: "I have studies that [may] go three years, but I don't
have a *lifelong* involvement. I don't have a *whole* body involvement. . . . So my
scope of interest in their lives is very narrowed, much more so than a private
care physician." Although this may seem to contradict his earlier point that
physicians have the time to educate patient-subjects about their illnesses, the
parameters of the interaction are nonetheless confined by the study protocols.

An important restriction on physician-investigators' relationship with
subjects is that they cannot make suggestions about alternative treatments or
lifestyle modifications to patient-subjects unless physicians recommend that
patient-subjects withdraw from studies. By making other recommendations,
physicians would risk leading subjects to deviate from the protocols. For example, two types of drug studies that are extremely prevalent are for obesity and
irritable bowel syndrome (IBS). Both of these conditions can be significantly
improved by making changes to diet and exercise. Physician-investigators,
however, cannot counsel study subjects to make these lifestyle changes unless
they are explicitly included in clinical trial protocols. Pharmaceutical companies are generally seeking data on the effectiveness of their product compared
with a placebo in the *absence* of lifestyle changes. By advocating for behavior
modification, physicians could put the results of the trial at risk (particularly
for the results of subjects on placebo). Thus, investigators must focus on the
pharmaceutical product regardless of their own personal beliefs about effective (holistic) treatments for illnesses.

Not only are physician-investigators constrained in *how* they interact
with subjects, they are also often faced with ethical dilemmas regarding the

recruitment of subjects, particularly their own patients. Most physicians see
that there is the potential for unintentional coercion—or more subtle "seduc-
tion"—embedded in the process of recruiting directly out of their own patient
population. One physician explained,

> The relationship between a physician and a patient should not be
> coercive. That's the number one problem [in private-sector clinical
> trials], that a patient's going to be coerced. It isn't going to be coer-
> cive off of some ad you run in the paper. It's going to be *your* doctor
> saying, "Jill, this is a great study for you because you happen to have
> that [illness]." What is likely is that you will worry about saying no
> to him: "I don't know what to do! Will he see me anymore if I don't
> do the study?"

The conflict between research and care within a private practice is intensified because there is a risk that physician-investigators will be unduly influenced by the financial conflict of interest from their study contracts with
pharmaceutical companies and will make poor clinical decisions about their
own patients. These problems are aggravated, many physicians claim, by the
strict timelines that pharmaceutical companies give for enrollment. One physician offered an example that he felt was typical of the conflict private-practice
physician-investigators face daily:

> The problem is the sponsor's timelines. It's great as long as that quota
> of seventeen patients has no expectations on *when* I need to get them.
> In that case, well sure, whenever they come through [the clinic], that
> perfect patient, I'll be happy to enroll them. But if you ask me to find
> them faster than they come through, then I have to *create* them. And
> I have to make a treatment decision based on what [study] I know is
> coming up. For example, if I've got a naïve diabetic protocol[57] coming
> up. You're seeing me on Thursday, and I know the site initiation visit is
> next week [to commence the study]. Do I delay starting your treatment
> because I got a protocol for a naïve diabetic coming up? ... I think
> once you take an aggressive timeline from the sponsor, and you *make*
> the physician fulfill it, you're asking for issues. You're asking for those
> gray areas of patient consent process: coercion of patients drawing off
> their physician-patient relationship to fill a study.

The risk that the physician identified about recruitment becomes an ethical critique of the logic behind the relocation of clinical trials to the private sector.

The physicians I interviewed understand that pharmaceutical companies want to work with them because of their patient populations, but many physicians prefer to recruit subjects through media campaigns, such as print and radio advertisements. For these physicians, the risk of coercion is eliminated when recruiting from the general population rather than from their own patient populations and, thus, the ethical dilemma disappears. One physician declared, "If you're driving them in with a radio ad, then there's no [ethical] issues, but if you're not, then there's issues." This particular investigator was unique among physicians I interviewed because he had retired from his practice to conduct studies and took the stance that subjects should *only* be recruited externally through advertisements and databases. He told me that he wanted to see recruitment become the obligation of the pharmaceutical companies themselves:

> I would love to see the industry go toward the sponsor taking all responsibility for recruitment. I think it's *their* job to find enough patients to screen wherever their sites are and whatever they have to spend on database drops and radio advertising and television commercials to find those patients. They should bear that burden, and they should ask us just to investigate and be available to see the patients when they send them in. Not to actually find them.

Although this physician's view of recruitment was extreme compared to other investigators, it articulates a well-recognized problem in the clinical trials industry. The dilemma for most physicians is not perceiving of their patients as research subjects but making ethical choices within the context of a clinical trials business, a business that makes revenue based on patient-subject enrollment. In order to make clinical trials profitable, physician-investigators need to enroll and retain patient-subjects. Physicians who are employed as investigators by SMOs and CROs particularly experience pressure from administrators to quickly meet the enrollment quotas in their contracts. This pressure induces physicians to experience the "ethics" of conducting drug studies more profoundly. A full-time physician-investigator working for a CRO complained,

> Obviously, there's an ethical standard that the physicians will be following, but of course, everyone knows, there's *shades* of pressure around your proper ethical behavior which may be trying to push or negotiate certain decisions that the physician is making or certain opinions that they're forming, to comply or go along better with others who are pressuring him/her.

Thus, the subtle—and perhaps at times, not so subtle—pressures regarding recruiting subjects can present ethical dilemmas rooted in the conflict between research and care.

The constraints associated with drug studies conflict with the identities physicians actively construct about themselves as entrepreneurial agents. By conducting pharmaceutical studies, physicians are seeking more professional autonomy in the health care delivery system, but they relinquish much of their professional authority when they agree to conduct studies. Rather than expanding the scope of care that physicians can offer to patients, physicians are reduced to executers of research protocols and providers of investigational pharmaceutical products.

In the role of what can be thought of as pharmaceutical emissaries, investigators are dispatched on behalf of the pharmaceutical companies to represent and advance the industry's specific interests rather than the interests of patients. Physicians in their duties as investigators no longer have the goal of curing or ameliorating individual patients' diseases; their goal is to ensure the safety of human subjects during the testing of new pharmaceutical products. Through their association with the pharmaceutical industry, physician-investigators come to represent the types of products that they are testing and therefore communicate to patients a strictly pharmaceutical answer to the problem of illness.

Although physicians might appreciate the service that clinical trials perform for underserved populations who have limited access to medicine, they are also cognizant of the blockbuster-seeking mentality that propels the pharmaceutical industry in its R&D. What this means to physicians is that the companies for whom they are working are developing largely "me too" drugs that are designed to capture market share rather than revolutionize medicine. In reflecting on the types of clinical trials he had conducted for various pharmaceutical companies, one physician remarked,

> During the nineties, we did lots of research on osteo anti-inflammatory drugs; we did research on all of these COX-2 selective ones: Vioxx®, Celebrex®, Bextra®. And I'm still doing work on ones that are going to get marketed at some point in time. None of them—the new ones—are more efficacious than the others. They're safer on the gut, but they're not safer on the kidney and what have you. But the bottom line on those drugs is that they don't change the disease state, so the whole idea of developing new ones is a *marketing* issue; a company wants to get a piece of the market share.

This is not to say that physician-investigators do not believe in the products with which they are working. Quite to the contrary. In fact, most investigators tout the contribution they are making to "medical progress." In general, they believe that pharmaceutical research leads to newer drugs that are more efficacious, have fewer side effects, and/or can be taken less frequently than older ones. Their criticism of the search for blockbuster drugs indicates that physicians are savvy about the profit motives that shape pharmaceutical companies' research agendas. What physicians seem far more hesitant to admit is the role they play in advancing the pharmaceutical industry's profit-driven agenda.

Conclusion

Some physicians respond to the political economy of health care in the United States by conducting pharmaceutical contract research. In doing so, these physicians try to gain a different type of control over their practices, primarily through a change in their sources of revenue. In the role of investigators, physicians construct professional identities as entrepreneurial agents. The move to contract research is entrepreneurial because physicians can increase their incomes and their status within medicine, and can provide a service to their patients and communities. In addition, physician-investigators see themselves as playing a key role (especially compared to academic physicians) in the execution of clinical trials and the success of drug development.

Physician-investigators who succeed in the clinical trials industry surely deserve credit for their entrepreneurialism, but they also concede much of their power to the pharmaceutical industry in the process. While there is much to gain from their participation in pharmaceutical research (namely, money and status), physicians do not obtain more professional autonomy. The structure of the research enterprise limits physicians' decision making regarding individual patients' treatment to the choice between enrolling and not enrolling them in studies. Moreover, investigators must contend with ethical conflicts generated by their dual roles as physicians and researchers and with increased liability as a function of their contract with the FDA. By relegating their role as physicians to the pharmaceutical industry under the identity of investigators, doctors relinquish their own authority in decision making for the health and welfare of patients. The pharmaceutical industry in return gains emissaries to promote current and future products from development to market.

Chapter 4

Coordinating Clinical Trials

Ruth,[1] a charismatic white woman in her early fifties, welcomed me into her office in the clinical research facilities of a large, successful obstetrics and gynecology private practice. Having worked at the investigative site for more than eight years and at another site for several years prior to that, Ruth had much to tell me about the clinical trials industry. Ruth juggled several roles at the site: research coordinator, recruiter, and "regulatory specialist." At the time of my second interview with her, she had recently been promoted and was transitioning to the position of site director.

Ruth explained to me that clinical research necessitates the involvement of people like her and the other coordinators at the site: studies have the potential to be cold and impersonal, but she and her colleagues provide a warm, compassionate context for that research. Ruth understands that the primary responsibility of coordinators is to ensure that pharmaceutical companies obtain the data they are seeking from subjects in clinical trials. This means finding and enrolling subjects for the studies through recruitment of private-practice patients or community members and then encouraging those subjects to be compliant and continue with the protocols. The pharmaceutical companies assign quotas to the sites for how many subjects they need to recruit and in what time frame they need to be enrolled. This is no small challenge when, in Ruth's experience, only about 10 percent of the interested potential subjects actually pass the protocol requirements for eligibility and decide to enroll. With those odds, coordinators need to make the active recruiting and screening of subjects a major thrust of their jobs.

At the same time, Ruth explains, another important responsibility of coordinators is to ensure that individual patient-subjects are treated ethically and commit themselves to the research process. She insists that she is not looking for "subjects" to be in the studies but "research partners." For her site, there is an "ideal" patient-subject, and the difference between who is or is not ideal is based on active, rather than passive, participation in the studies. For example, she receives a fair number of responses to mass media advertisements. Oftentimes people who are motivated by ads to contact her site are primarily interested in how much financial compensation they could receive for their participation in studies. She told me that most of these people are not ideal subjects because it takes more than money to encourage people to be compliant with the study protocols (duties often include writing symptom diaries and coming in frequently for appointments). She says that the best participants are those who embrace the education that she and the other coordinators provide to subjects about their medical conditions and about the details of the studies in which they are enrolling.

The dual nature of the job that Ruth pointed out—the need to meet the pharmaceutical companies' quotas and the selection of active, engaged subjects—is a theme that was woven throughout the narratives of most of the coordinators I interviewed. Fortunately for Ruth, she does not perceive these two tasks as competing with each other. Nonetheless, through my conversations with her and other coordinators, it became apparent that there is an underlying tension between these approaches to the recruitment and retention of human subjects that is rooted in the conflict between research and care. What is more, this tension can be seen as constitutive of coordinators' professional identities.

Dual Roles of Research Coordinators

The job description for research coordinators varies widely by investigative site depending on the amount of specialized division of labor in which the site has invested. The basic tasks that need to be done in order for sites to participate in clinical trials include recruiting patient-subjects, screening and enrolling patient-subjects into particular studies, managing the regulatory documents like IRB submissions and FDA forms, and overseeing the financial end of contract negotiation and fee collection. In general, the smaller the investigative site, the more likely it is that these activities all fall within the purview of individual coordinators; at larger sites, these activities are divided up among various employees. Despite this variation, coordinators are always responsible for direct contact with patient-subjects.

At its core, the coordinator position is premised on the role of nurses in health care delivery. Like nurses, the vast majority of coordinators are women, many of whom have come from nursing or other health-related positions. And like nurses, coordinators have the task of educating patients about clinical trials, getting patients to consent and enroll in studies, and alleviating patients' fears about medical research.[2] Unlike any other position in the clinical trials industry, coordinators are very much the face of pharmaceutical drug development. It is primarily through coordinators that patients interact with the clinical trials industry and come to trust that they are being cared for.[3] Coordinators understand that the quality of their interactions with patients and the rapport they build with them affects how well they are able to recruit, enroll, and retain those patients in studies.

In addition to its influence on the tone of coordinators' interactions with patient-subjects, nursing has shaped coordinators' status within the organizational hierarchy of the clinical trials industry. Like nurses, coordinators have less status, are responsible for the most onerous and challenging tasks, and are rarely credited for the expertise that they have. In short, coordinators often suffer the same professional problem as nurses: their work tends to be invisible and undervalued within the clinic as well as within the larger organization of pharmaceutical studies.[4]

That nurses and coordinators are women is not incidental to the devaluation of their work. In fact, the gendered dynamic is pivotal for both professional groups because their work is often framed as unskilled women's work rather than work requiring specialized knowledge and expertise.[5] In other words, nurses and coordinators are not devalued because their work is seen as unnecessary but because there is a perception that any woman could replace them. Of course, this is not true. In the quotidian operation of clinical trials, coordinators are often described as the most important member of the clinical research team because they must ensure that studies are conducted efficiently and diligently.[6] Yet the credit that is given to coordinators is more often that they are attentive workhorses rather than the specialized professionals and clinical trial experts that they are.

The coordinator position is premised on nursing but with one important difference. In clinical trials, "care" work is disconnected from nurses' traditional role in the health care team of providing individualized treatment to make sick patients well.[7] This is not to say that care must be absent from drug studies. In his study of nurses, sociologist Daniel Chambliss describes four definitions of "care" that emerged in his research: "face-to-face working with patients, dealing with the patient as a whole person, the comparatively open-ended nature of the nurse's duties, and the personal commitment of the nurse to her work."[8] All these functions could still be present for coordinators, yet the context of that care is crucially different. Coordinators, even more than investigators, experience a conflict between research and care.[9] "Ethics" becomes a tool that coordinators mobilize to navigate that conflict.

Coordinating as a Job

The purpose of coordinators in the organization of clinical trials is to facilitate the conduct of studies. Studies must be done according to protocol, and data must be faithfully recorded. The coordinators oversee and execute both functions. The role imposed upon coordinators by their job description is to serve the pharmaceutical industry through their service at investigative sites. From the industry's perspective, coordinating requires attention to detail and organizational skills, not any medical expertise or experience per se.[10] As a result, much of the expertise developed by coordinators is not acknowledged. Their specialized knowledge and skills get overlooked because of their gendered position in the industry and because of the broader political economy of drug studies, particularly the weak participation of physicians as investigators.[11]

Most coordinators have come to their positions by default rather than by intentionally pursuing this career path. As part of the pitch from pharmaceutical companies or ancillary clinical trials companies about conducting clinical trials, physicians are advised to name someone in their staff—such as a nurse or technician—as a coordinator to run the studies. As a result, many coordinators feel that they were chosen for the position because they were in the right place at the right time. As Ruth herself explained,

> I think I got into research basically the same way every woman or every staff member does: you just happen to be a person who's there and who seems willing and able to learn and likes learning new things. So when something comes along, a physician says, "Okay, here's what we need. We need . . . you to be a clinical research coordinator." . . . But most of the people who do clinical trials and have done them just more or less *fell* into the work. But if you have more than one brain cell, it comes together and you think this looks fun and interesting. Let me learn!

The pervasiveness of explanations like Ruth's about becoming involved with the clinical trials industry reveals much about the coordinator position.

First, it illustrates the extent to which coordinating studies is gendered because Ruth first identifies the similarity in job entry for all *women* before she clarifies that she means staff members. Second, describing her start as falling into the role emphasizes luck or serendipity rather than prior skill, competence, or expertise. The only thing required for being selected as a coordinator, according to Ruth, is exhibiting the willingness to learn. Finally, Ruth's comment about "having more than one brain cell" implies that coordinators do not need to be particularly smart to succeed in their jobs, that their enthusiasm counts more than intelligence. A statement like this one echoes what an SMO told a private practice that they were recruiting to conduct clinical trials; the coordinator recalled, "When our SMO came to us, they basically said that any idiot can do clinical trials." Of course, almost exclusively the person cast in this "idiot" role is the coordinator, not the investigator. Thus, when coordinators discuss "falling into" clinical trials in terms of luck rather than skill or experience, it may be symptomatic of coordinators' internalization of industry rhetoric about how easy it is to run drug studies.

From the outset, coordinators' jobs are devalued through a discursive deskilling in which they too engage. What is rarely mentioned is that the majority of coordinators have medical expertise as nurses, technicians, and physician assistants that provides a basis for the work that they do managing drug studies. In part, this expertise is ignored because (1) these positions are already lower status, (2) these positions are not seen as prerequisites for coordinating, (3) the subsequent promotion of office assistants and receptionists to coordinating has a further devaluing effect on the position, and (4) the role is overwhelmingly filled by women. Even the development of certification programs has not led to better pay or promotions for coordinators who become certified. Instead, the certification of coordinators has become a tool for investigative sites to display their legitimacy over other sites. Coordinating clinical trials is an emergent form of women's work wherein coordinators have heavy workloads, relatively low pay,[12] and little recognition.

The experiences of *male* coordinators reveal the extent to which gender is built into the organizational structure of the clinic and the broader industry.[13] As is often the case in nursing, male coordinators are rare enough in clinical trial work that their experiences and professional identities are quite different from those of their female counterparts. The most striking difference is that even when male coordinators have similarly "fallen into" the profession, they stress that they see their jobs as temporary. One male coordinator emphasized,

"You know, ultimately, professionally, there are future goals *obviously*. I enjoy the work, I do. I love patient relations, and I love patient care, but I have higher aspirations. . . . I want to be here for a while, but I'm going to get as much as I can out of it, learn as much as I can, and then be my own business, start my own company." In contrast, not only did most of the women coordinators I interviewed emphasize the luck they had to stumble into their jobs, but also none framed their jobs as transitional.

Similarly, male coordinators interact differently with investigators and with pharmaceutical company representatives than do female coordinators. Male coordinators are more likely to be treated as physicians' peers. In response to a question about how he saw his gender affecting others' perceptions of him as a coordinator, one coordinator told me, "Trust me, the physicians and I had to, more often than not, many times bond to keep me sane." Thus, with physicians, male coordinators seem to have more status than do female coordinators within the clinic. Moreover, because male coordinators are so uncommon, pharmaceutical company representatives often mistake them for physician-investigators at industry meetings. A male coordinator explained this common occurrence: "I went to an investigator meeting back east, and on my reservations and everything, they had me listed as an MD. . . . I don't mind it, and I wish I had the paycheck to go with it. . . . Sometimes it's beneficial when you're trying to get back to see your patients and your family, and they're trying to bump you from a flight." The mistaking of male coordinators for physicians underscores the low status of coordinating because it implies that it is better to err on promoting men to higher ranking, more prestigious positions than it is to assume that a man is employed in women's work.

Coordinator training—or more often, the lack thereof—further illustrates the sentiment so prevalent in the clinical trials industry that anyone can be a coordinator. Regardless of gender and the status associated with coordinating clinical trials, after falling into their positions, coordinators must learn the job. In the process of becoming a coordinator, many never receive any formal training at all.[14] This is especially the case for private practices initiating studies for the first time. Although coordinators in this situation may receive a small study-specific manual or verbal instructions from project managers or monitors at pharmaceutical companies or CROs contracting out to their site, many coordinators must simply learn by doing. One coordinator described the process as "initiation by fire." Another coordinator reflected back on learning the position on his own:

What training would I have liked to have gone through? Basically, I would have wanted someone to sit down and go over everything step by step with me. There's a lot involved in research from progress notes, drug accountability, safety concerns, serious adverse events, how to report those. . . . So to have somebody actually go over that with me when I started—not to mention direct patient care!—that would have been unbelievably beneficial.

While it is fairly common for coordinators at small sites to learn the job on their own, coordinators who work at larger or more established sites generally are introduced to the job and receive training through hands-on experience with another coordinator. The apprenticeship model of training is an effective way for coordinators to learn the mechanics of the job as well as the professional identity associated with the work.

But this limited training betrays a neoliberal streak: it is coordinators' own responsibility to learn their jobs and new markets have opened up to meet this need. Specifically, there are now a plethora of course offerings in clinical research available through professional organizations and community colleges.[15] In the last few years, it has become common for sites to encourage new coordinators to take these courses when available. While these educational opportunities seem invaluable, only the largest sites pay for the cost of courses, and coordinators working for all other sites are told to pay out-of-pocket.[16]

Another aspect to the neoliberal trend in coordinator training is that the industry stresses *ongoing* education. The variations in study protocols and expectations of different pharmaceutical companies and CROs add significantly to coordinators' perceptions that training can never be complete. One coordinator with a year and a half experience in her position explained this feeling: "Boy, I still, on a daily basis, feel like I'm new. I mean there's just so much to learn in research. The training I got was very site specific and study specific. . . . It continues to be a learning process on a daily basis." Thus, the burden is on coordinators to learn their jobs through continuous training and education that they likely pay for out of their own wages.

Whether their skills are learned in formal training sessions or in the course of doing their jobs, there are many components to coordinating clinical trials. So what is it that coordinators actually do? The labor of "coordinating" a study includes two stages: screening/enrolling subjects and maintaining study protocols. During the screening stage, coordinators meet with each patient-subject who has been referred by a physician or has responded to an advertisement. At these visits, coordinators go through informed consent forms and answer any questions potential volunteers might have about a study. Only after patient-subjects have signed their explicit consent do coordinators complete the screening process by taking patients' medical histories and completing all laboratory work (such as blood draws and urinalysis). This information about patient-subjects is used to determine whether they are eligible to enroll in studies based on the specific inclusion-exclusion criteria set by the pharmaceutical companies. The screening and enrolling process is often described as the most time-intensive part of clinical trials, particularly for studies that have very short enrollment windows.

Those patient-subjects who qualify are then enrolled in the clinical trials. This means that coordinators must follow the explicit instructions detailed in the protocols for randomizing patient-subjects into the different arms of the studies. Once subjects begin studies, they enter the phase of study "maintenance." Coordinators must ensure that patient-subjects are compliant not only with the study medications but also with attending all study visits and completing associated diaries or other instruments designed to collect data on their symptoms. One of the most important functions of coordinators during study maintenance is retention; it is important for the pharmaceutical companies' data that patient-subjects who are enrolled in studies complete them.

In addition to their direct interaction with patient-subjects, coordinators also have the major task of documenting everything that happens as part of the clinical trial. As one coordinator said, "[The coordinator is] the one that needs to write everything down and tell the story of what happened so that the investigator can evaluate the adverse event or whatever the situation is." These narratives are written in the patient-subjects' charts—called the "source document"—and then specific information requested by pharmaceutical companies is transferred to "case report forms" that are sent to the pharmaceutical company or its CRO.

According to coordinators, the work of documentation has intensified over the years, with pharmaceutical companies requesting that more and more information be included as part of the case report forms. Increased paperwork reflects trends in health care delivery generally, where documentation can have a more central role than patient care. In clinical trials in particular, the paperwork associated with the protocols is contingent upon the purpose and length of study visits with patient-subjects. Coordinators informed me that documenting interactions with subjects requires double to triple the amount of time actually spent with those subjects. One coordinator elaborated this point: "Say you have a patient visit that takes about an hour; you're going to have two or three hours of paperwork after that visit. You'll be getting it all together, transferring data from the source document to the CRF [case report form] and then from the CRF into a computer program or getting it faxed or getting it sent to regulatory documents." In other words, there are multiple steps—and versions—of the documentation process. First, coordinators must fill out a thorough narrative of the study visit in the source document. Next, they create a digested version of that narrative in the case report form. In some cases, that is the last step before faxing the forms or filing them for the pharmaceutical company. More often, however, coordinators have a third step of inputting the information from the case report form into software designed for "electronic data capture."

The time it takes coordinators to complete the documentation of drug studies is on the rise because protocols are requiring more procedures. More procedures mean more time with patient-subjects, and more time with patient-subjects means more time spent on paperwork. A coordinator explained,

> The work that we do now compared to many years back is more detailed ... Before where it might have only taken us maybe fifteen, twenty minutes to see a patient, now we're usually utilizing a whole hour. And even when we do the first visit, the screening visit—when we have them come in to see if they would qualify for the study—that's a guaranteed two hours at the least. You have to have time for the patient to read the consent form, and you're doing multiple tests and stuff, so it is time consuming. It is very time consuming!

The intensity of the procedures, time spent with patient-subjects, and documentation can become overwhelming for coordinators, and it is often the paperwork component specifically that makes them feel overworked or overburdened by their jobs.

In spite of this workload issue, many coordinators feel that the amount of documentation necessary for studies is justified by its purpose. All the paperwork that coordinators fill out becomes the data for the clinical trials. Because coordinators understand that pharmaceutical companies need the data to be complete and clear, they appreciate the fact that the paperwork is not merely bureaucratic. A coordinator commented,

> There'll be times that I think the paperwork will seem a little stupid. For example, you have to try to remember why [subjects] need to sign

this third consent [form] because a word was misspelled previously. That seems like you're overdoing it, but you are so that you don't *underdo* it at an important time, you know what I mean? . . . So I don't mind [the documentation] because there's a reason for it. I can *understand* why we're doing it.

Careful documentation is also vital for the financial success of the investigative site. Coordinators with experience are well aware that the better they follow protocols, fill out forms, and organize all study documentation, the more satisfied study monitors and their respective pharmaceutical companies or CROs will be with the performance of the site. Study monitor satisfaction directly influences the sites' ability to secure future studies with those corporations because monitors have an interest in enlisting sites that produce "clean" data. Monitors' recommendations of sites are critical during the site selection phase of new studies. A coordinator described this dynamic:

> You want [monitors] to come back and repeat business with you. I used to work with Merck, and I called myself "the Merck queen" because all I did was Merck studies, and they kept coming back because I was very knowledgeable. I'd been doing [studies] for a long time, and I knew what they wanted and could fill out their case report forms pretty good. . . . So they would bring more studies repeatedly.

Thus, coordinators must take study documentation seriously because their sites' success—and their own job security—very much depends on this part of the job description.

Clinical trials often lead to work intensification for coordinators because investigators have fairly low levels of involvement in the daily operation of drug studies. The delegation of the bulk of the labor associated with study protocols to coordinators requires that they be on top of their own job responsibilities as well as reviewing the tasks that the physicians must complete. Specifically, coordinators must keep track of meeting with patient-subjects, filling out case report forms, and filing all regulatory documents. Coordinators must ensure that physicians sign all necessary forms and perform all required procedures within the time frame and guidelines of the study protocols. In other words, they coordinate the studies by making sure that *all* the details, including those that physicians are responsible for, are being attended to. One coordinator explained her role in keeping physician-investigators on track: "Coordinators are . . . at the bottom of the rung, but they're probably the most valuable thing that a physician will have because my job is to *police* my doctors to do this study right." Whereas delegation often means that those who are given work are supervised by others, coordinators instead ensure that physicians are following the protocols and conducting the procedures appropriate to specific studies.[17]

A revealing example about the ways in which coordinators must intervene to help investigators properly run studies involves the recruitment of patient-subjects. Coordinators report that private-practice physicians are not as cognizant about their current and enrolling studies as they should be when they see patients. This leads to two different problems. First, physicians may refer patients to coordinators for studies that are no longer enrolling or that do not match the patients' conditions.[18] In these cases, coordinators may spend an inordinate amount of time with patients who are not eligible for any studies. The second problem, which is more common, is that physicians do not remember to recruit patients as they see them during their regular appointments. To compensate for this, many coordinators will complete initial reviews of the charts of all the patients who have appointments in a given day in order to identify in advance patients who may qualify for studies. If patients seem like potential study candidates, coordinators make a note on the charts to indicate to physicians to discuss clinical trial participation with the patients and to refer interested patients to them. Because coordinators are much more familiar with their current studies and the preliminary eligibility requirements than are physicians, they often need to intervene in this way to aid in the recruitment of subjects from physicians' patient base.

The broader clinical trials industry acknowledges the problem of "phantom investigators," or low levels of physician involvement in studies. In industry discussions about increasing physicians' participation, the problem is normally framed in terms of individuals or of sites (that is, how to increase *specific* physicians' involvement). What is rarely mentioned, however, are the ways in which the clinical trials industry *as an institution* actively encourages the delegation of the majority of study tasks to coordinators and simultaneously contributes to physicians' ignorance about the study protocols. One key manifestation of this occurs at "investigator meetings." The purpose of these meetings is to explain the protocols to all the investigators and coordinators who have been contracted to conduct a particular study for a pharmaceutical company. Inculcating who is responsible for the day-to-day operation of clinical trials, these events consist of a series of lectures about the studies that coordinators are required to attend in their entirety while physicians are often given free time or even a day off. A coordinator described an upcoming meeting she was slated to attend with an investigator:

> *Coordinator:* I'm going to Puerto Rico in April.
>
> *Fisher:* That sounds exciting.
>
> *Coordinator:* Well, for me, it will not be exciting because I'm the nurse, and I'll be doing the nurse work. Dr. X and I are leaving Thursday night. He and I both have to do the Friday part. Saturday morning he gets to play a round. Actually, he doesn't play golf, that would be Dr. Y, [but] he's got a *free* morning and *I* don't. And I'm thinking, wait a minute . . . could he fill out a case report form if he had to? . . . I think that the pharmaceutical companies should just make the investigator a little more responsible than they do sometimes.

In structuring their off-site events this way, the pharmaceutical companies make it clear to both investigators and coordinators who is ultimately responsible for appropriately conducting the studies.

The issue I want to underscore here is that physician-investigators' disconnection from conducting the studies leads to work intensification for coordinators. Although it may be unintentional, physicians frequently contract with pharmaceutical companies and CROs to do more studies than is appropriate for the number of coordinators at the investigative site. One particular physician who was more involved in his private practice than in research was accused by two of his coordinators, whom I interviewed, of being hopelessly out of touch with the operation of the clinical trials business. One of these coordinators explained his style of taking on studies and delegating them to his staff, especially to her: "The doctor of course just says [the coordinator] will do whatever study comes our way. Sometimes yes, sometimes I'm just not . . . [she pauses]. Sometimes I have to go in there and say, 'No more. I'm at my capacity.'" At a different site, an experienced coordinator was hired by a private practice that wanted to start conducting clinical trials for the first time. The physicians had hired her explicitly for her experience coordinating studies. Yet, because of their inexperience and lack of interest in the details of conducting studies, they felt frustrated by the low volume of patient-subjects scheduled for appointments each day. The coordinator explained why that position was short-lived:

> They thought they'd just hire someone who'd do everything and they could reap the benefits. . . . And I was just supposed to start making

money [for them]! Obviously there's more to research than just seeing
the patient, and for somebody who didn't know that, they didn't understand why I could only see two, three patients a day. What was I doing
with the rest of my time? So it only lasted a year. They actually closed
down the research. They said it just wasn't making enough money, and
I left there.

In contrast, physician-investigators who are more involved with the
studies tend to be more sensitive to the demands of coordinators' work.
These physicians are generally able to delegate work more effectively. For
instance, one physician who was quite involved in the day-to-day operations of his research clinic said,

> I think, because I do this full-time, I'm very attached to my coordi-
> nators, rather than unattached to them. I see how busy they are, I
> watch them cry, I watch them laugh, and I'm very in tune to what
> their work level is. I know what they can handle, and we talk openly
> about it: "Yeah, I can be busier" or "No, I can't be busier." And so
> we've done that.

Physicians who are more aware of coordinators' workloads are less likely
to take on more studies than the investigative site can handle. Thus, working with investigators who are involved in the studies they are conducting
provides coordinators with the double benefit of not having to compensate
as much for the physicians' low levels of involvement and of having a more
manageable number of studies at any one time.

Coordinators understand that all physician-investigators are not the
same. Many coordinators with whom I spoke were aware of the variation in
physicians' level of participation in studies either through their own personal experience or through their interactions with other coordinators at
investigator meetings. Those coordinators who were in positions in which
the physicians were particularly involved felt adamant that they would not
tolerate any less from investigators. One veteran coordinator who had been in
the industry for two decades and had worked for many physicians over the
course of those years told me,

> I wouldn't work for [an investigator] that didn't participate [in the
> studies]. I would leave. . . . There are some physicians that they get the
> study and the coordinator runs the whole show, and the physicians
> don't do a lot of things. I mean we talk amongst coordinators, OK? I

don't have that here. And if the physicians didn't [get involved], I told
them I'd be gone out the door in a minute.

Although all the coordinators I interviewed did not feel so strongly entitled
to work with physician-investigators actively engaged in research, those who
worked in that environment described how lucky they felt to have physicians
who were available and accessible to them.

Because coordinators' workloads depend on the degree of active participation by physicians in clinical trials, there are patterns of coordinator
job turnover that map onto investigators' attitudes and involvement. A study
monitor explained:

You only see a high turnover at some sites, but if you do see turnover,
you see it a lot. So you know that it's probably a management thing,
maybe they're overworked. A few of the sites really do try to overwork
their coordinators, give them too many protocols, and they don't pay
them very well. But you know again it more often really depends on the
PI, the physician that they work with, whether or not they like him.

In other words, physician-investigators have a tremendous impact upon coordinators' satisfaction with their jobs and their dedication to the research
enterprise.

Another factor affecting coordinators' perception of their positions is the
extent to which they experience a conflict between research and care. Coordinators are asked to understand that the primary purpose of their jobs is
to deliver patient-subjects and data to pharmaceutical companies. However,
this role is not without conflict for coordinators. Because they interact with
patient-subjects as individuals rather than as case report forms alone, they
cannot help but see their job as helping those individuals. Moreover, what is
often unsaid but is widely understood within the clinical trials industry is
that relationships of trust facilitate the recruitment and retention of patient-
subjects in drug studies. Because coordinators are the ones establishing those
relationships with subjects, they become invested in patient-subjects as individuals. As a result, having direct ties with patient-subjects creates difficulties for many coordinators to justify putting the interests of pharmaceutical
companies before the interests of the sick individuals coming to their investigative sites for help.

Relationships of trust between coordinators and patient-subjects are
developed through the amount of time coordinators spend with prospective

subjects and the quality of the interactions they have. As with nursing, there is a strong emphasis placed on the interpersonal skills of coordinators for establishing trust quickly. Specifically, coordinators must be able, in a short time, to make potential patient-subjects feel comfortable with the research process and answer all subjects' questions about the study in an encouraging way. Thus, dialogue between coordinators and subjects becomes a large part of the job.

Several coordinators I interviewed impressed upon me the importance of establishing the right tone in the first conversation with prospective human subjects. One coordinator who does most of her recruiting through media advertisements explained the importance of establishing rapport with individuals during the initial phone conversation when they are responding to an ad:

> Usually what we do is we talk to them over the phone, so we kind of build that relationship. I'm not one to say, you know, I only have five minutes over the phone. If they have questions, I'll answer anything that they have. . . . So I think over the phone, we kind of build that relationship to where 90 percent of the people that we talk to over the phone will come in. If they're undecided as far as the phone conversation, I'll just tell them, "Come in, meet with us, see our facility. Definitely it's all voluntary, you don't have to participate. You can come in, spend an hour with us, and decide you don't want to do it. It's strictly up to you." So I think they feel comfortable that way.

Similarly, a coordinator at another site emphasized the personal tone to recruiting and enrolling patient-subjects during initial phone contact:

> I try very hard to be very compassionate and understanding. I listen to them. It's not about "Hello, yes, we're doing a clinical trial, what zip code do you live in?" You know, "Can you do a, b, c, and d?" That's just not the way I personally recruit. The way I recruit probably takes a whole lot longer than some, but I'm a friend of that woman before she ever walks in the door. And when she does, I'm delighted to say, "Oh Mary, I remember speaking with you. It's so good to get to meet you now." So to me, it's very, very personal.

The importance of the relationships that coordinators build with patient-subjects is not limited to the recruitment phase but must be maintained and built upon over the course of the entire study. One coordinator explained her approach:

We work very, very hard at building good relationships. They're not
numbers here, no one's ever treated like they're W24601 [the number
assigned to the human subject during the study]. That does not happen. . . . So that's that personal element that as much as it is *science*
and we use the word *subjects* and protocols and things, they're people
and you know I can't get around that.

Although coordinators' practices could be seen as merely effective
recruitment and retention strategies from the perspective of pharmaceutical
companies, coordinators are sincere in their efforts to build these relationships with patient-subjects. The length of studies also contributes to coordinators' investment in patient-subjects as individuals. As they get to know
subjects over months or years, coordinators cannot help but place value on
the relationships they are establishing with those subjects. For example, a
recruiter who had been a coordinator for many years said,

It's really neat too because of the length of our studies—we have trials
that can go on for years: three, four, five years—you get to know those
people over time. You know, that's what I miss about coordinating
because you get to know those people. You see them through deaths
and weddings and birthdays. You see them through those events, and
you actually become a part of their family, a step back, but you get to
go through all those changes in their life.

The investment of coordinators' time and energy into relationships with
human subjects, however, leads to a heightened conflict between research
and care. Instead of simply seeing their role in relation to subjects as facilitating the collection of pharmaceutical companies' data, coordinators begin to
evaluate the drug studies in relation to the needs of patient-subjects. In one
coordinator's articulation, "Unfortunately, we have some studies right now
that are not a good option. For me, it's difficult when I have a conflict between
whether this is really the best thing for the subject or not."

One of the harder lessons for coordinators, especially those who were
trained as nurses, is that research is not care. Even with experience conducting the various aspects of clinical trials, many coordinators encounter
a conflict between their job description and their role vis-à-vis the patient-
subjects. I spoke at length about this issue with a coordinator new to the
industry. Because she had only been in her position a short time and because
she had been a practicing nurse for decades before entering the clinical trials

industry, she keenly felt the struggle to understand her role in research as separate from care.

> I'm going to see a lot of the same things [that is, illnesses] that we had in family practice. It's just getting that thing in your head that it's *not* a patient-doctor or -nurse relationship. It's a *participant-research* [relationship] and making that clear—which I feel like in these informed consent [forms] they *try* to make it very clear. The people I work with here ... try to make that real clear at the start. That, "Yes, you're important as an individual, but it isn't a doctor-patient relationship. You have to realize that you're signing up for a double-blind study."

She emphasized that it is often very difficult not only to make this distinction clear for herself but for the patient-subjects. She offered an example in which she had learned that one of the patient-subjects she had enrolled in a study had not understood the implications of the research process:

> Well, an example would be the participant we had that was doing this [study] for psoriasis. It was unfortunate that out of the four people that have [been enrolled in the study], he was the one [whose condition] was the worst and had been getting worse—which was why he came in. Well, we were almost sure he got the placebo. He got no effect. And he's only twenty-two, he's young. He felt, even though he'd read the informed consent and we'd explained it to him, he didn't understand it well, "How would they pick me to not get the drug when I'm so bad?" After he didn't get [the active drug], he went off the study. He still seemed a little dumbfounded by it because you're in a medical setting, *sort of*. So, you know, you just have to make that very clear to some people. And even if you think you've made it clear, it isn't always clear. We're doing medical tests and they're still expecting medical treatment *appropriate* for their [conditions], even though you've told them otherwise.

The coordinator recognized that randomization means that a patient-subject who very much needs medical treatment might instead receive a placebo as part of a clinical trial. Yet her narrative about the patient revealed that she felt that it was important that he get help for his illness, rather than emphasizing the importance of remaining in the study for the sake of the pharmaceutical company's data.

Separating the goals of research from care is crucial for coordinators to accept as part of their positions, yet it creates a role conflict for many who have come to know patient-subjects as individuals. In other words, the relationships that coordinators develop with patient-subjects to encourage them to enroll in drug studies also create conflict over determining to whom they have obligations, the pharmaceutical companies or the patient-subjects. Thus, the role imposed on coordinators as part of their job descriptions—producing data for the pharmaceutical industry—is not sufficient for most coordinators' professional identities. Instead, coordinators actively construct an alternative role that situates their work in terms of mediating the ethical conduct of drug studies through their care for patient-subjects.

Coordinating as an Identity

Care is central to coordinators' understanding of their jobs within the clinical trials industry. Perhaps because coordinating is premised on nursing, the technical aspects of the job are often relegated to care work in coordinators' construction of their professional identities. Yet because care cannot take precedence over coordinators' obligations to recruit and retain patient-subjects in clinical trials, coordinators have responded by developing an explanation for the importance of care work within a discourse of research ethics. Rather than simply caring for the health of patients, within this frame, coordinators ensure the protection of subjects within the clinic. Coordinators' mobilization of ethics departs significantly from codified principles contained within the regulatory system or discussed within the field of bioethics. In those frameworks, procedural matters such as informed consent figure prominently. In contrast, coordinators' formulations of ethics manifest in highly gendered language about the relationships they develop with patient-subjects and is grounded in their concern for patient-subjects as individuals.[19] Coordinators' articulation of care work through the lens of research ethics is powerful because it provides a moral justification for coordinators to put the needs of patient-subjects before their obligation to the pharmaceutical industry.

Research ethics are not an explicit part of coordinators' job descriptions. The only institutionalization of ethics associated with the job stems from federal regulation and the FDA's requirement for investigative sites (and therefore, coordinators) to follow "Good Clinical Practice" (GCP) guidelines. In the first case, federal regulation requires clinical trial protocols to undergo ethical review by IRBs and for human subjects to be given informed consent forms, which subjects must sign to document that consent has occurred. For investigative sites to abide by federal regulation, their responsibility rests in submitting necessary paperwork to IRBs and completing informed consent. If both of these actions are consistently taken, it follows—according to the regulatory framework—that studies are being conducted in an ethical fashion.

For the FDA requirement, the emphasis of GCP guidelines is twofold: protecting subjects in trials and producing valid data from the protocols. GCP guidelines instruct investigative sites on the importance of and details on how to conduct clinical trials properly. The protection of subjects is not framed in the guidelines in terms of ethics, but the process and practice of informed consent is thoroughly described as a way of ensuring that human subjects' rights will be protected. As is the case with the federal regulation, the implication is that if sites follow the GCP guidelines, the resulting research will be ethical. Thus, the only official recognition of ethics that is necessary for investigative sites is procedural. This framing of ethics could be seen as implying that the primary responsibility of sites is to the pharmaceutical companies and to the government, not to human subjects.[20]

Coordinators with more seniority—those who have been in their positions for more than ten years—acknowledge that a focus on ethics was not always associated with their work. In the early 1990s as private-sector involvement in research was just beginning, coordinators recall that no one ever talked about research ethics. At that point, the emphasis was on learning how to conduct studies and meeting their recruitment quotas. Some coordinators described in embarrassed or horrified tones how different their engagement with the protocols and patient-subjects was when they were first starting out. For example, one coordinator said,

> [Back then] it took about two years before you got the real gist of what you were doing. Now looking back on it, I think, oh my goodness, how dangerous that was, how dangerous! But again, fourteen years ago, I don't think that there was the emphasis put on [subjects'] safety and the ICF [informed consent form] that there are today. So, but looking back, it's like *oh* my goodness, I'm surprised we're not all in jail by now!

In interviews, coordinators described how because of a steep learning curve, no one in the past had time to consider ethics, but with experience the focus of their work has changed. For example, a coordinator reflected,

> So it's all about, "Yes, we want the patients in the trials," but your ethics are more involved now. [You ask yourself,] "*Should* this patient be in the trial?" . . . For me, coordinating is based on ethics now, I think.

Where before it was get the patient in, get them on the study, I think now it's more patient protection and ethics. That's the bottom line.

Coordinators cited the end of the 1990s as the moment when ethics became a central concern for them. Although they did not offer an explanation for why a change occurred, several factors, including professionalization efforts and a surge of negative media coverage, may have contributed to coordinators' reorientation toward their positions. Formal mechanisms to professionalize coordinators began to take off in the second half of that decade. Specifically, the Association for Clinical Research Professionals (ACRP) used the certification of coordinators as a way to bring recognition to the skills and knowledge necessary for conducting clinical trials. The first group of coordinators were certified in 1992, but the first five years of the program only resulted in the certification of about three hundred coordinators per year. After ACRP engaged in significant organizational restructuring in 1997, certification has since attracted approximately one thousand new coordinators per year.[21] By engaging in or becoming aware of certification efforts, coordinators may have begun to think of their roles within the industry differently. Ethics is not an explicit focus of certification, except for the obligatory discussions about informed consent, so certification alone is probably an insufficient explanation for the widespread shift in coordinators' awareness of ethical issues.

The end of the 1990s through the early 2000s were also a time of dramatic media coverage of clinical trials gone awry. In 1999, print and television news outlets reported high-profile cases of fraud perpetrated by physicians and coordinators in pharmaceutical clinical trials.[22] Several months later, Jesse Gelsinger (age eighteen) died in a University of Pennsylvania gene therapy experiment and two years after that, Ellen Roche (age twenty-four) died in a Johns Hopkins asthma study.[23] That both of these people were young and had volunteered as healthy human subjects added to the sense of tragedy in the media coverage. These reports led to major federal investigations by the FDA, Office of Human Research Protections (OHRP), and the FBI, as well as congressional inquiries and the appointment of presidential advisory committees. According to a physician-investigator, these events were responsible for "creating a very bad shiner for the industry that to an extent is very difficult to overcome." Given that all of these incidents involved what could be conceived of as ethical breaches that led to the harm or deaths of human subjects, coordinators may have responded by focusing on their own ethical practices in the day-to-day operation of investigative sites.

Regardless of the cause, coordinators' identities began to shift away from prioritizing the management of clinical trials to caring for patient-subjects recruited for or enrolled in drug studies. Coordinators' mobilizations of ethics depart significantly from formalized, institutionalized ethical principles and norms. While informed consent is still a central part of the process of enrolling patient-subjects into studies, coordinators do not make it the centerpiece of their ethical code. Instead, coordinators apply a traditionally feminized—and often maternal—sense of right and wrong to their interactions with patient-subjects.

Guiding coordinators' sense of what is ethical in clinical trials is often explained both explicitly and implicitly by popular articulations of the Kantian categorical imperative. They often mention the Golden Rule and view their responsibility towards patient-subjects in personalized tones, thinking about how they themselves would like to be treated in the same situations. A coordinator stated,

> Recruiting a patient for a clinical trial, or in fact we should say "subject" for a clinical trial. It's just like with everything, it's the same value I use with my everyday life, *it's what I raised my boys on*. It's to treat other people the same way you want them to treat you, and that is something that I strongly hold dear to my heart *even* in clinical research. I am not going to say or do anything to another woman that I wouldn't want them to say or do to me.

When operationalizing the implications of this orientation toward patient-subjects for clinical research, coordinators often talk about how they should only recruit strangers into studies, if they would enroll someone from their own families. One coordinator said, "I wouldn't do something to anybody else's mother [that] I wouldn't do to my own." If they would not enroll their own family members, coordinators indicate, they should question the ethics of their involvement with those studies. Another coordinator who actually had enrolled family members in studies declared, "If I wouldn't put my own mother or father or brother or sister or children in a study, then don't do it. And I won't, but I would, and *I have*."

An important aspect of coordinators' sense of ethics involves determining if a potential patient-subject is too ill for a given study. In other words, patient-subjects may be eligible to participate in studies by meeting all the inclusion-exclusion criteria detailed by study protocols, but coordinators may determine on their own that the studies are not appropriate for some subjects. Coordinators are most likely to do so when patient-subjects have illnesses for which there are effective treatments already available by prescription. Several coordinators explained that for some patients, it is not worth the risk that they might be put on a placebo as part of a clinical trial given the severity of their symptoms before the start of the study. One coordinator who primarily conducted studies on depression and anxiety drugs was especially adamant about this point: "A lot of people think that research might be a way to go, [but] it's not. If they're too sick, I don't want them in the study. They need to seek help. Even if they can't [access health care], we'll pick up the phone and call services in [the city] here that will provide services or at least can get them pointed in the right direction."

The question could become how coordinators *ever* justify enrolling patient-subjects in clinical trials when effective treatments are available in standard medical care. By trying to evaluate which patient-subjects may be better off being steered away from clinical trials, coordinators are not implying that all patient-subjects should avoid clinical trials. To the contrary, a crucial piece of coordinators' identity constructions and their view of ethics is their understanding of their work and clinical trials more generally in very altruistic terms. Coordinators emphasize the importance of having an ethical orientation towards their work that includes the desire to make the world better through improved therapies for diseases. As one coordinator explained,

> [Coordinators] want to do these trials because [patients] have a need for it, or [coordinators] want to do it because they want to improve science or add to the body of knowledge of science. . . . We do it just because frankly I get excited over the comparisons of some of the drugs that I'm doing right now, or a new drug that is going to probably make these [patients'] quality of life better.

From coordinators' own perspective, they are always already engaged in what they see as the "big picture"—the advancement of medicine for the benefit of humanity. In one coordinator's words, "You really have to see the *very* big picture. . . . We [coordinators] are women who are dedicated to wanting the world to be better for our children [and] our grandchildren." In order to conduct their work for these broader goals, it behooves coordinators to follow the drug protocols and enroll eligible patient-subjects.

Simultaneously, coordinators' emphasis on the big picture infuses their interactions with patient-subjects with its own ethic of care because coordinators see themselves as bringing medical progress directly to those individuals who enroll in drug studies. In one example of altruism manifesting in this way, an African American recruiter, who had been a coordinator for many years, described her experiences of bringing profound medical benefits to the patient-subjects: "You know to be able to *see* the outcome of research, working with your patients! Think of the RA [rheumatoid arthritis] patient that came in totally debilitated, in a wheelchair, could hardly walk or ambulate at all, and then to see that patient walking and skipping and hopping out the door after a while, then it's very much worth it for me." Because of these perceived benefits to individuals and to humanity, the recruiter told me that it became important for her to focus her energies on recruiting. She explained that as a recruiter, she could facilitate community outreach programs for minority populations who are often not included in many types of clinical trials.

In her experience, many minority groups, especially African Americans and Native Americans, are suspicious of research because of the sordid history in the United States of using members from these groups as human guinea pigs.[24] She said, "Unfortunately, the past has not been a good example of research. And just speaking, going out into the community and speaking to people, I'm a big advocate for getting a lot of the ethnic minority races and groups into research, and a lot of the stigmatism is still there. People are thinking about Tuskegee, and some other things that happened in the past." In spite of ethnic minorities' disinterest in pharmaceutical studies, the recruiter discusses with them the benefits to them of their participation, especially when individuals have illnesses that can be helped by clinical trials. She believes that those populations should be involved in studies because there are many benefits to be reaped from the research, not least of which is a form of access to health care. From her perspective, minority groups must be involved in clinical trials so that they will help find treatments for the illnesses that are prevalent in their own communities. She explained her view:

> But with the government agencies on our side now [regulating human subjects research], it's making it a lot more feasible for a lot of people to go into research. And once we go out and we educate more people and let them know, "Hey, this is for the good of your parents, your grandparents, your children, your children's children. We're benefiting each other on this, and it's a necessity." . . . You know, I liken medications to pantyhose, one size does not fit all; what's working for John Doe is not going to work for Ella Mae, so we need to do the research! Because I know that diabetes is prevalent in African Americans. I know it's prevalent on Indian reservations and part of the Indian population. I know

that the Asian community suffers from osteoporosis. So that's why I make it *my* business and *my* battle to go out to those communities and inform these people, "Hey, this is going on, you know, for your culture. Let's treat this right now, let's take care of this right now, so that you can have that future. You will have those children, grandchildren, and your line will be able to carry on. Let's take care of this right now." So I make that my passion, my personal passion, my personal goal.[25]

In their own narratives about their jobs, coordinators' (and recruiters') sense of altruism spills over to generate an imperative that altruism should also be the motivation for patient-subjects to participate in medical research. The recruiter quoted above emphasizes not only the individual benefit that subjects can obtain by participating in clinical research but also the benefit to their children and grandchildren. Her message is that only through their participation in clinical trials today will the diseases that plague those minority groups be treated or cured tomorrow.

In other cases, coordinators discuss the need to *teach* individual patient-subjects to be altruistic. Many patient-subjects do not explain their participation in terms of altruism, which is rarely the motive that brings them to investigative sites. Yet coordinators described the necessity of infusing trial participation with altruism, regardless of patient-subjects' initial motivations. For example, a coordinator explained her frustration with the term "guinea pig," and her desire to get people to think with other terms:

When everyday people call about our studies, I hear patients say, "Oh, I'm a guinea pig!" But I think we just need to basically make the community more aware that you're not being guinea pigs. We have to stress that this is definitely to help people and hopefully just try to make it easier for their kids growing up. For example, if their kids have to deal with depression or whatever, this clinical trial [that they are volunteering for now] will be something that's going to help those kids in the future.

Coordinators understand that patient-subjects have a variety of motivations for wanting to participate in drug studies, but they feel that altruism is crucial for patients to become good, compliant subjects in a clinical trial. According to a coordinator,

There are very few people that enter our studies that are altruistic, except at the end, then they really become altruistic because we try to teach them what research is about. It's not about being a hamster, and you joined a study. You want to learn . . . why this is done, what the principle behind it is. And at the end, they're like, "Wow, I really helped some other people." "Yeah, you have." But they didn't [think] that, typically, going in.

Because altruism is central to their identities and to their construction of ethics, some coordinators even go so far as to try to discourage patient-subjects who seem to be only motivated by money from participating in studies. In other words, coordinators may prefer to eliminate prospective subjects who are motivated for the "wrong" reasons than to work with subjects who may challenge their view of the "big picture" of pharmaceutical research and development. A coordinator shared her view on what type of subjects she wants to enroll in studies:

> When I begin consenting a patient and one of her first questions is: Do I get paid? No, not really. You know, maybe at other sites, and I know because of advertisements from other study sites that it's a real focus. But *I* am looking for participants who care about their body, their daughters, their granddaughters. If they have a problem that potentially participating in a clinical trial could help better—and again I emphasize potentially—I want them to be interested in the *science* of this and the progression of health care, not because you're going to get $50 for coming in and a pap and pelvic for free and that sort of thing.

This last quote emphasizes coordinators' desire for patient-subjects to both see and buy into the "big picture" of medical research and scientific progress. When patient-subjects do so, it affirms the ways in which coordinators form their own identities as part of the clinical trials industry.

Having an altruistic orientation to clinical trials thus has become a key part of coordinators' construction of ethics. For many coordinators, the desire to help individuals and humanity will direct them to make ethical choices in the clinic. Without this concern for others' welfare, the studies could begin to matter to them more than the people who are enrolled. With altruism as their guiding ethical reference, patient-subjects' value cannot lie in meeting their enrollment quotas. As one coordinator stated, "It's more than just good PR to have somebody care about you as a person, you know? I mean, that's what we're about. The studies don't matter to me; it's this person."

Because of the caring role they assume in relation to the patient-subjects, a final element that has become a dominant identity construct for coordinators is the theme of motherhood. Coordinators are cognizant of the ways in which the role of mother seeps into their work. One coordinator laughed about her relationship with her colleagues and patient-subjects: "I tend to be a mother to everyone. I have five children, and I have something for everyone." In addition, they frequently establish explicitly maternal relationships directly with patient-subjects. Another coordinator explained, "Yes, we do a lot of handholding. Sometimes we get accused of being mothers. But a lot of [patient-subjects], they do become our brothers or our sons." Coordinators find themselves embodying even the negative stereotype of a nagging mother: "So my job is to educate them [to be compliant]. In a nice sort of way that doesn't come off as an angry mother. It's challenging." Coordinators also talk about the maternal impulse to protect the patient-subjects by making sure they do truly understand what clinical research is all about. As one stated, "I wouldn't want a woman to take a medication or undergo a procedure, that *I* didn't *know* for sure based on my personal conversation with her that she *really* understands what she's doing and she wants to do that."

What coordinators' construction of the ethical treatment of patient-subjects reveals is that they see their responsibilities toward those subjects in ways that IRBs and traditional ethicists do not. Coordinators, simply put, have developed a different code of ethics than what is imposed by IRBs and bioethics more generally. For IRBs, the focus is on preventing coercion or deception in the researcher-subject relationship, while for coordinators, the focus is providing patient-subjects with care in exchange for their participation in double-blind, placebo-controlled studies. This underscores that coordinators' sense of responsibility to the patient-subjects, or to humanity, often takes precedence over their responsibility to pharmaceutical companies.

There are signs that coordinators' informal construction of ethics is slowly becoming formalized. For instance, coordinators transmit ethics to new colleagues through on-the-job training and local educational opportunities. In addition, some coordinators use ethics as a basis for intervening into the types of studies conducted at their sites and for critiquing the pharmaceutical industry. These examples indicate that coordinators' discourse of ethics might bring them more power within the clinic.

Unlike coordinators who began their careers in the early 1990s, newer coordinators described how they are learning ethics in the clinic *and* in the classroom. Many coordinators report that ethics is being integrated into their on-the-job training by more experienced colleagues. In that training, coordinators emphasize that the job involves care for subjects as well as knowledge about study protocols and paperwork. Moreover, experienced coordinators have begun to develop curricula around ethics, and they teach courses at community colleges and professional organizations. One of the greenest coordinators I interviewed had signed up for a coordinator-training course at a local community college. She reported that the instructor, a coordinator herself, was teaching the class about the history of human experimentation as a way to highlight why it is the responsibility of coordinators to do their jobs in an ethical fashion: "Right now, we're doing ethics, ethics, ethics, patient informed consent, the history of Tuskegee and the Nuremberg Code and the whole thing. So it's a good foundation, and I feel like I'm getting a good *beginning*, a real good beginning" to understanding the job. In this way, novice coordinators learn the mechanics of the job with explicit attention to research ethics built into the curriculum.

An interesting reaction to coordinators' study of the ethical misconduct of past researchers is that they are often critical of the activities of their counterparts in those studies. In the Tuskegee syphilis study,[26] coordinators are drawn to the portrait of Eunice Rivers, the African American nurse who worked with the Public Health Service for the length of the study and was even a coauthor on publications resulting from the research.[27] Rivers has become a famous example of a coordinator through the HBO depiction of her in its film about the Tuskegee study *Miss Evers' Boys* (Rivers was renamed "Evers" in the original play and subsequent movie). Through their identification with Rivers, many coordinators who learn about Tuskegee are more critical of her role in the study as coordinator than they are of the physicians who were involved or of the U.S. government. For example, a coordinator complained about the HBO portrayal of Rivers:

> You know what has always sort of bothered me about *Miss Evers' Boys*? I think, what kind of nurse was she that she didn't create more stir and turn them in? I mean call somebody and say, "What the heck is going on here?" So you know, in some respects HBO paints her as a saint, but I'm thinking, I'm not sure that I agree with that, that she quite deserves sainthood. *I* would have been saying something, but you know, I don't want to take anybody's honors away from them. I just don't know why she didn't *do* something about it.

This coordinator and others blame Eunice Rivers because she did not intervene in the study to terminate it or to inform subjects that an effective treatment for syphilis had become available. While it may indeed be true that HBO's depiction of Rivers romanticizes her role in the Tuskegee study, these coordinators ignore how little power Rivers had to shape or stop a federally funded project of that scale and scope.

Nonetheless, coordinator intervention into studies has become a manifestation of research ethics. Although coordinators are not going to be able to shape the research and development agendas of the pharmaceutical industry, they can shape the types of studies that their investigative sites take on or avoid. One particular coordinator effectively convinced the investigator with whom she was working to stop accepting contracts from all pharmaceutical companies for a particular type of new drug. From her experience with multiple studies in this clinical and pharmacological area, the coordinator began to see negative effects on patient-subjects. She recounted,

> A while back, I'm going to say about three or four years ago, we were doing some studies with a medication that was out. It was kind of a new classification [of drugs], and we had worked with three different pharmaceutical companies. And it just seemed like this classification of drugs just had really *a lot* of side effects. . . . Well, I finally got to the point where I said, "No, I don't want to do these studies." And so I had to talk to Dr. X and say, "You know these meds? We're supposed to be here helping mankind and these medicines aren't. They're making them worse and [causing] a lot of pain. That's not what we're here for, so I don't want to do these studies. If you want to do these studies, that's fine, but you'll need to find somebody else to do it for you. Because I can't legitimately give people these medications, knowing that it could cause them more pain when that's what we're trying to help them through. . . ." After I had talked to Dr. X about that, he said, "Hey, you know what, you're right, we're not going to do any more of these studies." And we didn't do any more of those studies. . . . When I know things are not going like they should, I need to say, "Whoa, I'm done. We can't do this. I don't want to endanger somebody's life."

She also told me that because coordinators have more direct interaction with patient-subjects than do investigators, they have more knowledge about side effects that might occur.[28] As a result, she concluded, coordinators are ethically obligated to bring those problems to investigators' attention.

Experiences such as this coordinator's have the potential to lead to coordinators feeling disillusioned with the pharmaceutical industry. Yet few coordinators I interviewed made any general criticisms of the pharmaceutical industry, the process of drug development, or the products in the pipeline.

This is not to say, however, that coordinators have no critiques of how studies are run or about the companies for whom they were conducting studies. Because of their own views about ethics and their responsibilities to their patient-subjects, some coordinators raised issues about how pharmaceutical companies make decisions about the details of the studies.

Most of the time, criticisms of pharmaceutical companies were not direct attacks but were framed instead as coordinators' desire for studies to operate differently. For example, some coordinators were particularly concerned about the lack of aftercare given to patient-subjects at the completion of a study. In one case, a seasoned coordinator did not mince words over her frustration with the pharmaceutical companies:

> The one thing that I find really troublesome is that most of our studies have to have a rescue medication that's already on the market. When we're done, we throw all that away. Well, we have to confiscate it . . . and [the pharmaceutical companies] throw it away. They throw it in the garbage after we ship it back. Those medications are destroyed because they say nobody can use them. That bothers me because I feel the pharmaceutical companies should be able to say, "Let the patients have it when they're done with a study, when the study's done."

The critique of the pharmaceutical companies' practice of destroying unused medications reveals that coordinators see an ethical breach by those companies. Even though it would violate FDA rules, those pills represent for coordinators the possibility of providing care for patient-subjects after the close of a clinical trial through the use of those already-marketed drugs. That the pharmaceutical companies destroy pills rather than offering a temporary treatment for patient-subjects' conditions at the conclusion of studies is viewed by coordinators as companies' unethical choice that cannot be justified on the grounds of good scientific practice.

These brief examples of the ways in which coordinators' construction of ethics are slowly beginning to be formalized indicate that their professional identities are still in formation. While coordinators may not continue to develop critiques of the pharmaceutical industry, their focus on ethics can be seen as putting them in opposition to the companies for whom they are conducting studies. Ethics becomes one effective way in which to prioritize care work and the needs of patient-subjects over the demands of the industry to which they are accountable.

Conclusion

Research coordinators' construction of their professional ethics illustrates the interplay between gendered role identities and a system of pharmaceutical research that both clashes with and exploits those identities. The importance of gender is underscored by the extent to which it is woven through coordinators' narratives about who should be a coordinator, especially in how they frame the relationships they form with patient-subjects. For example, empathy and compassion are coded both as the domain of women and as the human element coordinators add to clinical trials. And it is those characteristics of their professional identities that coordinators claim are the necessary foundation for research ethics in the conduct of clinical trials.

In contrast to investigators, who actively construct their identity as entrepreneurial agents based on their motivations to conduct trials and who discount the degree to which this arrangement makes them emissaries of the pharmaceutical industry, coordinators actively construct their identities in response to and as a form of resistance to the role that is imposed on them concerning their duties to the pharmaceutical industry. On one hand, the job description is clear that the function of coordinators is to facilitate the process of obtaining and reporting data from human subjects about pharmaceutical companies' investigative products. On the other hand, the experience of the job itself frequently compels coordinators to prioritize the needs of the subjects over those of the pharmaceutical industry. This is because coordinators have intensive contact with patient-subjects and much more limited contact with the companies sponsoring the studies. Coordinators attempt to resolve these competing interests by mobilizing a discourse and practice of research ethics that justifies the insertion of an "ethic of care" into the work that they do. By framing their interactions with patient-subjects in terms of ethics, coordinators balance their responsibility to the pharmaceutical industry with their responsibility to patient-subjects.

While this orientation toward clinical trials is clearly laudable, it is also problematic. Of course, it should be the goal of human subjects research to treat study volunteers with respect and care, but coordinators' orientation toward ethics simultaneously serves the profit motive of pharmaceutical companies. The relationships that coordinators build with subjects enable the recruitment, enrollment, and retention of those subjects in drug studies. Moreover, coordinators' focus on the "big picture" of medical progress benefits pharmaceutical development in two ways. First, it paints a false picture of the benefits that individuals can gain from their participation in clinical trials. Every patient will not experience a "magic bullet" cure as did the arthritis patient who entered a study in a wheelchair and ended it by "skipping" out of the clinic. The orientation toward benefits also obscures the research component of clinical trials by rhetorically erasing the presence of placebos in study protocols and the indeterminacy of the safety and efficacy of the products under investigation.

Second, coordinators' mobilization of altruism can lead to the further exploitation of disenfranchised groups. Rather than patient-subjects participating in clinical trials out of instrumental motivations, coordinators want subjects to participate for the greater good, a good that they might never benefit from if they are living in poverty or have no health insurance. By making subjects' participation about altruism, coordinators are inadvertently condoning the pharmaceutical industry's instrumental use of disenfranchised groups, which coordinators never problematize. The African American woman employed as a recruiter to increase the involvement of minorities in pharmaceutical research is an example of how trying to do good for individuals and communities also benefits the pharmaceutical industry in disturbing ways. In sum, coordinators add a softer, maternal face to the demands of drug development. Through their work, coordinators ensure both current and future consumers of pharmaceutical products—as nurses have traditionally ensured compliant patients—within the system of medicine and health care delivery.

Chapter 5

Monitoring the Clinical Trials Industry

One Wednesday evening, I drove to an airport hotel for an interview with Evelyn,[1] a clinical research associate, or "monitor," at a large contract research organization (CRO). Her company was based in another region of the country, and this was the last evening she was in town before returning home from a two-week trip during which she conducted three site visits in three cities in the Southwest. Because her only "office" while in town consisted of a back room at the investigative site she was there to monitor, she suggested we meet for the interview in the hotel lobby.

Evelyn, a Latina in her late fifties, was a nurse who had been recruited nine years earlier into study monitoring by a friend and former nurse colleague. For a number of years, she resisted going to work for the CRO in spite of her friend's adamancy that she join her at the company. She explained that she was afraid of giving up the patient care that had defined her professional identity for over twenty years in order to take on an "auditing" type of position. Eventually, however, she gave in, interviewed for the job, and found herself on a plane the very next day to accompany her friend on a site visit. Since that first trip, she informed me, she has doubled her salary and has never once missed nursing.

At the time of our meeting, Evelyn was a designated team leader on a large phase III, four-year clinical trial of an investigational weight loss product being tested at sixty-five clinical sites in the United States. Her role as team leader made her the primary contact person between her CRO and the sponsoring pharmaceutical company, and she oversaw other monitors who

were each assigned several sites to monitor. She described in excited tones
how she had been responsible for designing the SOPs (standard operating
procedures) for the study, including testing and using the weighing scale for
the trial. In addition, she had designed the case report forms that were given
to sites to fill out with the details of patient-subjects' participation. Evelyn
had brought a large bag with her to the lobby, and she pulled out many forms
to show to me (after verifying that they did not contain any proprietary or
confidential information) and thoroughly explicated the duties and responsibilities of monitors.

Although monitors themselves may have a plethora of responsibilities
within their companies, monitoring clinical trials involves three stages: site
selection (also known as site qualification), site monitoring, and site closing. As these names indicate, the task of monitoring is configured in relation
to the investigative sites conducting the studies. Site selection, the initial
stage of interaction with sites, requires that monitors visit the site to assess
its appropriateness for specific study protocols. During these visits, monitors
meet with study staff to discuss their clinical trial experience and get information about the sites' patient populations or past recruitment successes. In
addition, monitors will inspect the facilities to ensure that relevant equipment needed for studies is present. Monitors are also frequently the individuals with whom site staff will negotiate details of the budget and contract.

Once sites are selected and clinical trials have begun, study monitoring
begins according to the schedule laid out in the protocol. Although studies'
significant differences in length and complexity impact upon the amount of
time monitors must spend at each site, as a rule, monitors travel to each site for
a few days every six weeks. During site visits, it is the monitors' job to verify
that the site is being compliant with study protocols, that source documents
match case report forms, that informed consent has been obtained from each
patient-subject, that regulatory documents like IRB submissions are up to
date, and that the inventory of investigational drugs or devices is appropriate.
Most sites create office space for monitors to do their work during a site visit,
and at the conclusion of monitors' review, they meet with coordinators, and
less frequently physician-investigators, to discuss their findings, particularly
any errors or omissions.

At the conclusion of each clinical trial, whether the study lasts only a
few days or a few years, monitors return to sites for a closing visit. At that
time, monitors review any remaining documentation that has been produced
since their last study visit, retrieve all materials and equipment that is the

property of the CRO or pharmaceutical company, retrieve or destroy remaining investigational drugs or devices, and review the site's study file to ensure its completeness in case of a sponsor or FDA audit. Monitors also review with coordinators and/or investigators all policies regarding storage of files, IRB requirements, and publication agreements with which the sites must comply. Evelyn added that site closings are very busy with activities that monitors have to complete, but these site visits are often sad, too, when they mean saying goodbye to staff that she has gotten to know well during lengthy studies.

Monitors' relationships with sites are complex. While there is much work associated with monitoring clinical trials, the primary function of the job, Evelyn reminded me, is to ensure the integrity of the pharmaceutical companies' data, particularly to detect any fraud that might occur. This means that, on one hand, monitors encourage a collaborative atmosphere to help sites conduct studies well. Through this process, monitors can, and often do, develop strong bonds with individuals working at sites. Evelyn referred to this process as becoming the coordinators' "best friend." On the other hand, monitors are performing an audit function and have control over what information about sites is reported back to the pharmaceutical companies. This role can, and often does, lead to antagonism between the monitor and site staff, particularly when the site is new to clinical research and more prone to making mistakes.

Adding to the complexity of relationships between monitors and site staff is the ambiguity of their authority over sites. A major problem in the industry is that monitors are supposed to be the representatives of the sponsoring pharmaceutical companies (even when they are employed by CROs), but project managers and others at those companies too frequently communicate directly with sites and cut monitors out of the information loop. Evelyn described how frustrating it is to be conducting a routine monitoring visit and find out from coordinators that a pharmaceutical company has made a significant change to the study protocol. When this happens, monitors are delegitimized because they do not have the full information about the studies they are overseeing, and subsequently, sites feel encouraged to sidestep monitors and speak directly to managers and administrators higher up in the chain of command.

Although Evelyn had incredible insights into monitoring and the clinical trials industry after working nearly a decade in the profession, she seemed less aware of the more intangible, or even symbolic, aspects of her role. Harder to see from the inside is the extent to which the role of monitoring is reflective of the broader political economy. With women predominantly filling the ranks, monitoring, like coordinating, is feminized labor that the industry considers unskilled. Monitors are the embodiment of neoliberal audit culture within clinical drug development, and they lack the resources or authority to craft the rules within the norms and logics of that managerial culture. Moreover, the trend for pharmaceutical companies to hire CROs to manage clinical trials means that CRO monitors become symbols of outsourcing for sites. Any frustrations that investigators or coordinators have with outsourcing, especially with CROs, are routinely blamed on individual monitors.

Monitoring and the Political Economy of Pharmaceutical Studies

The system of monitoring clinical studies is unique to pharmaceutical product development. Federally funded clinical grants do not require the same type of oversight of research as do private-sector drug and device studies. The distinction between the types of research is made on the basis of the market. The clinical testing of products to be reviewed by the FDA for prescription sale has different rules than do investigator-initiated grants through government agencies. Having a robust system in place to oversee the activities at and data produced by investigative sites is a source of pride for many within the clinical trials industry because it illustrates their commitment to safety and data integrity in a way that is different from publicly funded projects.

The FDA does not mandate that pharmaceutical companies have designated *employees* to monitor the clinical trials that are conducted as part of the drug approval process. What the regulation stipulates is that the pharmaceutical companies oversee the progress of clinical studies to ensure the safety of human subjects and to verify the integrity of the data. This means that the system of monitoring as it is now organized by the clinical trials industry is technically voluntary. The FDA has, however, developed its own system of "guidance" that stipulates that individuals should be selected as monitors for particular studies to aid in the selection of sites and perform periodic site visits to verify the appropriateness of those sites and to systematically review all patient-subject records.[2] Pharmaceutical companies are ultimately allowed to design their own system of monitoring, but if not done thoroughly, they risk the possibility that the FDA will deem their oversight inadequate and refuse to review their new drug applications.

Hiring individuals to monitor the progress of clinical trials makes a lot of sense to pharmaceutical companies in an era of outsourcing to hundreds of private-sector and academic sites. Whether the pharmaceutical companies use their own employees or outsource the task to CROs, they are able to build neoliberal audit culture into the distribution of labor to maintain control over the drug development process.[3] Monitoring becomes a mechanism to enforce rationality and accountability onto a process of clinical development that is distributed among many places and to many contract researchers and their staff. Pharmaceutical companies may not be able to determine the extent to which they can trust that investigators and coordinators are collecting data honestly and according to protocol. Having monitors conduct frequent site visits and review all study documentation helps to structure site compliance and provide frequent feedback about sites' performances to the pharmaceutical companies.

A key objective of monitoring is to prevent or detect investigator fraud. Clinical trials can be a very profitable activity for investigators, particularly if their enrollment of subjects is high. While the majority of investigators do not engage in gross misconduct, there have been high-profile cases of fraud in the industry. Interestingly, the most extreme case of fraud occurred in spite of the system of monitoring already in place, and dozens of monitors failed to discover the problem.

Although it took three years to come to public attention, June 1996 was a monumental month for pharmaceutical clinical trials. The events that came to light catalyzed what was to become the biggest FDA investigation in the history of drug research. During that month, Susan Lester alerted the FDA to the fraudulent practices of Dr. Robert Fiddes and his company, Southern California Research Institute (SCRI), in Los Angeles. She reported that Fiddes had been committing fraud for several years in his clinical trials business and endangering patient-subjects in the process. At the time of her initial contact with the FDA, Lester had resigned from her coordinator position at the company because she could no longer participate in what she saw as the unethical and fraudulent practices demanded by Fiddes.

Lester was not the first coordinator to quit her job because of disapproval of Fiddes's activities. One year earlier, Dawn Simons had been assigned to a hypertension study into which a seventy-year-old woman was enrolled. During the course of the study, the patient-subject's blood pressure became dangerously elevated, so Simons made an appointment for the woman to see Dr. Fiddes. His response to the situation was to prescribe two marketed hypertension drugs and to instruct her to take those in conjunction with the study pill (either an investigational medication or a placebo). Of course Fiddes's action violated the study protocol, but by all accounts, he wanted her to continue in the study. Within a matter of days, the patient-subject's heart had nearly stopped, and she was brought to the clinic with slurred speech and unable to walk. Fearing that the woman would suffer from cardiac arrest and die, Simons pleaded with Fiddes to drop the woman from the study. When he refused, Simons instructed the woman to go to the hospital. At that point, Simons copied all of the patient-subjects' records, gave them to the woman in case she wanted to sue Fiddes, and resigned from her position. In the eyes of Simons and Lester, Fiddes was not only defrauding the pharmaceutical companies but also seriously jeopardizing the health and lives of the patients enrolled in studies.

Through the course of an extensive eight-month investigation, the FDA and FBI verified that Fiddes and his staff had committed criminal fraud. According to an official FDA report, under Fiddes's direction, SCRI had:

- Made up study patients entirely. For one vaginal yeast infection study, Fiddes falsified virtually all the results, using data from old patients' charts to make it appear that more than twenty-five patients had participated in the study when only one patient was actually enrolled. In a birth control study, employees made up information to continue medical records of patients who had actually dropped out of the study. In that study, too, patients who remained in the study were told to stay on the birth control they were already using.
- Failed to conduct required physical examinations on some patients and falsified the results of physical exams on others. Some physical exams were skipped altogether. In one study for an osteoarthritis drug, Fiddes documented normal x-rays as abnormal, saying they showed bone spurs or other signs of disease.
- Substituted medical information of an SCRI employee for a patient's true data. For example, an employee substituted her own high-protein urine for the urine of various patients who did not have protein levels high enough to qualify for a diabetes and high blood pressure study. Also, employees used their own blood samples for three fictitious patients in a birth control study.[4]

In September 1998, a U.S. District Court found Fiddes guilty of fraud, sentenced him to fifteen months in prison, ordered him to repay $800,000 to several pharmaceutical companies he had wronged, and debarred him for a period of twenty years. In a formal letter of debarment to Fiddes, the director of the FDA Center for Drug Evaluation and Research wrote, "Your actions reveal that you were not concerned with the drug regulatory process or the welfare of the subjects who participated in the studies or of the public at large. The Agency finds that you displayed a wanton disregard for the public health and the drug regulatory process."[5] Many in the clinical trials industry felt that justice had been served because the doctor had been caught, prosecuted, and imprisoned.

However, when the *New York Times* printed a story on the case, it called public attention to the limitations of the government's and pharmaceutical companies' entire system of oversight of clinical trials.[6] Most disconcerting was Fiddes' statement that he had been behaving no differently than other doctors who were similarly using drug studies to supplement or replace revenue of their private practices. News media picked up the story, airing exposé style reports—including one on *60 Minutes* as late as April 2001—and questioning the safety of drugs in the United States given the outsourcing of studies to the private sector. In response, the FDA claimed that no concern about the safety of marketed drugs was justified. They argued that there was adequate data about the drugs that Fiddes had worked on, collected from other sources, so the FDA approval of those products was warranted.

The Fiddes scandal revealed to the pharmaceutical industry, the FDA, and the public a fraud of disturbing magnitude. To make matters worse, monitors from pharmaceutical companies and CROs had been routinely making site visits to SCRI and inspecting source documents and case report forms. That no one suspected that Fiddes and his staff were perpetrating fraud meant reevaluating how monitors should engage with the documentation produced by investigative sites. Rather than verifying the data for each patient-subject enrolled in studies, monitors were asked to compare the data *across subjects* for patterns in reports of vital signs, blood counts, and other tests as well as in the signatures of subjects on informed consent forms. Thus, monitors' roles shifted from primarily verifying that the data from each patient-subject was complete and accurate to assessing whether the data produced originated from separate individuals. The Fiddes case led to the amplification of monitors' duties to make fraud detection the primary objective of site visits.

Dual Roles of Pharmaceutical Monitors

Monitors are the link between investigative sites and pharmaceutical companies. They become the ambassadors of the pharmaceutical companies by having regular personal contact with and physical presence at the sites. Monitors have a dual function: one that is work intensive and one that is symbolic of outsourcing. The function of working with all the data cannot be overstated. Evelyn described this as the "nitty-gritty" of monitoring. Nonetheless, the symbolic function should also not be underestimated. Official industry sources highlight the complexity of monitors' roles. A primer on monitoring states, "The CRA [monitor] must be able to act as a cheerleader and coach, as well as an 'enforcer.' These are difficult roles to perform all at the same time."[7]

"Nitty-Gritty" of Monitoring

Monitors, or clinical research associates (CRAs) as they are formally called, are recruited from the ranks of coordinators, nurses, and—increasingly— pending college graduates. Like coordinators, the majority of monitors are women.[8] As a profession, it has the aura of cutting-edge work in the pursuit of medical progress with the benefits of excellent salaries and potential for travel. Additionally, it is an attractive career because there is little emphasis on prior experience. This portrayal of monitoring clinical trials is not inaccurate as such, but it does not convey the hierarchies and nuances of an industry increasingly focused on outsourcing and accountability.

The structure of the clinical trials industry is such that monitors can be employed in three ways. First, they can be on the staff of specific pharmaceutical companies and do the monitoring of clinical trials for that company. Second, they can be hired by CROs and assigned to the clinical trials of any pharmaceutical company using their services. Third, and least common, they can operate as independent contractors and work directly for any pharmaceutical company or CRO that hires them.

The majority of new monitors are recruited and employed by CROs, so it is through CROs that most monitors receive training and experience. As a result, positions with pharmaceutical companies are considered more prestigious than those with CROs, and most CRO monitors are anxious to be recruited by pharmaceutical companies. Independent contract monitors have the ability to make much more money than can either of the other two types, but because there is so much instability associated with this type of position, few monitors take this employment risk. On this hierarchy, a CRO monitor explained:

> Well, it was always like the dream of the monitors at [my CRO] that eventually we would move on to the pharmaceutical companies. The perception is that any of the CROs are a stepping-stone up to being a monitor at the pharmaceutical company level. And then eventually from that, if you were ambitious enough, you would become a

contract CRA. That's where you made "the big bucks." But it was a general perception that being a monitor at a pharmaceutical company was not only a better job, but you made more money. . . . I've never been a monitor for a pharmaceutical company, but it was definitely what we all aspired to do.

The structure of monitor employment encourages high turnover because horizontal movement between companies can greatly increase monitors' wages and benefits. As a result, it is common for monitors to jump from CRO to CRO and then from pharmaceutical company to pharmaceutical company. Most drug studies with a duration of more than six months will have at least one change in monitor over the course of the study, and it is not uncommon to hear about four or more monitors assigned to studies that last more than a year. Monitor turnover often causes periods of disruption as sites adjust to newly assigned monitors.

Currently, very little experience is necessary for people to qualify for jobs as monitors, especially with CROs. Although having experience in medicine is seen as an incredible asset for the individual monitor, there are few requirements that limit who could be employed in the position. The groups most heavily recruited by CROs, however, are coordinators, nurses, and college graduates with degrees in the sciences. The targeted groups illustrate different emphases of what characteristics make good monitors. Coordinators are advantaged by already having a sophisticated understanding of clinical trials and of the industry itself. Like some coordinators, nurses are well qualified for monitoring because they are already familiar with medical terminology and procedures, and they typically have specific expertise about one realm of medicine or illness that can be useful when assigning specific studies to monitors. A pharmaceutical company monitor explained,

> It's definitely better, in my opinion, [when] you know the disease better and the history of the medications you're working on. It's a whole new language, every therapeutic area that you're in. And if you've never worked in oncology before, and you try to monitor an oncology program, just the drugs alone, it'll take you months to study up and be familiar with it.

In comparison, monitors with college degrees in the natural sciences possess an understanding of research protocols and the importance of data through their training in scientific methods. As a CRO monitor with a science degree said,

Being a monitor doesn't require a whole lot of medical knowledge. Typically, any life science degree will get you in. Biochemistry is almost a little too specific. I mean, I knew people I worked with, with psych degrees, even like animal husbandry or something, something random like that. . . . I never felt ill-prepared or anything. It really wasn't a job that I think you could learn outside of it; you just sort of learned as you went.

As this monitor indicated, none of the groups is already prepared for the job without training. Monitors must learn how to read the case report forms that sites fill out and to anticipate what formal "queries" that data entry employees will have before the fact. This means that they need to develop a deep understanding of the specific protocols to which they are assigned and also have at least a basic understanding of how the qualitative case report forms become quantitative data.

Training for monitoring positions differs from company to company. Some pharmaceutical companies and CROs have formal classroom-style training whereas others assign new employees to work with more experienced monitors to learn the system and skills. A veteran nurse turned monitor was trained by working with an experienced monitor for several months. She explained why she did not receive any classroom instruction:

Well, as a nurse, I think I was probably trained a little bit differently because I already knew medications from my experience with medications. I knew what certain conditions were, so I didn't have to have that kind of training in medical terminology. Monitors do come into it without all of that training; like I've worked with some people that might have a degree in biology, that kind of thing, so they might have to go through that extra training.

Other monitors pay out of pocket for training courses offered by the Drug Information Association (DIA) or the Society of Clinical Research Associates (SOCRA) as a way of obtaining formal credentials and increasing their marketability towards the top CROs or pharmaceutical companies. A monitor who had done so said,

I went back East and took an entry-level clinical research associate class through the Drug Information Association. They have entry-level, intermediate, and advanced classes, and I paid for that out of my pocket, but that was kind of how I learned about what exactly it was. And it got my feet wet in it. It was a three- or four-day class. Then I knew somebody within [a major pharmaceutical company] and he said, "Oh, we're looking for people who are entry-level people." It was that I kind of happened to be in the right place at the right time sort of thing. . . . I've never worked for a CRO, and from what I understand, I'm lucky!

Role of Gender in Monitoring

The hiring and training of individuals in monitoring positions is highly influenced by gender roles and norms. Monitoring is a feminized profession in part because the majority of those hired are women but also because of the extent to which "feminine" characteristics are seen as assets for the job. The predominance of women may simply be due to the large number of coordinators (who tend to be women) who are recruited by CROs and pharmaceutical companies to become monitors with the promise of higher salaries and more status within the industry. An additional benefit is the possibility of promotion, unlike most coordinator positions: monitors have more opportunities for advancement within CROs and pharmaceutical companies. A male monitor who had recently quit his job to begin his own company explained the extent to which the managerial team at his former CRO was female:

> [The clinical trials industry] is actually a very female-oriented industry. All my managers were female at [CRO]; all my managers' managers were female. It seemed like a lot of the management, I mean, and not even the management, just the workforce itself. [This CRO] had to be at least 75 percent female I would say. . . . In my office, almost the entire managerial tree was female. Now you get up towards the upper echelons, you know, in the world headquarters, and I think that that was still mostly men.

The position is often discussed explicitly in terms both of its suitability for women and its challenges for women.

Many monitors argue that monitoring is a job for which women are better candidates than are men because it requires attention to details, intuition, and interpersonal skills. First, monitoring requires an appreciation for fine details and the patience to be systematic and thorough. Many in the clinical trials industry believe that women are better suited to the work than men because most men would view the tasks as too tedious or onerous. As Evelyn explained, "I guess it appeals to a person who really likes little nitty-gritty.

You have to become obsessive-compulsive and look at tiny, little items . . . so it's very good [work] for nurses."

A second component of the gendered construction of monitoring is the importance placed on intuition which is framed as an essential element in monitors' ability to identify fraud in the industry. For instance, monitors are said to need good instincts about the sites and also to know how to ask the right questions. In their descriptions of their work, monitors talk about how intuition gets folded into their training to find sham data through errors and omissions in the case report forms. A monitor explained the technical side of trying to detect fraud: "We're taught to learn how to look at data that's given to us and look for patterns of fraud, and to make sure there are indeed patients, that it looks like patients are going in and out [of the clinics], and the data looks correct."

However, technical training is often not enough for monitors to be able to detect cases of fraud, and most monitors have experiences of being assigned to clinical trials in which one of their sites was later revealed to have engaged in fraudulent practices. Monitors argue that fraud is very hard to detect because monitoring is disconnected from patient-subjects' visits in order to protect subjects' anonymity and privacy. Even with specific training to look for signs of deception in the data reported by sites, it is often hard to find. For example, a monitor confessed,

> There was one [fraudulent] site when I first started out that I went to. I had no idea! That was right in my very first year and actually like in my second month of working, and I was out with another monitor who was teaching me. And actually there were two investigators, it was over in Georgia, and they both went to jail for fraud, and it was very well known in the research area. . . . I can't remember exactly what the fraud was, but I know that it was not something that I picked up. I was too new to have any feeling about it, but even the experienced monitor that I was with, she had been going there for a while, for over a year at least at that site, and she didn't know it either, so they can be really good [at covering it up].

Another monitor with whom I spoke had been monitoring Fiddes's site when it was tipped off to the FDA, and she helped investigate the data that had not been destroyed by Fiddes and his staff:

> The first site I ever went to when I was a monitor ended up being, I don't know if you've heard of the whole Fiddes façade. You heard he

was creating patients? Yeah, that was my first site I ever went to. And they had multiple sponsor audits, they had multiple FDA audits. That was the first site I ever went to, and I ended up helping close that site out, and you would have never known! I mean, they were really good [at covering it up]. So you do see it [fraud]. I've seen some more *minor* cases, you don't see *that* sort of [major] fraud very often.

Because gross examples are so rare and so well disguised, monitors admit that there is no foolproof way of detecting fraud. Although they talk about the systematic ways in which they routinely check the data for accuracy, they place a very strong emphasis on their intuition or feelings about sites. A monitor explained,

> You sort of get a *feel* for—when you see patients really go in and out of the site—you get a feel for whether the site is a legit site or not. And I think that, I don't know, part of that just comes with intuition and feeling about whether it feels right or doesn't feel right. If it's a big clinic, a big set up, and you see people going in and out, that gives you a good, good feeling that everything's okay. . . . If you sort of don't believe the physician, and there's just something that you've got a *feel,* and I think a nurse particularly would feel that because most nurses have that kind of intuitive ability anyway.

This emphasis on intuition or a "feel" also manifests in monitors' interpersonal skills. It is not only the signals they get about sites but being able to translate their interpretation of those signals into appropriate, nonthreatening questions. In one interview, a monitor explained that she focuses on how "real" patient-subjects seem to be through their data:

> It's partially a gut instinct, but there's definitely red flags to look for. You know you just look for trends in the data to see if it's all starting to look the same. There's a lot of different ways you can do it, but it's a lot of it asking the right questions of the coordinators, talking to *them,* because they're really the eyes and ears of the site. And if they come to you and say "We kind of have a little problem," then you've got to ask the right questions.

An interesting ramification of this approach is that when patient-subjects appear suspicious in the case report forms, monitors will warn the sites about those cases. They are very cautious about accusing sites of malfeasance, so they often broach the subject in guarded terms. From the sites' perspective, this approach by monitors can be frustrating. A coordinator explained how it feels to be on the receiving end of these warnings, "We've had some monitors that come in and say, 'You shouldn't have picked this patient because I don't feel that this patient is very real.' They're not accusing us of the patients not actually being *present,* but they say things like, 'Maybe you shouldn't have picked this patient.'" Yet from the monitors' perspective, this is one way in which to test the waters about a site's conduct. They talk about how important it is never to accuse coordinators outright of any fraud. Coordinators, however, interpret the monitors' warnings as a judgment of the appropriateness of patient-subjects.

Monitors' emphasis on intuition in assessing sites and relating to coordinators highlights the importance of interpersonal skills for the job. Another aspect of the need for these skills is that monitors must be able to communicate to investigators and coordinators regularly about the mistakes that they have made. And industry insiders insist that *women* are better able to give this information in a less threatening and more diplomatic way. According to one female monitor,

> Coordinators have an extremely difficult job, and I think that's one of the reasons I work well with them because I can *see* that they have a very hard job, you know? They're balancing a lot of things. And in most cases, they're trying to do a good job for their patients. . . . Most men wouldn't be able to see that. [Besides] the women that I've worked with . . . when we have our phone calls, we always say, "Well, what are you doing this weekend?" So it's become kind of a personal basis.

Additionally, women monitors are said to place more emphasis on cooperation or teamwork. Another female monitor explained that women "work more closely with the sites to help them. We're not there just auditing them and saying, 'This is bad, this is bad!' You know, it's kind of a *team* effort. So if we work together, I always say, 'If you work with me, I'll try to make you look good and you can make me look good, and we'll work. It'll be a great team that way.'"

Given that monitors technically have authority over those working at sites, including the physicians, it is often emphasized that women are better at not *appearing* to have more power. This is important, according to monitors, because the best working relationships with physicians, who are predominantly male, occur when monitors do not boss them around but make suggestions that physicians and their staff *want* to take. A monitor described the gender and power dynamic:

There are some monitors—especially men, but, you know, not always—
that for some reason think they've been appointed by God to do this work
or something, and . . . they can come in, just power hungry or something,
and they come in and really make people's lives very miserable to get the
things [done] that need to be done. I don't think that that's necessary. . . .
I know that some PIs, some doctors, don't want people coming in and
bossing them around. *They're* the boss, they're the boss in *their* offices,
and they don't like somebody coming in and wielding their power with
them. I always try to respect what they do. They *are* the boss, they know
what they're doing. And I try to get done what I need to have done without doing it [wielding my power] because that's really not necessary. . . .
There's always people in every area that just really get off on power, and
being a monitor can give you power. I mean you're coming in, you're
really kind of the boss to say to the site, you need to do it this way, this
way, and this way, *but* you don't have to make it *appear* that way.

The sense that monitors, especially women monitors, should not flaunt
the power that they have over investigators is a carryover from traditional
doctor-nurse relationships. It is not surprising that monitors who were practicing nurses before they entered the clinical trials industry maintain this
style for interacting with physicians to get their own goals accomplished.[9]
What is interesting is that monitors learn this mode when they have less institutional power and rank than physicians but continue using it when they
have more institutional power.

While women may seem well suited to the job of monitoring because of
their "innate" skills, those in the clinical trials industry often discuss it as a
very difficult career. Most monitoring positions involve considerable travel,
which is seen as an obstacle to having a happy and fulfilling personal life. A
female administrator at a large SMO described how monitoring can be difficult for women:

[Monitors have] a very demanding travel schedule, and frankly I haven't
met that many monitors who seem to love their jobs. . . . They seem to
be very stressed as far as deadlines and the amount of work that has to
be done and the amount of travel and verge of exhaustion. I'm sure a lot
of them burn out also. . . . Many times *men* can travel, or it seems that
the way our society is set up, especially the majority of women monitors are *single* women; you see very few married with children. However, you see a lot of male monitors married with children, but then

someone's still staying at home with the kids or whatever. So there's *that* dynamic, the travel thing makes it a little more complicated . . . It's not exactly a lifestyle for relationships, for married people, I would say, or family life.

Motherhood, especially, is considered a major obstacle to being a monitor. One female monitor related what she has seen among her colleagues:

Men make excellent monitors just because they don't have to worry about childcare most of the time now. Young women, it's very hard, some of them work and some of them have young children, and it's bad . . . when they try to take care of kids. . . . I have one of my team members that has an adorable little girl. She's about this big, and my company . . . was in [a particular city], and she really just got tired of the travel [because of] that baby. That baby was really hard; the baby would cry and say, "Mommy, don't leave me, don't leave me!" And it was really horrible, so she took a [different] job.

Monitoring is also perceived as being difficult for single women because of the strain it puts on their dating lives. None of the monitors I interviewed discussed this themselves, but many younger coordinators used this as a reason why they would not want to become monitors in spite of the offers they have received from CROs. A female coordinator described the impact of monitoring she has seen on women's social lives:

It is a burnout career for a CRA, or otherwise a monitor, because they are flying, they're young, they have no life, no social life. They can't have a boyfriend when they're spending four days here, of building a relationship and having that, and so there's this overturn of CRAs . . . I can understand it. You have a boyfriend, and you're out of town for two weeks, and he's lonely. And there's troubles in paradise, okay? [she winks] . . . I feel sorry for them, especially the young ones.

The message is that monitoring is a job that is perfectly suited for the skills that women (inherently) have, but that the demands of the job require a lifestyle that is not compatible with the needs of women and their families. This contradiction associated with monitoring is one of the ways in which gender is constructed and made central to the profession. By enabling (if not creating) the conditions in which women monitors are manipulated into believing that they are valued for their gendered skills, yet it is their sex that

makes the job a problem for them, the clinical trials industry does not need
to adapt the demands of the job so that the system is flexible for its workers,
whether men or women.

Instead, the industry inculcates the value of worker flexibility so that
monitors will internalize the demands of the job without being externally
managed. For instance, a female CRO monitor proudly asserted,

> I think I'm at the point now where nobody has to tell me I have to do
> it. It's my job, it's my team, and I work with the sponsor, and I just say,
> "We'll get it done." Then I just do it; I'll look at my schedule and do it.
> But it's part of what makes a good monitor is you don't have to have
> somebody beating you over the head to tell you this is what you have
> to do; you *know* what you have to do.

Her statement underscores the extent to which many monitors have internalized the postindustrial logics that shape the clinical trials industry. A training manual for monitors emphasizes these values in its explanation of the
role of monitors in disciplining themselves to achieve success:

> So what type of person makes a good CRA, and what skills are required
> to be successful? A CRA should be someone who is a self-starter with
> good interpersonal relationship skills, who is detail-oriented and a good
> writer and speaker. A CRA must be self-confident, flexible and adapt-
> able to a changing environment. He or she must also be focused, manage
> time well and follow through on problems and commitments.[10]

The primer continues,

> Most CRAs spend a significant amount of time working away from the
> office without close supervision. It can be very easy to sleep in or go
> shopping, or involve yourself in any number of other diversions when
> your supervisor isn't around. Good CRAs maintain the same discipline
> and work habits on the road as they do in the office. . . . You must ask
> yourself: . . . Do I do an honest day's work, in or out of the office? . . .
> Do I travel well? Do my personal commitments allow me to travel with
> a clear conscience?[11]

While this description of the right worker for the job could be used for many
positions in many sectors of the U.S. economy, the point here is to show the
extent to which the clinical trials industry relies on monitors to adapt to the
demands of the position by being flexible workers who have internalized their

responsibility to the companies for which they work. Moreover, monitors must do this without clear lines of authority drawn for them within the broader organization of the clinical trials industry. Structurally speaking, the gendering of the task of monitoring pharmaceutical studies serves to maintain hierarchies and power dynamics in a dispersed industry that is interested in creating systems of accountability for outsourced labor.

Symbolic Functions of Monitoring

Monitors are simultaneously seen as symbols of protection of the public's health and welfare, as coordinators' "best friends" to help in the process of reporting back to pharmaceutical companies, and as disruptive representatives of outsourcing. The symbolic framings of monitoring come from the FDA, pharmaceutical companies, and CROs as well as from investigators and coordinators. Monitors may embrace or reject these symbolic roles, but these less tangible functions of monitoring should be seen as institutional impositions on the work that monitors do.

For much of the industry, monitors symbolize the FDA's and the pharmaceutical industry's interest in preserving public health and safety. In order to bring new products to market, the data on which the FDA makes its decisions must be valid and robust so that the government can predict those products' effectiveness and concomitant risks to the general population. Because monitors are helping to make the data generated from studies more accurate, many people in the clinical trials industry have a deep respect for monitoring. Specifically, physicians and coordinators value the public health implications of monitors' work. A site administrator in an SMO articulated this focus:

> I think all of our purpose is to produce data that will protect public safety. I mean public safety is depending on our data being *right*. And so when you look at it that way, would you want to have extra eyes [the monitors'] there to help make sure that your mother who's taking that medication is going to be taking a *safe* medication? So I think we all kind of look at it as our relatives, or *we*, could be taking these medications. People *will* be taking these drugs once they get out on the market. So it's more than just data, it's the public safety at stake. So I don't think you can have too many people helping to monitor that process.

This perspective justifies the invasiveness of regular monitoring visits to sites. It is not that the sites are being singled out but rather that monitoring underscores the importance of their work in drug development.

This is not to say that sites are enthusiastic about monitors' visits. Quite the contrary. Most of the time, coordinators have considerable angst about these visits because they want the sites and themselves to look good to the monitors. Because most coordinators are invested in the quality of their work, they do not want to make mistakes. For example, a coordinator confessed, "I don't know, it's kind of weird. I mean, they come here and actually they're looking for mistakes. Who likes to make mistakes? So of course, I find it to be a stressful time, very stressful actually. Only because I want everything to be right." This is not to say that those coordinators who find the process stressful feel persecuted and are not able to see the purpose of monitoring. In spite of the personal anxiety that monitoring may bring to individuals, coordinators still know that the system is in their own and the public's best interests. Another coordinator explained, "You know, it obviously doesn't *feel* good to have your mistakes pointed out to you, but it's done to improve the quality of the data as well as make data more accurate, and keep things in check and in line to varying degrees."

Perhaps as a discursive way to combat the bad feelings that could result for coordinators who feel picked on when their mistakes are pointed out, there is a strong sense in the industry that coordinators should see monitors as their "best friends" during the course of a drug study. This phrase is often deployed to mean that monitors can be seen as people who will be there for coordinators when they need advice, guidance, or even sympathy. In addition to monitors' site visits, coordinators are encouraged to speak with monitors over the phone or to communicate by e-mail. A coordinator explained how she views her contact with study monitors:

> [Monitors] are like our best friends because a lot of times if we're doing something where we have patients here in the office, that usually is our first line of contact [with the pharmaceutical company] is to contact them because they're very knowledgeable in the protocol and what they want to obtain. And if you have a problem patient and we're not sure what to do, you can call them, and they let us know what we need to do, so we interact with them quite a lot actually.

Part of being "best friends" includes assumptions about the quality and kind of interactions that monitors should have with coordinators. Specifically, monitors are framed as being on the side of coordinators, rather than being critical or confrontational. In her description of "good" monitors, one coordinator seemed to be employing the word "good" to simultaneously convey moral value to monitors as well as to recognize that some may be better at their jobs than others.

> A *good* monitor will just sit with you and be very nonjudgmental, I think, and say, "You know, this is fine, but *this,* you want it this way." . . . So I really think that most of our monitors, we really like them. We have a really good relationship with our monitors because they're there to help you; it's not like they're there to say, "You've done this! Shame on you!" I mean, they're there to help you do a good study as well, and they want a good outcome as well as everybody else, and so do we. . . . This person's here to help you out, to help *you* become a better coordinator as well.

In other words, competence is not enough to make good monitors. They need to have the right attitude and interaction with coordinators.

Also imposed upon monitors is the view of them as examples of the problems with outsourcing. CROs have become major players in the clinical trials industry when it comes to project management and monitoring for pharmaceutical companies. In 2004, the pharmaceutical industry reported outsourcing 57.5 percent of their studies to CROs.[12] Investigative sites have many complaints about CROs, and instead of blaming the pharmaceutical industry or the management of the CROs, monitors become scapegoats for many of coordinators' and investigators' frustrations. The theme that was the most predominant in interviews was that monitors often become a disruption or an obstacle to the work that sites need to complete. Although my interviewees usually qualified their criticisms of monitors in terms of public health and the good of the industry, most investigators and coordinators nonetheless had strong opinions about two related problems with monitors: their high turnover and "personality quirks."

Roughly 60 percent of all monitors change companies within three years, and nearly 80 percent of all monitors are no longer in monitoring positions at all after five years.[13] Higher salaries entice monitors to change jobs, and the intensity of the travel often compels them to abandon the profession all together. The perception of most people in the industry is that the turnover is significantly worse at CROs than at pharmaceutical companies. According to one coordinator, "Some of those CRO monitors, they are swapping CROs so often, and they're always getting new employees. I think that CROs train a lot of new people and then they go on to get another job at another CRO making more money." An investigator voiced his opinion about the problem:

"With CRO personnel, the monitors seem to move around a lot more than monitors with a pharmaceutical company. Pharmaceutical companies stay put much more so. CROs, they flit in, they flit out. I don't know in how many studies that we've had two or three or four different monitors during the course of a study."

While it is true that CROs do have a higher turnover of monitors than pharmaceutical companies, it is not as great a difference as many believe. According to 2001 statistics, about 66 percent of all CRO monitors and 59 percent of all pharmaceutical company monitors change companies within three years.[14] Pharmaceutical companies do better at retaining monitors longer because of the perception that those companies are more desirable places to work than CROs. This does not mean, however, that monitors at pharmaceutical companies will not look to see what options for employment they might have at other pharmaceutical companies.

Whether or not CROs are the problem, sites do experience difficulties because of the high turnover of monitors. One result is that monitors can be inexperienced and uncommitted. The inexperience of monitors is also often seen as a symptom of outsourcing, and sites assume that pharmaceutical companies hire individuals with more prior clinical trials experience than do CROs.[15] However, rather than seeing the responsibility of CROs or pharmaceutical companies to appropriately train new monitors, investigators and coordinators generally fault monitors themselves for their lack of expertise. In a sense, monitors come to represent the shortcomings of CROs and the industry more generally.

High monitor turnover does mean that monitors may not be as well prepared for the job as they should be. Coordinators report being put in a position to give new monitors direction on what they should be doing during study visits. The director of a site that was part of a national SMO vented,

> You get a lot of untrained, well, I shouldn't say untrained, but really new, inexperienced monitors with the CROs. They tend to need training when they come to the site. And oftentimes they're learning from the coordinators what needs to be done, which is not really okay. It doesn't give us a great sense of peace because our expectation is that they should know *more* than us in general. We're depending on them to help us make that data as clean as possible, so we're wanting their expertise to come in, review our data make sure everything is being done exactly according to the regs and guidelines. And if we don't feel a high level of confidence in them, it's a little scary.

In addition to inexperience, a characteristic that sites associate with new monitors is a literalness with which they do their jobs. From the perspective of those at sites, monitors who are new to their positions tend to be unforgiving about small errors and omissions that are easily correctable when pointed out. The owner and director of a local SMO joked about the problem: "We kind of call the new monitors our 'baby monitors,' and the 'baby monitors' tend to sometimes be overzealous. They can be challenging to work with. [She laughs.] But if you understand [the process], I would rather have somebody who's overzealous than someone who's lax."

A second and more common disruption associated with high turnover of monitors is the confusion that is created when monitors change during the course of a study, particularly if this occurs multiple times. With a change in monitors often comes a change in expectations for the sites' performance. Because different monitors from the same companies should have similar expectations for the same study, both investigators and coordinators often interpret any differences in monitors' work as being due to personality quirks. A physician described his sense of the problem:

> They [monitors] might interpret [differently]. It's always a question of interpretation. You know, there's a hundred and one things that you're doing, and they think that you've got to write it in a certain way. And we say, "No, the last monitor said, it's not supposed to be written that way, you're supposed to write it this way." It's really silly. When you come right down to it, it doesn't make a hill of beans.

Although investigators find these problems irritating, the burden of monitor turnover and any differences in personality or style falls on coordinators. These "silly" differences between monitors create hours of work for coordinators because they need to make changes to all the documentation in order to satisfy replacement monitors. Given that most changes are not problems with the data per se, coordinators become very frustrated by the disruption of having to make many minor changes to what they see as finished work. For example, a coordinator explained,

> The majority of monitors have their little quirks, and a monitor wants it done this way, so it's do it that way or else. [A] real big frustration is when you have a monitor that changes or you get a different monitor in the progress of a study. One monitor wanted it done one way, the next one comes and they want it done a different way. And it's just monitor

quirks, so that can be very frustrating. You know, I *hate* dealing with
monitor quirks, so it's generally good if you can get one monitor consistently throughout the entire study. Then there's monitors that have
been doing it for a long time, and some of them are, I'd say, very, very
quirky. They have it so it has to be done their way absolutely, and there's
no other right way. Those are the ones that are frustrating to work with.
I like it when the monitor's a little more open. . . . But generally, well,
some of the quirkiest monitors actually will know the protocol the best
though, I will say.

The difference among monitors does not necessarily imply that one is better
than another at her job but that the difference is in style. Yet, interestingly,
the coordinator also claims that monitors who seem the "quirkiest" seem to
know the studies or products the best.

Coordinators and investigators frequently conflate their frustrations with
outsourcing, or the use of CROs, with the specific monitors with whom they
interact. This may be because in addition to complaints about the inexperience of CRO monitors, sites often find that CRO monitors expect much more
of them than do those monitors coming directly from pharmaceutical companies. Therefore, the monitors from CROs seem to be placing undue demands
on coordinators and investigators compared with monitors from pharmaceutical companies.

Some extra demands may be a result of individual monitors, but it is
likely that the difference between CROs and pharmaceutical companies is
based on organizational goals. Whereas the pharmaceutical companies simply want the sites to produce good, valid data, CROs need to impress the
pharmaceutical companies hiring them in order to win future contracts.
CROs may create additional demands on sites through monitoring to do so.
One veteran investigator who began conducting pharmaceutical studies in
the 1980s commented that he was still trying to get used to CROs. Unlike the
vast majority of my informants, he immediately applied an organizational
analysis to the difference between the types of companies.

I much prefer working directly with the [pharmaceutical] companies.
CROs, it seems, always have to prove to the company that they're doing
a nice job, and they look at minutia so much so that in some ways can
kill you. And really pharmaceutical companies are much more, I don't
want to say loose because they're not loose, they expect a lot from you,
but *petty* things are just not on their agenda. Whereas the CROs, many,

many times, they make you jump through all kinds of hoops because they actually report back to the big boss [the pharmaceutical company] to show they are getting you to do the job.

There are dozens of CROs for pharmaceutical companies to contract with, so CROs feel the need to exceed the pharmaceutical companies' expectations in order to continue to get contracts from those companies. The problem for sites is that this CRO agenda translates into more work and more frustration for them with no added value for them or the patient-subjects.

In spite of organizational explanations for differences between CROs and pharmaceutical companies, the most common and vociferous complaints are made against CRO *monitors,* not CROs or the pharmaceutical companies. Monitors stand in for all the problems with outsourcing and are vulnerable to heavy criticism while the pharmaceutical companies doing the outsourcing remain blameless. CRO monitors are particularly attacked because of their institutional position and limited authority.[16]

Even though monitors are the main point of contact for sites with pharmaceutical companies (this is true regardless of who employs the monitor), CRO monitors often do not have the authority to make decisions regarding specific studies and therefore more often play the role of go-between for sites and pharmaceutical companies. Moreover, CRO monitors do not always have specialized knowledge about the particular pharmaceutical products whose testing they are overseeing. According to a coordinator, "One of the downfalls to having CROs as opposed to working directly with the sponsor is that [monitors] are not always as knowledgeable . . . about that particular protocol because they don't always work with the same company or with the same drug. They are monitoring this study, and just last week they were monitoring another." Another coordinator articulated other limitations of CRO monitors: "You know, CRO monitors . . . can only do so much. They can't give you protocol exemptions, waivers, things of that nature. They can acknowledge it and push you on to somebody else, and they appreciate being kept in the loop so to speak, but the direct ultimate answers always come from the sponsor."

An important implication of CRO monitors' limited authority is that communication can be impeded about investigational products or about study protocols. CRO monitors tend to be the lowest point on the chain of command for obtaining the necessary information. In a sense, they are information gatekeepers for pharmaceutical companies. Their function is to provide basic information to sites and then judge whether questions are important enough to be taken to project managers and others at the pharmaceutical companies.

This means that coordinators and investigators get information much more slowly than if they were to speak directly to individuals at the sponsoring company. This reveals the limited authority that CRO monitors—and perhaps to a lesser extent pharmaceutical company monitors as well—have in making decisions about their studies. In the experience of a coordinator,

> If we have a situation, it goes to the CRO, but then it still has to go back to the sponsor, so you have one more person involved there. And it's slower. It's a slower process. Like I wanted an answer on a kid today, and it's got to go back to the sponsor. They probably won't be able to get back to me with an answer today, maybe tomorrow. If I were able to call the sponsor directly, I'd have an answer right now. Someone would make a decision. The CROs are very slow.

I asked her why, in a case like that, she could not contact the pharmaceutical company directly. She replied, "[Monitors] prefer not. I mean you're really under a contract to work *through* them; otherwise you would have all of these investigators calling people at the sponsor, and that's not fair. I mean, that's why they *hired* these people."

In a similar example related by another coordinator, she felt frustrated by the bureaucracy because the safety of a patient that she had enrolled in a study was in question. She complained,

> But now they've gone out and they've hired CROs. . . . I think there are too many fingers in the pot. I just had a patient call me a few minutes ago, stating she has shingles. I have put in *two* phone calls to the sponsor's CRO company. Nobody has called me back to tell me whether this patient can remain in the study being on a drug with this particular illness, okay? The communication is *lost*. And more time consuming! . . . There's too much that can happen in that amount of time. . . . Now I'm going to leave here tonight, at my given time, and I have no answer. And that's because we're dealing with a CRO. Now I can get mad and call the sponsor, and I may get somebody and I may not, to make a decision, but that makes a CRO company look bad. And then they're mad at you for going over their head. So there are some *very* bad things about this situation.

In addition to slowing down communication between sites and sponsors, it can happen too that pharmaceutical companies do not keep CRO monitors in the information loop. This is not uncommon when changes are made to study protocols during the course of a clinical trial. A coordinator related an example of this occurrence:

> Sometimes the right hand doesn't know what the left hand is doing. Like a sponsor might call the site directly and say, "You need to start doing EKGs at every visit." So of course, we are like, "Okay, do EKGs at every visit." The monitor will come and say, "Why are you doing EKGs at every visit?" "See this piece of paper, this is why." "Well, I didn't get that." Yeah, I mean, it's not all the time . . . but sometimes monitors don't know.

This type of interaction seriously undermines CRO monitors in the eyes of coordinators and investigators because it makes them question the utility of conducting business through the monitor rather than skipping the chain of command and speaking directly to those managing the projects at the phar-maceutical companies.

A final criticism that is made of CRO monitors is that they do not have a sufficient medical orientation: their training emphasizes business processes, such as negotiating contracts. Some coordinators claim that without a back-ground in medicine, CRO monitors do not have enough respect for the work of the site. A coordinator exclaimed,

> They need to educate the CRAs more that come here. Like I said it's usually the first job, and they come in with an old gal like me and ham-mer you over the head like you're a kindergartner. . . . It's like they're reading it off a clipboard, you know? "Okay, this, you gotta do this, you gotta do" . . . When you come to a ripe aged principal investigator and coordinator, you should get a good sense of what that person is about and know that *they* know what they're doing.

Other coordinators are frustrated because, from their perspective, CRO moni-tors do not necessarily appreciate that some mistakes are inevitable, especially when it comes to patient-subjects following every single detail of a protocol. Because many monitors from CROs are so keen on everything going perfectly, coordinators perceive that those monitors behave irrationally about errors that are an everyday part of human nature. For example, a coordinator said,

> Things happen in life. Like in other words, to be blunt, you know, shit happens, it really does. Like could you walk across the street and drop the study medication out of your pocket? Absolutely. Can you lose your bladder diary [to record your symptoms while on the trial]

somewhere? Yeah. How many diaries, and I mean I lose things a lot sometimes, my own personal things. . . . I've had patients that have called up and said, "I lost my diary." And then of course [the CRO monitor] really goes ballistic.

Another aspect of this criticism about the business orientation of CRO monitors is that they are not as flexible about the protocols as are pharmaceutical company monitors. Many coordinators and investigators have had pharmaceutical company monitors grant "exceptions" when patient-subjects have failed to follow the study protocol perfectly or mistakes are made. In contrast, they find that CRO monitors do not have the authority to do this and often request that sites just stick to the parameters of the protocols. This was a point of real frustration for one coordinator:

> The doctors sometimes they need to fudge the protocol a little bit for the benefit of the patient. And sometimes the CRO [monitors] lose the fact that we're trying to help these people. Because in a lot of the protocols, there are a lot of inclusion/exclusion criteria where it should be left to the opinion of the doctor, but the CROs don't really respect that fact. Even the doctor will say, "Well, it's in my opinion that even though this patient might not have this inclusion A or exclusion A or exclusion B, it's in my opinion that they're perfect for this study, and they should stay in." And the CRO [monitors] just ignore that fact [because] they're just stuck on the fact that "Oh, but [the patient-subject] violated this exclusion" or "this lab value is .0002 out of range." So then the doctor says, "Oh, that's okay, they're okay for this study." And that's usually the biggest issue. . . . Usually the pharmaceutical companies' [monitors], they're more understanding about that, and they usually defer to the doctors a little bit better.

This last quote highlights a difference between coordinators' and investigators' frustration with CRO monitors. Coordinators are frustrated because they often do not receive answers quickly enough to help their patient-subjects or because their personal experience in clinical trials is not appropriately valued. Physician-investigators, however, seem frustrated because working with CROs monitors undermines their status in the industry compared to working directly with pharmaceutical companies. One physician declared, "I want to see sponsors, which means pharmaceutical companies, get rid of CROs and deal with investigators directly. That's the grand source of irritation for me, is dealing with ditzy CRAs working for CROs."

The construction of CRO monitors as "ditzy" is not uncommon from investigators who argue that they should not have to work with CROs at all. What tinges their comments is an elitism and sexism that underscores their sense that working with CROs devalues them. Several investigators stated that CRO monitors do not show them the proper respect and recognition for their station as physicians. Investigators often feel that the pharmaceutical companies treat physicians better by making them feel valued when they are assigned to clinical studies. For these reasons, physicians' egos might get a little bruised from their dealings with CRO monitors. One investigator said,

> When you're working directly with the pharmaceutical company, you get access. And people who you know and who know *you*. . . . I do a lot of work with Merck, and they know me personally. I know all the people at Merck. I know the people, and they have a couple of studies with CROs. When I call up a CRO [monitor] working for Merck, it's like they've never heard of me, they don't know who I am, and so I say, "Listen, I don't want to fill out the form, just speak to Merck, they know who I am and they want me on this study, *they* want me."

The problem for CRO monitors as they are currently situated within the clinical trials industry is the ways in which their authority is compromised by their companies. This is even true for monitors working directly for pharmaceutical companies, even though CROs are criticized more often. Monitors are charged with the responsibility of overseeing the accuracy of the pharmaceutical companies' data by making sure sites are following the directions given by those companies. Although they are granted the authority to have coordinators and investigators make changes to their practices and correct mistakes, they are not given much authority to make decisions about the study protocols or their conduct. The limitation to monitors' authority to provide information or make decisions, especially for those working at CROs, systematically delegitimizes them.

Conclusion

Monitors, like investigators and coordinators, are caught between two roles. One role is the responsibility for nitty-gritty details: traveling to sites, pouring over hundreds of pages of study documentation, and being attuned to any malfeasance or fraud. Because monitors are predominantly women and because the skills necessary for their position can be seen as "female" attributes, monitoring is a feminized profession. The flexibility that is called for by the job is not atypical of the "helping" professions, such as nursing, but it is also part of broader trends in the economy reflecting postindustrial values in the workforce. The role itself and how it is constructed is critical in the political economy of pharmaceutical clinical trials. When the organization of clinical development privileges outsourcing to hundreds of private-sector clinics, monitors are needed to provide the oversight that is necessary to keep sites conducting studies honestly and robustly.

The other role imposed upon monitors is a multifaceted symbolic one: protector of the public health, coordinators' "best friend," and scapegoat for the problems of outsourcing. Their existence signals that the data being produced in clinical trials are accurate and therefore ensure FDA approval of only safe and effective products. Second, the framing of monitoring in terms of friendship with coordinators conveys a partnership in the process of drug development that is highly gendered. Rather than researchers at sites taking on a more active role themselves in the development of new pharmaceutical products, they are instead made to feel part of a team through specific relationships with monitors who are in the clinic as representatives of the pharmaceutical industry. Finally, monitors, especially CRO monitors, stand in for all the problems investigative sites experience with the outsourcing of study management from pharmaceutical companies to CROs. That pharmaceutical companies maintain authority over the details of clinical trials while outsourcing the responsibility of conducting them to CROs gets represented as shortcomings of individual monitors or at best CROs rather than an institutional problem that is generated by the pharmaceutical industry.[17]

Monitors are in a difficult position. Like investigators and coordinators, monitors have developed their own mode of dealing with role conflict. In brief, investigators disconnect from conducting the studies, coordinators construct their own ethical codes of conduct, and monitors privilege job mobility and salary before they leave the position altogether. It is no wonder that monitors have a high job turnover rate and that most monitors' careers in the industry are fairly short. Monitors have been given much responsibility to provide oversight of a complex industry. They work long hours and travel frequently. However, as representatives of a system of neoliberal audit culture, monitors are granted little authority even as they are asked to exercise the power that their positions denote.

Chapter 6

Recruiting Human Subjects

Early in 2005, I received a message on my answering machine. The call was from a company specializing in clinical trials on healthy human subjects and was part of a general recruitment campaign for their facility in the southwestern United States. The woman calling reminded me that I could earn money by enrolling in any of the company's active recruiting studies:

> This message is for Jill Fisher. We are [a clinical trials company], calling just to advise you of current studies we have available that you are qualifying for. They are very good studies currently running, and it's good, easy, fast money to make for the New Year. If you want further information, feel free to give us a call. Our number is 1–888–xxx–xxxx. Thank you.

Several weeks later I received a postcard from the same company. The card wished me a happy birthday, and it offered me an additional $25 for screening for any one of their studies during the month of my birthday. The card informed me that studies pay up to $3,200 in exchange for my participation.

I had become part of the company's database a year earlier when I had tried to enroll in a study for the purposes of participant observation.[1] The study for which I passed the phone screening—meaning that I met the basic qualifications of age, weight, and so on—was a three-week, in-patient, randomized, double-blind, placebo-controlled study to test the "pharmacokinetics, safety, and tolerability of multiple dosing regimes in Healthy Subjects of an investigational drug being studied to treat rheumatoid arthritis" with a $3,000 stipend.[2] The clinic was located in the most impoverished part of the city, known for its predominantly Latino population. I arrived at the appointed time as one of two hundred screening to fill forty-two study slots, and found that I was one of very few women (about 20 percent) and one of the few who spoke English. Informed consent was done in groups based on language, and the English-speaking consent group was significantly less than half of the total.

After being weighed, measured, and having my vitals checked, I was sent to the phlebotomist's station. It was at this point—unfortunately for my research[3]—that I was disqualified from the study because my veins, I was told, were not good enough for research. The phlebotomist explained that they need to take blood samples in sixty seconds or less, from tying the tourniquet to applying the final Band-Aid. Because they have more people who are interested in studies than they can enroll, she said they did not need to bother with cases of more difficult veins. Indeed, they had 25,000 participants in their database, of whom nearly 10,000 individuals screen for healthy subject clinical trials each year. More than 3,000 enroll in studies at this in-patient facility with over one hundred beds. In my case, my veins were labeled as uncooperative, I failed the screening visit, and I was told to go home.

Who participates in pharmaceutical clinical trials? How are they recruited? How do the demographics of participants differ depending on the types of clinical trials (for example, type of illness, healthy subject, and so on)? And what are the reasons that people give about why they enroll in drug studies at all? Human subjects' decisions to participate in clinical trials are influenced primarily by their need for medical treatments or income. Although there are important differences based on the race, class, and gender of subjects, the clinical trials industry takes advantage of disenfranchised groups by offering them "access" to the medical establishment or large stipends in exchange for access to their bodies to test new drugs.

Political and Economic Contexts of Human Subject Recruitment

Since the late 1970s, the period in which neoliberal political and economic policies began to infiltrate the provision of health care in the United States, poverty rates and health insurance coverage have shifted. According to a U.S. census report, in the second half of the 1970s, the poverty rate was roughly 12 percent (25 million Americans). By 1983, that rate peaked at 15.2 percent (35.3 million Americans). Over the next twenty years, the poverty rate fluctuated up and down, but in 2002, it returned to its 1970s average at 12.1 percent (34.6

million Americans). Of course, poverty is not distributed equally among racial groups in the United States. As a group, people who are white and non-Hispanic have the lowest poverty rates (8.0 percent in 2002). In contrast, currently about 22 percent of all Hispanics and 24 percent of blacks live in poverty.[4]

Although the number of people living in poverty has declined since rates peaked in the early 1980s and again in the early 1990s, the number of Americans without health insurance has risen. In 1987, 12.9 percent of the population (31 million) did not have health insurance. By 2005, the percentage of uninsured Americans had risen to 15.9 percent (46.6 million). Examining the trend by racial and ethnic categories, the percentage of uninsured white non-Hispanics increased from 9.8 percent in 1987 to 11.3 percent in 2005 and of uninsured Hispanics from 30.7 percent to 32.7 percent. Black Americans actually experienced a slight decrease in the percentage of uninsured from 19.9 percent in 1987 to 19.6 percent in 2005. Most Americans regardless of race and ethnicity receive health insurance through their employment, and the growing number of uninsured is due to fewer employers paying for or subsidizing health insurance. With the loss of many jobs since the 1980s that provided health care benefits to workers, many citizens have begun to work in jobs that do not have any benefits, or they are employed as part-time workers who are not eligible for benefits. In 2005, 17.7 percent of all full-time and 23.5 percent of half-time employees did not have any health insurance. As some compensation, government programs like Medicaid have increased the number of recipients to cover the poorest segment of the population. Medicaid coverage increased from 8.4 percent of the total population in 1987 to 13 percent in 2005.[5]

This quick presentation of poverty and insurance status statistics is meant to convey some of the context for pharmaceutical clinical trials in the United States. In order to enroll patient-subjects more quickly in their studies, the pharmaceutical industry developed the strategy of conducting clinical trials in locations where they could recruit individuals who would be motivated to participate in exchange for income or access to health care. Mobilizing the logic of medical neoliberalism, the clinical trials industry applied the term "ready-to-recruit" to the scores of willing subjects in local communities that they envisioned would sign up for drug studies.

In spite of the optimism of pharmaceutical company executives, the transition away from academic medical centers to the private sector has not led to surges of interested patient-subjects. Making clinical trials more convenient for potential human subjects helped but was not sufficient to fill studies. The pharmaceutical industry as well as CROs and other ancillary clinical trials companies had to develop more formalized tactics for recruitment. For example, advertising agencies that were successful at direct-to-consumer campaigns for marketed pharmaceutical products specialize in recruitment for drug studies. Online databases of clinical trials offer notification services that send e-mails to interested individuals when studies match their requirements. Other companies have crafted directed recruitment techniques that involve building searchable databases made up of patients who can be directly solicited about studies, effectively making recruitment into a rational "science."[6]

Although recruitment for clinical trials can take many forms, the dominant, public form has been mass media advertising. In large cities around the country, ads for pharmaceutical studies are present in public transportation, newspapers, radio, and television. In many places, the proliferation of ads has integrated clinical trials into everyday life, so that any aberrancy associated with participating in studies has been removed. This is not to say that advertisements alone encourage large numbers to enroll in studies, but it does mean that advertising normalizes trial participation. Consequently, advertisements serve a double purpose in clinical trial recruitment. First, they recruit potential patient-subjects into *specific* drug studies, and second, they sensitize communities to the possibility of participating in pharmaceutical research generally, regardless of the illnesses or conditions portrayed in the ads.[7]

The distribution of clinical trials around the country has made participation in drug studies seem like a viable choice for individuals who are interested in the income they can earn, in access to health care, or even in the possibility of an effective treatment or cure for an intractable illness. The neoliberal framing of choice, however, obscures the structural conditions that make patient-subjects feel like trial participation is the only option they have. This is not to say that individuals who volunteer for pharmaceutical studies cannot have positive experiences. To the contrary, many participants rave about their participation. Instead, I am interested in how the system of clinical trials itself, including the recruitment process, can be exploitative of individuals *and* groups, given the persistence of social, political, and economic inequalities in the United States.

The Recruitment of Pharmaceutical Study Participants

The demographics of participants in clinical trials depend to some extent on the type of illness for which the pharmaceutical research is targeted. Yet trial participation in the United States can be said to be gendered, raced, and classed. Efficacy studies that test the effects of investigational products on patient-subjects' illnesses attract primarily white middle-class women. Studies of this type that target relatively benign (that is, not life-threatening) illnesses attract mostly uninsured individuals, the majority of whom are also white women. In contrast, however, healthy subject clinical trials that test the safety of investigational products and pay large stipends to volunteers attract mostly low-income minority men. In the Southwest, these studies are filled predominantly by Hispanic, non-English-speaking men, whereas in other parts of the country, these studies are filled predominantly by African American men.

There are many possible reasons why these groups are overrepresented in pharmaceutical studies. First, that women are less likely to enroll in healthy subject studies than men may not be due to lack of interest but failure to qualify for studies.[8] Many of these studies have restrictions regarding women of reproductive age, including the frequent exclusion of all women of "childbearing potential" or women taking some kind of hormonal contraception. There are fewer restrictions placed on male participants in these studies. In other words, it is possible that more women would enroll in healthy subject studies if they were eligible for them.

Second, the two types of studies (healthy human versus targeted illness intervention) are structured very differently, and these structures may work better for certain groups of people than for others. In the case of healthy subject clinical trials, studies are often conducted as in-patient "confinements," wherein participants check themselves in to the clinic. Pharmaceutical companies and IRBs require subjects to remain in the clinic to be closely monitored because many of the new drugs have never been tested before in humans and may produce serious adverse effects.[9] The length of in-patient studies varies, but they can be as short as a few days or as long as one month. In general, the longer the confinement period, the larger the stipend that will be awarded to participants at the conclusion of the study. In contrast, the efficacy studies tend to rely on office visits to investigative sites that are scheduled at routine intervals during the clinical trial. Because most of these clinics operate during normal business hours, participants must be available for appointments on those days and during those hours.

The structural differences between clinical trials, therefore, imply different types of flexibility that are required from potential human subjects. In the case of healthy, in-patient studies, participants must have the flexibility to devote intense periods of time to clinical trials. This means that they cannot have regular paid employment and that they cannot have significant responsibilities within the home (like childcare). Healthy subject clinical trial participation, thus, may be possible only for people who are unemployed, self-employed, or work from contract jobs of finite lengths and who are not the primary caretakers of family members. Men are more likely to have the flexibility required for these studies. In addition, in the Southwest, the large numbers of Latinos who participate in healthy subject studies may also reflect the opportunities available to them to earn income. Because study participation is not contingent on legal resident status, healthy subject trials may provide an unparalleled source of income to undocumented workers through high study stipends.

In contrast, efficacy studies of investigational products require a different type of flexibility from human subjects. Participants must have the ability to make multiple, lengthy study visits during business hours. If participants are employed, they need to have positions in which they can arrange their hours or be granted time for medical care. If participants are unemployed, they cannot rely on study compensation for income because most stipends for efficacy trials are nominal (typically, $15 to $50 per study visit depending on the time and procedures required). Middle-class women may have the most flexibility in their work, either because they have sick and vacation leave available to them or because they are better able to negotiate their hours or for time away from work to participate in a study. For instance, women who tend to be primary caretakers of children and elderly parents may already be accustomed to take time away from work for their relatives' illnesses, and participation in efficacy studies would fit the same pattern for them.

In addition to flexibility, a third reason minority men and white middle-class women are overrepresented in healthy subject and efficacy studies respectively might be reflective of complex social and cultural norms. Men might be more willing to take greater risks with their bodies in exchange for income.[10] If motivated by severe financial hardship, the need to provide for themselves or their families might make the potential risks of trial participation seem minimal for many men. Because women are more predisposed to be health consumers than are men, they are probable candidates for enrolling in efficacy clinical trials. Women are more likely than are men to schedule doctors' appointments, so they are more apt to be recruited for clinical trials that are conducted by their personal physicians. In other words, white middle-class women are the most available group to recruit into efficacy studies.

The enrollment of the uninsured typically follows similar demographic patterns as those of efficacy clinical trials more generally. Advertisements for drug studies often emphasize the free office visits, tests and procedures, and medications that potential subjects will receive as part of their participation, so it is hardly surprising that these ads and hence the studies themselves appeal to people who do not have health insurance. Although both men and women respond to these ads, investigative sites enroll more uninsured women than men in studies, and the vast majority of uninsured patient-subjects are white. Similar to the social and cultural gender norms playing into women's recruitment from patient populations, white women, as a group, might already identify with the role of health care consumers, even when they lack health insurance and do not have access to the medical establishment. Thus it is likely that many uninsured white women who know that they have an illness needing medical attention might perceive clinical trials as a way to access care. This group may also be more aware of alternative health care opportunities than are white men or other groups.

These explanations for why certain people are more likely to participate in different types of clinical trials are partial and incomplete. Not only do the motivations and structural conditions of potential human subjects determine who will or will not participate in clinical trials, the perceptions and attitudes of recruiters, coordinators, and investigators also affect who is enrolled in studies. Indeed, industry staff construct their own "ideal" types of patient-subjects based on assumptions about gender, race, and class.

Before continuing, I must point out that the pattern of human subject participation I describe here does not hold for clinical trials that are testing investigational treatments for cancer and HIV/AIDS. Because these clinical trials are often the first type that people think of when imagining medical research, I want to explain that studies for these illnesses have differences from many others.[11] Specifically, most cancer research studies are filled by more affluent white men and women who pursue specific physicians or medical centers renowned for cancer research and therapy. The primary reason for this is that cancer research continues to be conducted primarily out of large academic medical hospitals or major medical centers rather than at private-sector sites. Cancer research is also different from most other clinical trials because procedures and office visits are usually billed to patient-subjects' insurance companies rather than paid solely by pharmaceutical companies. Because of this, there is evidence to suggest that people without health insurance are actually deemed ineligible for many cancer studies.[12]

HIV and AIDS research is also distinct from other types of clinical trials. Drug studies in this therapeutic area are common in the private sector, yet many sites that conduct these studies focus exclusively on HIV/AIDS and generally operate as nonprofit organizations. In addition, this type of research tends to cut across socioeconomic lines because of the perceived severity of the illness, enrolling a range of patient-subjects from the very wealthy to the insolvent.[13] HIV and AIDS research differs from other illnesses in attracting more men, especially homosexual men, than women. Sites attribute this trend to their community-based settings, which are often known as gay resource centers, so individuals infected with HIV/AIDS who do not identify as homosexual might feel uncomfortable about pursuing drug trials in those contexts.

Patient-Subjects' Participation in Efficacy Studies

To begin a discussion about why people decide to participate in clinical trials as possible treatments for their illnesses, it is important to examine what patient-subjects themselves say about their participation in efficacy studies. Four reasons emerge from patient-subjects' narratives about why they enroll in pharmaceutical studies: hope for a "magic bullet," access to health care, desire for "higher-quality care," and source of income. For purposes of description and analysis, each of these four reasons will be treated as discrete, but the patient-subjects with whom I spoke perceive multiple benefits of participating in clinical trials. Although most of the patient-subjects had a dominant reason that motivated their enrollment in a drug study, many had other overlapping reasons, many of which developed and became important to them over the course of the clinical trials. Because of the patterns of participation, or perhaps in spite of those patterns, research staff develop explanations for why middle-class white women are the ideal group for participation in pharmaceutical efficacy studies.

Magic Bullet

The pharmaceutical industry and the media often represent medical research and drug development in terms of wonder drugs and magic bullets. As a result, it should be no surprise that the framing of miracle cures is the most common conception of clinical trials in the public imaginary. The search for a magic bullet conveys the public's and individuals' hope that research will improve the lives of people suffering from fatal or debilitating diseases and illnesses. Although in my interviews this was not often the initial motivation of patient-subjects' participation in drug studies, this view nonetheless shaped people's expectations about clinical trials.

Individuals who were participating in pharmaceutical studies because of hope for a magic bullet to cure their illness had generally found out about the studies from and were recruited by their physicians. Because information about the clinical trials was coming from a trusted source, these patient-subjects felt that their physicians believed the pharmaceutical study to be the best option for their individual conditions. As one middle-class white female patient-subject with rheumatoid arthritis informed me, "I didn't consider *not* participating in the study when I was asked [by my physician]. At the time, I was very motivated to do *anything* I could to lessen the daily pain I was feeling. . . . I wanted to get better, and they were offering me that possibility."

A second middle-class white woman with rheumatoid arthritis was also recruited by her physician. In contrast to the other woman, she joined a drug study because she was not finding relief from drugs already on the market: "The rheumatologist that I have . . . asked me if I wanted to participate, and that's how I got in the study. . . . A lot of the stuff that I had been taking wasn't really working too well, and so I thought I'd give the clinical trial a try." Both women hoped the clinical trial would have the direct benefit of effective *treatment* for their rheumatoid arthritis. Additionally, it was important to both of them that the clinical trials were offered to them by their own physicians; in their minds, the drug studies became an extension of their care.

Similarly, an affluent, white woman who had been diagnosed with an incurable form of cancer explained that she felt that the study her oncologist offered to her was her only hope for remission: "I had a recurrence of my lymphatic cancer, and so the doctor at [hospital] offered me this clinical trial. And I believe that she is outstanding in her field and that the study was probably my best chance for maybe getting some kind of remission." As she framed the issue, her belief that the clinical trial was the best treatment choice was based on the fact that her doctor, in whom she had a high level of trust, had recommended the study to her:

> I had a lot of faith in her ability to know where I was at and what would be best for me. So I leaped at [the study] when she suggested it. My confidence was in my doctor. . . . She's someone who is truly on top of her field, and not just someone looking for accolades or monetary rewards, so I have enough confidence in her to feel that she's in it because she cares.

The root of the woman's trust in her oncologist was twofold. First, she believed that the physician was technically skilled, inspiring the patient-subject's confidence in the physician's ability to treat her cancer. Second, she believed that the physician was motivated to enroll her in the study because she cared about the woman as a patient, not because she might reap professional or monetary rewards from the clinical trial. Her confidence in the doctor's motives led her to believe that the clinical trial was her best chance for combating cancer.

Access to Health Care

Advertisements for clinical trials emphasize the opportunity to receive medical attention at no cost to the participant. This marketing is designed specifically to appeal to people who already know they have medical conditions but do not want to pay out-of-pocket costs to treat those illnesses. Clinical trials marketing highlights the possibility of a solution to the uninsured's alienation from the health care system.

For example, a clinical trial became the solution for dealing with insomnia for one uninsured middle-class white patient-subject in his early thirties. He told me,

> I saw an ad that had to do with insomnia. I didn't have medical insurance at the time, so it's not like I could go see a doctor because it really wasn't cost effective with prescription drugs and things like that. And I figured, well, the drug's not proven yet, but I just rolled the dice, and the study was great. . . . It was done in a doctor's office. . . . I had never thought about clinical trials [before seeing the ad], but I thought what the hell! . . . I didn't have insurance, so I didn't really have any other avenues or at least not that I could think of.

The man talked about his decision making in terms of a gamble that he feels he won. The specific clinical trial in which he enrolled had three parts in which all patient-subjects participated in varying order: a placebo stage, a low-dose of the experimental drug, and a higher dose of the drug. Because he knew that he received the active drug for the majority of the study, the patient-subject felt that he had been helped by the study and was sorry for it to end: "The drug is what helps me, except for those damn placebos. . . . [At the end of the study] they did write me a prescription for a sleep medication, but I didn't have insurance, so I had no way of getting it."

Similarly, a middle-class white man in his late twenties enrolled in an HIV clinical trial because he felt that he did not have adequate insurance to pay for the medications that would keep him healthy and stave off the progression of AIDS. He told me that his insurance was adequate for paying for his biannual doctor's visits, but the cost of drugs was a burden in spite of his insurance. He said, "You know, I can't afford Kaletra and Fortovase! I can't afford these drugs, so clinical trials help with that a lot. I know that's why a lot of us do these studies. Unfortunately, it just is." This particular patient-subject had been on multiple clinical trials over the course of five years, and he informed me that he intended to volunteer for another at the end of the current study.

One final example of a patient-subject who turned to clinical trials because of problems with insurance was a working-class white woman in her late forties with an overactive bladder condition. She described the anguish she experienced before enrolling in a clinical trial because of the embarrassment caused by her condition and her financial inability to pay for the treatment she needed. She frequently worried about what she would do at the end of the study, but her concerns were allayed when she received word that the study would be lengthened by an additional twelve months:

> [The study] was just scheduled for six months when I first started. Before I got into the next leg of it, I was talking to the gal [research coordinator] and said, "Gee, I'm going to hate giving these pills up because [before I had them], I really wet my pants, I mean, down my leg and in my shoe, and it is embarrassing!" She said, "Oh, you don't have to worry about that for a while. I was just getting ready to tell you that the study's been extended. So I guess you want to go on?" And I said, "Yes!" . . . It really is a blessing to have it.

As these patient-subjects' experiences illustrate, clinical trials allow the uninsured a certain type of access to health care. One physician-investigator articulated their situation: "They don't have any health insurance, and they need some contact with the health care delivery machinery." His use of the word "contact" is on target because the constraints of clinical trials greatly limit the type of access that patient-subjects can receive. They are not receiving treatments for their conditions; instead, they take either investigational medications or placebos as part of studies to test new compounds' efficacy.

"Higher-Quality Care"

The framing of clinical trials as offering "higher-quality care" forms the third theme in how patient-subjects explain why they enroll in efficacy studies. This rationale for participating is different from patient-subjects' hope for a magic bullet because it is rarely focused on the pharmaceutical product itself. What matters to these patient-subjects is the context of the clinical trial: the environment and people who are conducting the study. Often, patient-subjects explicitly compare their experiences in drug studies to standard medical care and find that they receive more "care" in clinical trials.

From the perspective of patient-subjects, clinical trials offer better care because patients have more face time with health care professionals than they have come to expect from standard medical care. As one middle-class white woman said, "There certainly was a lot more attention paid to me [in the clinical trial]. I mean I saw someone much more often. . . . And I got a lot more attention." In addition to the time spent with study staff, another benefit to participating in drug studies is that patient-subjects often spend less time in the waiting room at their study visits. A middle-class white man said, "I was sad when the study ended because I had started to get to know the nurses and things like that. It was really cool getting to be a regular, so to speak, and I never had to wait more than five minutes in the waiting room."

Clinical trials are also perceived as better for patient-subjects because they have more people monitoring their conditions more regularly. This was particularly important for patient-subjects who had serious medical conditions or who were undergoing complex procedures, like surgeries. For example, a female patient-subject with cancer said,

> I can see that you get more attention when you are in the clinical trial because I've been *not* in one and in one. First of all, there's a *team* on the clinical trial; [because of] that in itself, you don't fall through the cracks. There's a person who administers the whole protocol, and I meet with her . . . and we go through the protocol. And then I see the doctor's designated RN, and she goes through some questions for the medical trial: "How has the drug felt here? What happened on this day? How's your appetite?" You know, she has a battery of questions for me. . . . So I feel I have a whole *team* that supports my case, not just one physician, you know? The more the better as far as picking up problems!

Other patient-subjects echoed this woman's sentiments by describing coordinators as integral to the care they receive.

A third way in which patient-subjects perceive clinical trials as better than standard medical care is that they receive additional tests and procedures. Many patient-subjects felt that these tests provided more in-depth and more frequent information about their conditions. A patient-subject in an HIV study explained,

> I don't think people realize everything that the clinical trials discover medically about me. You know, they always do physicals and everything like that. I don't think a lot of people realize that information . . . will go to your primary doctor. . . . That's one of the things I really appreciate about the study. So when I go to see my doctor—which happens like once every six months just because it's like an oil change, you've got to do it—he has all my recent labs and everything [from the clinical trial] since he last saw me.

Patient-subjects who participate in clinical trials for a known condition also have the experience of being diagnosed with other conditions in the process. One middle-class white woman who had enrolled in a weight-loss study was found to be anemic during the clinical trial. At first, the research staff assumed it was from the study medication, but through the process of conducting several procedures and diagnostic examinations ordered by the pharmaceutical company,[14] it turned out the woman had colon cancer. This was a diagnosis that would have likely come much later if she had not enrolled in the clinical trial. Similarly, many coordinators and monitors reported high rates of detecting breast cancers in women who volunteered as patient-subjects for other, non-cancer drug studies.

What these three elements of "better care"—more time, monitoring, and information—mean for many patient-subjects is that they themselves and their medical conditions are not slipping through the cracks of an imperfect health care system. Because many patient-subjects do not know what to expect of clinical trials before they have been enrolled in their first study, this reason to participate comes up with repeat participants who find that they enjoyed or valued their experiences and want to participate in other studies. In particular, patient-subjects often discuss this reason as one on which they would base their recommendation of clinical trials to others.

Source of Income

Finally, some patient-subjects join efficacy studies for the small source of income they can provide. Aside from potential health benefits, drug studies usually include stipends, referred to as "compensation" or "reimbursement" depending on the language required by IRBs.[15] One older unemployed white woman without insurance described herself as a patient-subject motivated by the financial reward of participating in clinical trials. She said, "It's a good way to make some money right now because I'm waiting for social security to start, so it helps to supplement that a little bit."

Some patient-subjects are excited about making extra income because of a medical condition that they have. Although most studies do not pay large stipends, there are some studies that patient-subjects perceive as lucrative. Serial patient-subjects I interviewed described how the amount of money associated with completing a study enters into their decision making about whether they want to enroll. For example, a white woman in her thirties explained how diabetes is a condition that she has learned to profit from now that she has discovered pharmaceutical drug and device studies:

> For me, [I participate] because the money is good: $100 for an hour, you can't beat that! . . . But it's not *just* the money either; you kind of have to weigh how much *time* versus the money. For example, I've been asked to be in studies that were all day, and it was a good bit of money, but it also involved being stuck all day long with venipunctures, and I wasn't willing to do that.

This particular patient-subject estimated that she had participated in six studies in the last few years. She said she was more naïve about them at the beginning:

> The first study seemed like easy money, but it was a little more cumbersome than I thought it would be. . . . One of the study devices that I wore [for my diabetes] didn't work properly, and I was sick for a day. . . . But that's the risk that you can face I guess, and I have and will test again for that company even if there's a risk of getting sick. I've also tested products that didn't work and that were cumbersome and need a lot of work, but I guess I like being in the know [about new products], and I like being a guinea pig and getting paid for it!

There are certain medical indications that seem to attract patient-subjects for mainly monetary reasons, and the financial incentive may lead to patients faking the illnesses. According to some coordinators, many of the clinical trials offered within the domain of psychiatry seem to fall into this category because of the subjectivity of symptoms associated with illnesses like depression and anxiety. Although no patient-subjects I interviewed told me that they had ever faked symptoms in order to collect stipends from clinical trials, a coordinator who had worked solely on depression and anxiety studies described her experience:

I don't work on depression studies per se right now, but I *know* about them from past experience. And I guess the drug companies know as well that the majority of the subjects might not even be depressed. They might be doing it for money. They might be *actors* in this town, you know? It's not far-fetched. And maybe some genuinely are depressed, but it's easy enough for someone to figure out how to fake their way into a trial too. I don't know if people are doing it for money, but it could be a huge motivating factor. Where I used to work, they paid quite a bit, *unheard* of amounts [that is, $60 per visit] actually compared to other sites. . . . [Currently,] we pay subjects between $10 and $30 per visit.

In other words, the stipends offered by clinical trials do motivate patient-subjects to enroll in studies. Although the majority see money from studies as a fun benefit that can be gained from an illness that they already have, there is concern that patient-subjects could be taking advantage of the pharmaceutical industry to earn some additional income. Concerns about faking symptoms are high in psychiatry studies, but it is unclear to what extent $60 would motivate people to bother enrolling in clinical studies.

Researchers' Perceptions of Patient-Subjects by Gender, Race, and Class

Recruitment is a huge focus of clinical trials. Investigative sites need to enroll patient-subjects to get paid by the pharmaceutical companies, meet their study quotas, and continue to get offered contracts to conduct studies. As a result, coordinators, investigators, and other study staff leverage patient-subjects' motivations for participating to enroll more participants in efficacy studies. This involves using patients' trust in their physicians to interest them in clinical trials, framing studies as a type of health care for uninsured individuals who are ill, and describing clinical trials as a means to receive better "care" for those who enroll. Recruitment, however, has other layers to it as well. Investigators, site administrators, and particularly coordinators develop ideal "types" of patient-subjects based upon assumptions about which groups of people are most appropriate to participate in clinical research. These assumptions influence their decisions about enrolling patient-subjects into studies.

Middle-class white women as a group are overrepresented among the patient-subjects participating in clinical trials to test the efficacy of investigational drugs. During interviews with coordinators, investigators, and administrators, I asked why they thought pharmaceutical studies attracted more women than men and mostly white patient-subjects as participants. I found that individuals working in the clinical trials industry have developed gender-, class-, and race-coded explanations for who participates in clinical trials.

To account for the preponderance of women enrolling in studies, coordinators contend that two elements distinguish women from men: their open-mindedness towards and available time for clinical trials. Open-mindedness is seen as necessary for patients to agree to pursue an alternative to standard medical care regardless of how they are recruited for the studies. Coordinators insist that a basic difference between most women and men is that women are willing to entertain the possibility of participating in clinical trials while men are quickly dismissive of the suggestion. One female coordinator expressed her understanding of women's open-mindedness:

> Women are more open-minded to research than men are . . . because women are more interested in their health, you know? And if something's [a treatment] not working, they'll look for an alternative. Whereas men are just, you know, "Oh well, just give me this, I'll take it, and if it doesn't work, well, I'll try something else." Unless they're *very* open-minded, and I think the more educated men are more open-minded and apt to want to participate, but the noneducated ones are just, well, "Whatever my doctor tells me."

The implication here is that when men seek health care, they are not likely to deviate from the course their physicians set in a standard medical care setting, therefore their lack of interest in clinical trials.

In addition, "open-mindedness" is used to describe women's receptivity to the rigidity of study protocols and the risks associated with study participation. Women are perceived as being compliant, docile patient-subjects who express more trust in their physicians and the research enterprise than do men. For instance, one coordinator described men's and women's typical reactions to the logistics and risks outlined in consent forms:

> Men, a lot of times, they see those things [logistics and risks], and they're out the door. Yes, they're like, "I'm out of here." . . . I think women can tolerate more where men can't. . . . Every study's different, so every study has different requirements, and every study may have different side effects, and men are just like, "Mmm, I don't think I can, no, I don't want to do that, I don't even want to take a chance." You know, they're just more afraid of doing it, trying out for the study;

especially if they're already taking a medication that is working good for them, they may not want to do it.

An added gendered dimension to the differences that coordinators perceive between men and women is their framing of men as breadwinners. Clinical trials pose a risk to patient-subjects' time and energy, and this too is often a risk men are less likely to take than are women. A coordinator stated simply, "Men are usually the breadwinners, and so they don't want to have [study obligations] that will take them away from their work." Coordinators never contest the concept of "breadwinner," so they too frequently attach more importance to men's work than women's work, seemingly regardless of the particular cases. Perhaps this is because coordinators as well as many others in the clinical trials industry never question their assumption that men's work is qualitatively different from women's, both in terms of the labor force and the home.

Not just men's and women's work, but time too is often couched in very gendered terms about who can make or afford time for their health care. Specifically, women are seen as having flexible schedules into which clinical trials can easily fit. Only men who are self-employed or retired are seen as having the same type of flexibility in their day as do women. According to a female coordinator,

> [Men are] not necessarily geared to taking at least two hours out of their day. A current study we're doing is one to two hours every other week, so for men, we need someone who either has a night job and they're free during the day, like they're not working, and that's a little bit rare to find, or they're just kind of self-employed and they have time. But a *typical* situation is that women can be a little bit more available; they come after work, or let's say some jobs they can get away at lunch, or go in late to the office, or they don't work at all. So it still impacts women, but they *tend* to organize their day a little bit differently. And men can be a little bit more tied up. Typically, the men are like, "Hurry up, let's go!" They don't have time.

Another coordinator who explained why women's time is more flexible framed her answer in terms of what is considered socially acceptable for men and women in the workplace: "I think women are much more likely to [enroll in a study] because of the amount of time it takes to do something like this.

A lot of men are more work-oriented. You know that would be the last thing they'd say to their boss, 'Oh, I need to come in late because I'm in a study.'"

Interestingly, men, regardless of class, are seen fairly uniformly as having inflexible work schedules that become impediments to participating in clinical trials. However, the construction of women as flexible agents who are open-minded and ready to enroll in drug studies is tempered by research staff's assumptions about class. More specifically, the common portrayal of "women" generally refers to middle-class white women. When pressed to talk about socioeconomic differences, most say that their study participants are fairly homogenously middle-class. One site administrator mapped out the differences she saw between social classes:

> I think for the large part, clinical trials appeal to maybe the middle class and the lower middle class. They're real positive opportunities for the uninsured or the underinsured. . . . I find that the more affluent a patient is, the less likely they are to participate in a clinical trial. [That is,] *unless* they have something like they need an oncology type product, or it's more of a last resort kind of thing. . . . The very poor generally have very disorganized lives, trouble with transportation, and are less likely to be able to be relied on to come back for successive visits.

More than one interviewee described women of lower socioeconomic status as having lives that are prone to crisis. As one coordinator asserted,

> Lots of times poor women have children attached to them, and it makes it a lot harder. . . . But I think a lot of it is if you have a three-year-old at home and you take the bus, it's really hard to make a commitment [to take part in a study]. I mean we had one woman in a trial just recently, and she just had a family crisis and she couldn't complete the trial because of it. I don't see it that much with the other women or with men. So I think that those are the barriers that you see [to poor women's participation].

It is not uncommon for coordinators and others in the clinical trials industry to refer to poor women as having trouble making "the commitment" to clinical research. In a remarkable example, a coordinator explained why her site does not recruit low-income women into birth control or sterilization studies:

We're doing a clinical trial evaluating a non-incisional, permanent sterilization procedure for women who have completed their families and are certain they don't want any more children. You know, I would love to be able to go to our county hospital which is *overrun* by women who have lots of unplanned pregnancies and say, "Line up, come on over here, and let us do this for you." But that's not the way you do clinical trials. . . . Maybe sometimes it's unfair [to say, but] you have to have women who can understand *their* commitment toward the clinical trial that they're participating in. I mean it's not all about what *we* can do for *you*, and that's something I discuss with women.

The theme of "commitment" is a telling insight into coordinators' understanding of class differences in clinical trial participation. Not surprisingly, those patient-subjects who most closely resemble coordinators—middle-class white women—are seen as the most *committed* to the responsibility of being subjects. This provides further context to the importance coordinators place on treating patient-subjects the way that they themselves would want to be treated.

Those in the clinical trials industry—from coordinators at sites to project managers at pharmaceutical companies—have also come to label races according to perceived trends in those groups' participation. Placing these groups along a spectrum of receptivity to drug studies, they argue that Asians are not altruistic, blacks are suspicious, and Hispanics are compliant. For many at the site level, they find minority groups' fear of participating in clinical trials is a challenge to recruiting individuals from those groups. An African American recruiter said,

So it's just that a whole gamut of the ethnicities are just negative toward participating in clinical trials. So it's up to people in my department, recruitment people, to go out there to really open the eyes of the community and let them know, "You know what? This is a good thing! We're not here to harm you. Your rights are very well protected, and you have the *right* to say, 'Yes, I'm going to do this trial!' And if you sign up for the trial and you change your mind, you have every right to change your mind, and nobody's going to make you feel bad because of it."

Many sites have never enrolled any Asian patient-subjects in their studies, and investigators, coordinators, and administrators often believe that Asians are not altruistic as a group and that is why they are not better represented in clinical trials.[16] One physician had strong opinions about Asians' lack of participation:

> Asians ... don't participate in research. ... It's not part of the culture. That's why Japanese companies have to come here to do clinical research. Here we [Americans] have people who are willing to *volunteer,* which is something that's alien to their culture. We have folks who are willing to volunteer, participate as a study subject, and for their own reasons, their own motivation, want to be study participants. Some cultures can't really get their arms around that idea.

In contrast to Asians, African Americans are seen as suspicious and reluctant rather than being inherently unwilling participants.[17] Whereas Asians are constructed as ungenerous, most coordinators and investigators believe that because of past research abuses in the United States, black people have the right to be concerned about their health and welfare. Coordinators especially view their role to educate African Americans about the protections that the federal government has put into place in response to those past abuses to ensure ethical practices in research on humans. One white coordinator said, "African Americans are a very tough group to get [that is, enroll in studies]. I think that not recently but probably four years ago, a guy walked out and said, 'I'm not going to be any Tuskegee.' And so that's still back there in the minds of some of the older—probably the *wiser*—guys."

At the same time, African Americans are valued in clinical trials because their enrollment into studies is seen as a real recruiting success. As a white coordinator told me in excited tones, "I've had two black guys in one of my other studies, and I've got a black woman coming into this study that I'm currently recruiting for. So it's sort of like, oh boy, I get two points for the black woman because black and a woman. But they are rare, unfortunately." Ironically, although they have low involvement as patient-subjects in clinical trials, African Americans are one of the key groups in large urban areas to participate as healthy human subjects in early drug studies. Participation in those studies may reinforce some black people's impression that pharmaceutical research is extractive, rather than beneficial to them, and is better avoided.

Because of Asians' and African Americans' perceived antipathy toward clinical trials, many coordinators marvel that as a group, Hispanics do not seem suspicious of clinical research. Moreover, they find that Latinos are the most compliant group that enrolls in drug studies; so much so that many sites claim that this group's compliance more than makes up for hiring Spanish-speaking staff to cater to non-English-speaking patient-subjects. As one recruiter claimed, "I usually say that Hispanics are more compliant. They show up on time if not early. They show up for all the return visits. They always show up for check-in [for in-patient studies]. They're the compliant group. So our 'show' rates have been better [since we started enrolling non-English-speaking Hispanics]." Similar to rates for low-income urban blacks in the East, Latinos in Southwestern cities make up more than 50 percent of those volunteering for healthy human subject studies. Because these trials often involve long in-patient stays, sites specializing in those studies especially value Latinos for their perceived compliance.

These characterizations of race and ethnic group participation in clinical trials are problematic for several reasons. First, they frame people as belonging to homogenous groups. The expectations of individual patient-subjects' willingness to participate and subsequent compliance are based on the "norms" that have been constructed for that group. Second, each group is compared implicitly to the "norm" of white people's participation. This is troubling because a false sense of altruism can be credited to whites and Americans. This was suggested in the physician's quote above where he insisted that the United States has people who are willing to "volunteer" for clinical trials. By making these comparisons, differences among groups are interpreted as being rooted in *culture,* not social contexts. This move thereby makes invisible any instrumental or structural motives that patient-subjects have for becoming involved in drug studies.

Another important effect of characterizing different groups along gender, race, and class lines is that research staff mobilize these assumptions in the decisions they make regarding the enrollment of patient-subjects into efficacy studies. Although investigative sites are not supposed to make determinations about whom to enroll along any lines other than those outlined in the study protocols' inclusion and exclusion criteria, there is a loophole that research staff can exploit: individuals can be denied enrollment (or removed from studies) based on noncompliance. As one coordinator explained her way to disqualify people from studies, "I put down that the patient does not feel they could be compliant. And I wouldn't lie to them. [I would tell them,] 'You cannot be compliant with this . . . and I really think this study is *not* for you.' And I have said that."

Many coordinators claim not to make any unilateral decisions about study participation based on their assumptions about individuals. Many feel that as long as patient-subjects qualify for studies, that they must be given the opportunity to enroll. Yet in spite of this view, one coordinator said, "All you can do is hope they fail something, you know, [laughs] fail a pulmonary function or fail their blood work or something." Rather than simply refusing to enroll individuals, coordinators use the informed consent process to dissuade individuals from *wanting* to participate. A coordinator said she frequently used this technique on low-income women interested in participating in studies at her site:

> Usually you try to give them enough information that they do it themselves [decide not to participate], you know? Maybe I'll say to you, "Well, I don't know; these hours are not going to coincide with your work or with your lifestyle, you know?" Or "You've got such bad veins that I really don't recommend you get in this study, you know?" You look for something to kind of sway the thing [decision] to go in the other direction [of not participating].

To justify her process of discouraging low-income women from enrolling, she said, "It really is for the safety of that patient, you know? They are not going to make it [through the end of the study] because they don't have the tools to do it. And you don't want to tell them you don't feel that they're mentally capable."

It is hard to know how common it is for sites to dissuade patient-subjects from enrolling in studies. It is certainly not in their economic interest to do so because they get paid by the patient and have enrollment quotas to fill as part of their obligation to the pharmaceutical companies for whom they are conducting studies. Yet it is not unreasonable to presume that the differential perceptions of whites and minority groups, of different social classes, and possibly different sexes contribute to the polarization of the types of studies (efficacy studies for middle-class white women and healthy human subject studies for poor minority men) into which these groups enroll.

Healthy Subjects' Participation in Drug Studies

Money as the underlying motivator for participating in clinical trials is most often associated with healthy human subject studies because of the large stipends attached to these studies. Compared to the scale and pace of efficacy studies on patient-subjects, healthy human studies, especially first-in-human clinical trials, are a completely different breed of pharmaceutical research. The emphasis on the healthiness of subjects is important in these early clinical trials because that stage of clinical development is measuring, through blood and other testing, what effects investigational drugs have on the body. There are two primary types of studies conducted on healthy subjects: first-in-human and bioequivalency. An investigator at a large research facility explained,

> We do first-in-human studies. With those, it's kind of interesting to see what's been done in the animal studies, what effects to be expected in humans, and how the protocol's laid out. [We also do what's called] the [bio]equivalence studies where you're just giving a brand name single dose or the generic. Those are basically what's called a "bleed-and-feed study" because you just feed them for a day and take a lot of blood and compare how the two drugs are absorbed and metabolized. Those aren't very exciting, but that's part of the job that needs to be done.

First-in-human studies pay healthy subjects the most because they are more time intensive, require multiple doses of varying quantities of the experimental drug, and carry higher and oftentimes unknown risks to human subjects.[18] In comparison, bioequivalency studies generally do not pay as well because they are seen as benign comparisons of a brand-name medication to a generic that is seeking approval and because they take considerably less time and fewer doses.

Healthy subjects research is unique in its treatment of human volunteers and has different ethical issues associated with the work. The studies involve higher risk and no individual benefits other than the financial compensation, and subjects' participation is much more finite than most efficacy studies. The majority of healthy human clinical trials are conducted at study centers that specialize in those types of studies. Thus, the experiences of healthy subjects and the attitudes and perceptions of research staff working in these facilities are different from efficacy studies that enroll patient-subjects.

A Latina woman in her early thirties described her experience as a healthy human subject. Like the vast majority of healthy subjects, she had become interested in volunteering for a pharmaceutical study for financial reasons. She was a single mother with a low-paying job, and she thought that volunteering for a well-paying clinical trial could provide additional money to see her through a few months. She called the toll-free number of a local study center and was informed about several studies for which she prequalified—based on gender, age, and weight—and could select one for which to screen. One study was for an investigational drug being developed for vaginal endometriosis; participating in that study appealed to the woman because she had once been diagnosed with endometriosis and knew a little bit about it. She felt from her personal experience that women's health problems are not as well understood as they should be, and that being in that study would not only benefit her economically but was something she could feel proud of doing.

A problem occurred, however, when she showed up for her screening visit and was given the consent form for a study of an experimental drug for attention deficit disorder. She recollected,

> I had no idea when I got in there that they had signed me up for a different study. So I'm in the middle of filling out my paperwork, and I'm going, "This is for endometriosis, correct?" because that's what I thought I was in there for. . . . The administrator says, "Oh no, this is for attention deficit disorder." And I said, "That's not what I had signed up for." She said, "Well, you are qualified for this study at this time." . . . So I go, "Well, fine," and signed the paperwork. But I still didn't know what I was doing. . . . I knew the study I had come for paid $2,300. . . . I figured they made a mistake, but I'm just going to go through the process. . . . And it was basically the same amount of money for both studies.

The woman explained that she had been primarily interested in doing a study because of the money not because of the type of study, and given that she was already at the facility being offered the same amount of money, she decided to go ahead and participate.

Yet, as she waited in the facility for her blood to be drawn, her urine sample to be collected, and her vitals to be checked, she started thinking about what she was doing there. She described to me a room full of fairly young people who were going through the process with her, all there for the same reason: money. She said that she felt ashamed of herself because she knew she was not going to leave, and she felt disdain for the study center for exploiting people. She also wondered how the government allowed this to happen. She recalled her thoughts and impressions as she sat there,

> That day a light went on in my head, and I go, "I feel like a piece of crap sitting here." . . . I was going to hurt myself even though I realized that this research was not for me. . . . You could go through the whole process and know that you're not protecting yourself one bit. You're just

not. I mean, to me, it's a freaky thing, a freaky thing to do. . . . I think
everybody does it for desperation reasons.

Even having the realization that she should not be participating in the study,
she stayed for the money. Although the study did not harm her, the woman
decided that she was not ready to enroll in another study any time soon.

An interesting aspect of healthy human subject clinical trials is that
prequalifying and screening for studies by no means guarantees individuals'
participation. This is because study centers screen significantly more people than there are available slots. The centers do this because they want to
ensure they have enough people who will pass all the laboratory tests administered during the screening visit. These tests ensure that subjects really are
"healthy" as defined by the study protocol.

Not everyone who screens will be deemed healthy enough to enroll in the
study. Although study centers have an obligation to provide individuals with
information about why they did not qualify for the study, anecdotal evidence
suggests that this is not always done in practice. Another Latina woman in
her twenties who failed her screening and could not enroll in a study told
me, "You go through the whole [screening] and have them tell you 'no' [you
don't qualify]. Then you see, wow, I gave them my life's information [that is,
medical history], and all I got in return was a 'No, you're not qualified.'" She
said that the disqualification made her worry that she might have a serious
medical problem, and she began to call the center for information. She never
received a response. She told me, "But if you call again and say you want to do
[a study], they call you right back. But if you call again and ask them for the
results [of your screening visit], they're not going to give it to you. . . . I was
very disappointed that I couldn't get any information back. . . . I still would
love to this day to know how my blood work came out."

Many other healthy subjects do qualify for the studies but are not selected
to enroll. Because there are generally more people who qualify than there
are available slots in studies, study centers often use a competitive system
in which people are told to call in on a particular day at a particular time.
Qualified people are chosen to enroll in the studies based on the order in
which they call in. This selection process is considered to be a way to add
randomization to the study, and it saves the study staff from having to make
determinations about whom to enroll.

Interestingly, many individuals volunteering for healthy subject studies
do not feel inconvenienced if they are not selected to enroll. In part, this is
because they are paid to screen for studies. Although payment is usually a

nominal amount ($25–$100), potential subjects feel compensated for their time. In addition, serial healthy subjects know that screening means getting paid to give body samples without needing to take any of the experimental substances. More importantly, it means not having to wait the thirty-day period allotted for drug washout before screening for another study. Because healthy subjects must wait between completing one study and enrolling in another, they know that screening for studies can make them additional income until they are selected for the next study. If they were "washing out," they would not be eligible to screen for studies.

Additionally, some healthy subjects are asked to be alternates on studies. This means that they are admitted into the study and spend the first twenty-four hours of the study in the facility in case people do not show up or do not pass their lab work. Alternates are dismissed when the first dosing of investigational drugs has been completed and they are not needed to fill study spots. One white man in his forties who had been an alternate spoke about this as a good situation: "I've been really fortunate. As a matter of fact, I just did [a study] for a company recently, and it was great! They overbooked by two people and myself and another gal got paid $60 to leave!" Alternates are often not put out by being dismissed from studies because they are not exposed to investigational drugs and, thus, do not have to wait the thirty-day washout before screening for a new study. These opportunities to screen for studies or be alternates could be seen as subtle ways that healthy subjects can take advantage of the system; there is very little risk to them in those roles. It also means there are more opportunities to get income out of healthy subject research than if they enroll in a study that only pays moderately well and then have to wait thirty days before taking part in the next.

There is a common assumption in the clinical trials industry that serial human subject volunteers are indiscriminate about what studies they do and are motivated solely by the money they will receive from their participation. Although this portrait is not inaccurate, it is not complete. What is interesting to glean from human subjects at study centers is the ways in which they conceptualize what they are doing *and* what the study centers and pharmaceutical companies are doing. As one Latina healthy subject stated,

> Can you imagine what you're putting yourself through for that much money? So I knew there was a big amount of your health that you were giving up. . . . You're a guinea pig and you're a guinea pig. But I went through the process; knowing at the end . . . *prostitution* to me, this is what they're doing. They're paying a big amount of money to just

use our bodies for that amount of time, but the outcome of it all is not good for us.

It is not uncommon for healthy human subjects to have opinions about the types of studies that are being conducted. For instance, a white woman in her forties told me that the point at which she decides whether or not she will participate in a study is when she first hears what it is during the initial prequalification phone call. The focus for her decision was based on logistics (such as time commitment) and what type of drug was being tested. She said, "[The center] wanted people to come in and take the antirejection medication for either kidneys or liver, and I don't want to do that. I feel like I have enough bombarding my body, I don't want to put anything more in it. I'm almost fifty years old . . . so I'm not interested in those studies and going that far out on a limb." That time, she did not schedule an appointment to be screened for the study, but she asked instead what other studies she might qualify for. Another healthy subject told me that she would never participate in any heart studies because she has a family history of heart problems. Rather than seeing participation in healthy studies as a possible way to help herself or her family members later on, she felt those studies would be too high of a risk.

This is not to say that all potential volunteers would use the same criteria in making their decisions about whether or not they wanted to enroll in specific studies. Instead, it suggests that the decision-making process takes place before healthy subjects arrive at study centers and long before they view consent forms. The next chapter will discuss consent issues in greater detail, but this evidence indicates that healthy subjects might feel that they are already consenting to the study by making the appointment for screening.

Researchers' perceptions of differences between healthy human subjects also shape recruitment practices. Specifically, study center staff outline three types of participants that are associated with healthy subject clinical trials. Subjects are said to fit one of the following profiles: (1) first-time or "educated" participants who are inquisitive about the study process, (2) compliant serial participants who sign on to any studies offered to them, and (3) serial participants who are noncompliant and disruptive during studies. In any given clinical trial, human subjects fitting all three types tend to be represented.

In explaining the differences between the three groups, an investigator at a healthy subject testing center described his perceptions of subjects' motivations and interests. About the first group, he said, "The first time people and the more educated types of people tend to be more cautious and they want to really know about the drugs and studies." When asked if subjects in that group are less likely to enroll in studies than others, he replied,

> Usually they'll go ahead and take part, but it depends on the study. If it's a first-in-human or something like that, then they're less likely to do it if they have not been through the process before. And in fact, I kind of really discourage them if they've never been a participant before. I tell them not to be in those first-in-human or things where there's unknown side effects. They should do a couple bioequivalence studies first where you're just taking a simple dose of a generic versus a brand name, simple studies, you know? Give those a try, see how they do with those, and then if they don't mind it, don't mind being confined, don't mind the regimentation of blood draws, and having to eat at certain times and sleep at certain times, then go ahead get into another study.

Thus, first time subjects are no less likely to enroll in particular studies than are serial participants, but the investigator might encourage them to enroll in different studies than the ones for which they are screening. Those subjects who do not mind the experience are likely to go on to do future studies. According to the investigator, the main factor that determines subjects' willingness to enroll in additional studies is their experience with confinement in the facility during the study. He said, "The more *motivated* people that have done these studies already know they tend to get bored and don't like being confined."

Serial healthy human subjects who are compliant make up the second type, and they are the participants that form the majority of the study population at the center. In the investigator's view, because they have done multiple studies, they are not concerned about the details of particular clinical trials in which they enroll. He said,

> Then there's kind of a population of professional lab rats. This is kind of what they do, and they don't really seem to have any occupations. They do a study every month or two and live off that somehow. Those people seem to care less what they're going to take, and that's probably the majority of them that we see. It's the repeat business, the "professionals," that just do this all the time, and surprisingly they seem to be very uninquisitive about what they're going to be taking.

Not only are serial participants able to tolerate confinement during studies, they also seek out the longer in-patient clinical trials because those studies

pay significantly more than do ones requiring shorter stays. In the investigator's mind, pay is not the only motivation for those longer studies; he said,

> The professional type [that is, serial] participants like the long-term
> ones because they pay more. *And* they seem to like being here eating
> our food and sleeping in our beds. I don't know why. Maybe they're get-
> ting away from some bad situations at home or something, but that type
> *look* for the long-term ones, and they seem to be very happy watching
> TV all day long.

Serial participants also make friends during studies, and the friendships add
to their positive experiences during long in-patient confinements. According
to the investigator, there is a lot of camaraderie among serial participants:

> You see them here during screening. They've been on a few studies
> together, they're talking, and I understand that sometimes they all go
> out to breakfast together when they leave here, things like that. Sure.
> Yeah, the people who've been doing this for years know a lot of peo-
> ple. . . . They've got some friends and people to socialize with. They
> seem to make friends fairly easily.

In contrast to *compliant* serial participants, there are also those serial
healthy subjects who can be disruptive during studies. Subjects must comply
with specific diets and schedules during clinical trials, and they must not
deviate in any way from the protocols. Some subjects do not want to restrict
the foods they eat or the times they sleep. Noncompliant subjects become a
more serious problem for the study center when they are resistant to the dosing or blood draw schedules. Study protocols dictate when blood should be
drawn, and subjects are expected to be present when it is their turn. When
subjects fail to show up or are difficult to find, research staff must complete
additional paperwork to document protocol deviations. The investigator
described this group as troublemakers and explained, "If somebody *is* a trou-
blemaker, that's not getting along with people or staff, then we'll put them
on a do-not-use list, so you weed out the ones that don't do well in confined
situations or do get into trouble or complain a lot."

By examining the investigator's description of the three types of participants, some patterns emerge regarding healthy human subject participation
in clinical trials. In his description of the three groups, he polarizes them
so that the compliant and troublemaking participants are seen as lazy, poor,
and stupid without a care for what they are volunteering to do to their own

bodies, and the inquisitive people are seen as being "motivated"—not satisfied merely eating someone else's food and sleeping in their beds—and want to know about the studies and what they are agreeing to do with their bodies. Thus, there is different worth placed on the groups within the clinical trials industry. Even though—or perhaps because—they are not the most informed, the serial participants who are uninquisitive about the studies but are compliant with the protocols are viewed as the best trial participants.[19]

Conclusion

Human subjects volunteer for clinical trials for multiple reasons including their health conditions, insurance status, and mode of recruitment as well as gender, race, and class. What should be clear is that subjects' participation, although technically voluntary, is motivated by instrumental reasons that might be more important than their concerns about any risks of participating in specific studies.

Although the advent of regulation has been hailed as the end of coercive and deceptive medical research, the current system continues to exploit those who are most disadvantaged in society. In healthy subjects research, this is most obvious because the majority of volunteers are minority men who answer the call to earn "good, fast, easy money," as one study center promised on my answering machine. The studies are framed as a simple exchange of time for money. Yet, as my informant from a healthy subject study declared, this exchange commodifies the body in a way that is not distinct from prostitution. The logic of the system insists that everyone will profit from the exchange.

In efficacy clinical trials, the potential for exploitation might be harder to detect, but those studies are structured nonetheless to posture as a service to underserved and uninsured populations. While patient-subjects do receive medical attention as part of their participation in clinical trials, it would be a mistake to equate this with access to health care. Given the inflexibility of study protocols and the frequency with which placebos are used, the "care" that patient-subjects receive is confined to their interactions with coordinators and to a lesser extent physician-investigators.

The difference that emerges as part of the new regime of exploitation embedded in pharmaceutical clinical trials is that middle-class white women—both with and without health insurance—are now targeted. This is a major change from medical research structured by traditional medical paternalism in which women, especially white American women, were often explicitly excluded from research. Until the early 1990s, policies of exclusion were meant to protect women's reproductive systems and any potential fetuses that could be harmed by research.[20] The new inclusive regime of medical research enables a hegemonic form of exploitation wherein white women, as the primary health care seekers in the United States, are particularly vulnerable in efficacy studies. These women are ideal for pharmaceutical clinical trials because, as a group, they have the socialization encouraging them to be compliant with the inflexible demands of the study protocols, including finding the time necessary to participate.

The system is exploitative when it comes to the participation of this group of women who might not otherwise be seen as marginalized (even when they do not have health insurance) because many of these women have bought into industry rhetoric surrounding their participation. They experience coordinators preaching altruism, their personal physicians requesting they participate, and advertisements promising free health care and medications. The white women who are filling pharmaceutical clinical trials in the United States do not necessarily question the system or their participation in it but buy into it as health care consumers. This is evinced by the nearly unanimous "positive experiences" they have in clinical trials. This is not to say that they are duped, but that clinical trials are folded seamlessly into the neoliberal context of all health care available to them.

Whereas the minority men and others participating in healthy subject studies understand their participation as an exchange, women in efficacy studies do not claim to see the exchange involved. Instead, they mistake the neoliberal system—in which profit-centered "care" has replaced patient-centered care—for individualized treatment in their best interests. These women may argue that they as individuals are not being exploited by the system because they are receiving some benefit in exchange for their participation, but this reasoning has been mobilized in the past: the orientation of these women towards clinical trials echoes that of prisoners who petitioned Congress in the 1970s to continue to allow medical research in prisons. Those prisoners too felt that they were receiving personal benefit (that is, income, better food, reduced sentences) from a regime of medical testing in which prisons were a major source of human subjects. What Congress, led by Senator Edward Kennedy, understood this to mean was that something was not right with the prison system if prisoners embraced medical experimentation as entirely a benefit. Similarly, something is not right with our current system of health care if clinical trials are received solely in terms of individualized benefits to those who participate. In the meantime, informed consent has been offered as the solution to exploitative research practices, yet most often decisions about participating in clinical trials occur prior to the formal process of informed consent. Current U.S. regulation regarding human subjects research does not address the meta-level unethical practices that can result as part of pharmaceutical (and other) research.

Chapter 7

Mobilizing Informed Consent

During my fieldwork, I had the opportunity to sit in on an informed consent visit for a study to test the safety of an experimental treatment for Alzheimer's disease. The prospective human subject was a seventy-five-year-old Latina woman, who was accompanied by her middle-aged son. They had found out about the study through a print advertisement in a local newspaper, and the son had made the appointment for his mother to be screened. The clinical trial was being conducted out of a dedicated investigative site not affiliated with a private practice.

The tone of the informed consent visit was educational. The physician-investigator conducting the study spent an hour with the woman and her son to explain the disease itself and the history of the product being tested.[1] The most important information he gave them about the study was that the product had previously been tested in humans and had caused the development of encephalitis in many of the participants, leading to death in several cases. The current one-year study consisted of a retooled version of the drug, and the purpose was solely to test its safety. Unlike most phase I studies, which primarily use healthy populations, this study required that subjects enrolled were already diagnosed with Alzheimer's disease because of the risks associated with the product. The mother and son were told that the study would not have any therapeutic value and that the primary motivation for participating should be altruism.

After the physician finished presenting the information, he asked whether either the son or the woman had any questions. What occurred during the subsequent conversation revealed the assumptions that potential patient-subjects (and their family members) have about medical research. The son began by telling the physician how important it was to him to find an effective treatment for his mother. While this would likely be true for any individuals watching their parents deteriorate from Alzheimer's, the son had turned to clinical research because he had recently buried his father who had suffered for many years from the same disease. The possibility of losing his mother in the same slow way was unacceptable to him. His goal, in his explanation as to why he responded to the advertisement, was to find a treatment that would curb the progression of his mother's Alzheimer's disease.

In response to the son's explanation, the physician carefully reiterated that participants would not receive any therapeutic benefit from the study. He explained that while the study included a rigorous evaluation, including an MRI at the outset to establish the diagnosis of Alzheimer's disease, there would be no further tests during the course of the year to assess the deterioration participants had experienced due to their illness. In spite of being told explicitly that the study would do nothing to improve his mother's condition, the son actively continued to search for a therapeutic benefit for his mother.[2] For example, he hypothesized that his mother might experience an improvement in her illness if the treatment was later proved to be efficacious. He posited that even if the purpose of the study was not to help his mother, the drug could still work to that effect. The physician quickly replied that in order for the drug to have any effect, it would have to be administered regularly, and the study included only one dose and a lengthy follow-up.

After much more exchange between the physician and the son, it appeared that the son had indeed accepted that his mother would not improve from participating in the clinical trial. Instead of using this opportunity to thank the physician and leave, the son settled on the diagnostic benefits of participating in the study as sufficient reason for his mother to enroll. His mother had only the most basic health coverage through Medicare, and he was attracted to the idea that she would be able to have a very expensive MRI performed. Even though he had responded to the ad because he hoped for a miracle cure for his mother, the son instructed his mother to sign the consent form to enter a study with no therapeutic benefit and with significant risk.[3] It seemed that the son had made up his mind that his mother would participate in the study prior to hearing the details. What the informed consent visit achieved was to give him different reasons for justifying her participation.

After the woman and her son had left his office, the physician-investigator turned to me and requested that I pretend that I was with the FDA and try to find fault with his process of informed consent. Although the invitation sounded sincere, he immediately started telling me the things that he did right. I told him that I was surprised that he had not given them a copy of the informed consent form until the end of the visit and that he had not gone over the language in it. I wondered if that interaction would happen when they came back. He said that no one would specifically cover the language in the form because the forms are not conducive to providing a "productive confidence-building interaction." He contended that he told them all the information in the form in such a way that they would understand the protocol better than if they read the actual form. Although in some ways I agreed with him, the problem rested in the time allotted for each item. He had certainly not spent equal time on all the parts of informed consent that needed to be discussed, particularly not on the risks associated with study participation.

What I now see is that the FDA likely would find nothing wrong with the doctor's informed consent process. Technically, it was more or less flawless, even though one could make some minor improvements as I had suggested. However, at a broader level everything was wrong because informed consent, as it is conceptualized by U.S. regulation and by bioethicists, did not take place. The ideal "autonomous" individual that ethicists assume as the agent who makes a decision—who, based on informed knowledge of the research protocol, "consents" to become a subject—did not exist. In this situation instead was a son who was desperate to do anything to help his mother. Any kind of marginal gain—more precise diagnosis, a miraculous recovery based on one dose of an experimental drug, or increased health care access—was better than what he held at the time as an option for his mother. The act of consent can only occur in the context of choice, of having an option of not agreeing. But if one is desperately ill, very poor, or unable to access necessary health care, then one may feel no choice but to consent. Moreover, clinical trials are offered as a whole, as "take-it-or-leave-it" packages, so many subjects must make a "choice" that is ultimately not really a choice at all.

This story is illustrative of many of the complicated issues raised by the informed consent process in pharmaceutical clinical research. Regardless of social address, patient-subjects are similarly dismissive of the information transmitted through informed consent. In part, this is because patient-subjects have already made up their minds to participate in studies before "informed consent" takes place. Additionally, however, informed consent has been transformed by the clinical trials industry from a possible obstacle to subjects' enrollment to a tool to "educate" patients about being responsible research subjects. Through the neoliberal delegation of responsibility to patient-subjects, the informed consent process operates as a mechanism of power within drug development, particularly by facilitating the transformation of patients into subjects.

Informed Consent and (Neo)Liberal Subjects

Informed consent is often hailed as *the* corrective to the abuses of human subjects that occurred in past eras of medical research.[4] It is credited with increasing the amount of information available to potential human subjects so that they can make rational decisions about their participation without coercion or deception.[5] In addition, when treated as an ongoing process rather than a discrete event captured by a signature, it is commended for the respect it bestows on volunteers for their decisions to take part in the process of drug development.[6]

In spite of the accolades it has received and the importance placed on the process, informed consent in the clinical setting does not and cannot fully meet the expectations placed upon it by regulators and bioethicists. To begin to address weaknesses with the procedure, bioethics must refine its notions of liberal individualism to account for the complex realities of *neoliberal* subjects. The construction of the ethical principle of "autonomy" in bioethics is premised on the liberal assumption that individuals act as autonomous beings who make measured decisions about participating in research based on the information given to them.[7] Social scientists as well as some bioethicists have criticized this position by arguing that human subjects' decision making is a process that may include consent forms but that is situated in the broader contexts of people's lives.[8]

As the previous chapter has illustrated, human subjects volunteer for clinical trials for a host of reasons including access to health care, need for income, hope for a magic bullet, and interest in different types of care. Although other factors also motivate subjects to enroll in pharmaceutical clinical trials, the reasons for participation are reflective of or responses to the broader political economy in the United States. Given the political and economic realities of life in a largely neoliberal state, access to quality health care and economic security are not assured for all people living within U.S. borders. Millions of people each year perceive clinical trials as an opportunity for care or income.[9] While only a fraction of the population who are without health insurance or who are impoverished participate in clinical studies, the overrepresentation of these groups in drug development indicates a structural problem for which augmenting or respecting individuals' autonomy is not sufficient to protect the rights and welfare of those human subjects.

In addition to the neoliberal context of participation in clinical trials, the political economy of pharmaceutical drug development involves important constraints that limit the degree of autonomy human subjects can exert in their participation. In drug studies as in most medical research, human subjects have autonomy only over the decision *to* participate. They retain this right throughout their participation, so that they may discontinue the studies at any time. Yet once human subjects have decided to participate, they cannot choose *how* they participate. Similarly as for investigators, study protocols are take-it-or-leave-it options in which subjects are not given any rights to negotiate.

It can be argued that the stringency of study protocols is merely good science, that research must be done consistently to produce generalizable results. On many points of study protocols this view is correct; however, it ignores the multiple factors that influence the design of the protocols.[10] Specifically, all the decisions that pharmaceutical companies make in the design of clinical trials are not based solely on science. Introducing some procedures and practices into clinical trials also fulfills marketing missions by familiarizing physicians and other health care professionals with pharmaceutical companies' products. Many elements of study design serve as data for future marketing by establishing how subjects respond to certain procedures, restrictions, or even side effects.

Given the complexities of structural constraints, individual interests, and local contexts, the ethical principle of autonomy and the process of informed consent are too narrowly focused and do not capture the lived reality of most subjects' decision making. Rather than understanding subjects' participation in clinical trials through liberal constructions of individualism wherein there are no differences among people in terms of gender, race, class, and so on, we should instead recognize that individuals are neoliberal subjects who make decisions in light of their individual experiences of the broader political, economic, and social contexts of the United States.

Human Subjects' Reception of Informed Consent

What weight do human subjects attach to the process of informed consent? How does their engagement with informed consent correspond to their reasons for participating in clinical trials and the ways in which they are recruited for studies? The vast majority of potential subjects are generally uninterested in the information contained in consent forms. This is because most human subjects have already decided to participate in clinical trials before the informed consent process takes place. Informed consent appears to work as intended by regulators only to discourage patients from participating in efficacy studies that carry extreme risk or inconvenience.

The process of informed consent can be time intensive. Most sites conduct informed consent by following a set procedure: patient-subjects are given an overview of the project, they are given time to read the entire consent form, and then they can pose any questions or concerns they have before deciding whether or not to sign. The process generally takes an hour, but more complicated studies require up to two hours. The consent procedure is routinely delegated to coordinators as part of their task of recruiting and enrolling patient-subjects, but investigators may informally go over the details of studies with subjects after they have signed the forms.[11] It is rare for physician-investigators to be involved with informed consent because of the time commitment.

There are frequently two informed consent forms for pharmaceutical studies. The first is for the study protocol itself, and the second is for an optional genetic component of the study in which patient-subjects are encouraged to participate. Adding to the time it takes to complete informed consent is that the forms themselves are long and often dense. Regardless of the attention paid to reading level by institutional review boards (IRBs), the language in consent forms is not easy to comprehend. The increases in the length and the specificity of details in consent forms are in large measure due to liability issues associated with drug development. Pharmaceutical companies and IRBs are careful to include any and all information about clinical trials that is thought to protect them from lawsuits.

Patient-subjects show disturbingly little interest in the details of the consent forms.[12] Although some might argue that this is due to the impossible length of the forms or the difficulty of the language, it also is because of the reasons why patient-subjects seek out clinical trials in the first place. For some patient-subjects, the fact that their personal physicians asked them to participate in a clinical trial is enough for them to decide to enroll. According to an upper-middle-class white patient-subject in his sixties, "I didn't have to think the clinical trial over or know the details. I am a retired mathematician and research administrator so I have *always* known about medical research. . . . I accepted the trial as soon as my physician offered it."

For other patient-subjects who do not have health insurance and respond to clinical trial advertisements, most have already decided that study participation is their only means for treating a problem that they know needs medical attention. Patient-subjects' commitment to enrolling in studies is illustrated by the inconvenience some undergo to be able to participate in drug studies, particularly long-term clinical trials. As an example of this, a coordinator related to me a story about a patient-subject who had moved out of state during the course of a study:

> We've had one patient who used to live here. He was in what you call a long-term safety study. Before the study was over, he moved to [a nearby state], but he didn't drop out of the study. The problem was that he didn't have health insurance. He decided that it was cheaper for him to come here and get his medicine than to get something that was already on the market. Besides he was in the maintenance phase of the study where you're pretty much guaranteed the real thing [rather than a placebo]. So it was cheaper for him to get an airline ticket to fly here for his appointments than it was for him to buy medicines on the market.

Although I did not get to interview this patient-subject, the coordinator's story about him puts study participation in sharp relief: the cost of marketed drugs is so much of a burden that a major logistical inconvenience did not outweigh the financial benefit of receiving medical care through the study. Given the health and economic constraints influencing patient-subjects' decision making about clinical trials, it is no surprise that the details outlined in consent forms may matter very little to them.

Because the majority of patient-subjects have already decided to participate in clinical trials before they read consent documents, informed consent is not as effective a tool as U.S. regulation purports it to be. This has been reported in other empirical studies of informed consent, and coordinators in my study were quick to corroborate the finding.[13] For example, one told me, "Generally if they've responded to our ad, then they are interested in doing research and will enroll the majority of the time." Some coordinators even go so far as to say that when it comes to decision making, "The informed consent has no impact at all!" because they find that generally that by the time they are sitting across from patient-subjects, the subjects have already committed to enrolling.

From the point of view of many patient-subjects, a major problem with informed consent is that the most important question they have about efficacy studies is one that will go unanswered: Will I get the investigational drug? This is not to say that patient-subjects cannot appreciate the reasons why clinical trials are blind or even double-blind. What it means is that for many potential patient-subjects, it is the answer to that question that would affect their decision about whether or not to participate in a study. As one patient-subject said,

> Informed consent, to me, means that I give my consent upon having been informed of the possible unknown outcomes of my participation in the study. Honestly, I don't recall exactly what process of informed consent I went through. I'm sure I signed something, but I don't recall what it was. What I do remember is that I had only one question, which they could not answer: Was I on the placebo or the real thing? I felt free to ask whatever other questions I wanted to, but nothing else occurred to me that was of great significance.

This particular patient-subject did not remember what was told to her during the informed consent process, and what she did recall was not accurate: the form would have indicated the *known* risks associated with the study based on prior clinical trials. Unfortunately, this is not a unique occurrence. Many empirical studies of informed consent have found that patient-subjects have poor recall of the details of consent forms.[14]

The patient-subject's comments also illustrate the importance of what the consent form did not say versus what it did say: informed consent could not answer her primary question or concern about participating in the study. People who are interested in clinical trials because they do not have health insurance might be deterred from participating if they knew that they were going to receive a placebo. In contrast, people who are primarily motivated by money, especially in healthy subject studies, would likely prefer not to be randomized to the investigational drug arm of the study. In other words, in addition to the scientific principles on which randomized controlled clinical trials are based, blind studies are also advantageous for pharmaceutical companies and sites in their efforts to recruit and retain human subjects.

In addition to the problem that consent forms do not inform patient-subjects about whether they will receive active drugs or placebos, another reason for patient-subjects' disinterest in the content of the forms is that they are unable to negotiate any part of their participation. Clinical trials are a take-it-or-leave-it option to whomever they are offered; patient-subjects can either accept the terms of the clinical trial or they must refuse to participate. There may be parts of the study that are not convenient or may even be uncomfortable or painful, but if patient-subjects would like to participate in the study, they must consent to all of it. For example, by enrolling in a study, a woman in a cancer clinical trial had to undergo procedures that she would not have had to undergo in the course of standard treatment for her cancer. The woman explained,

> There are certainly things in the study that were a little bit distaste-ful. I would have to submit to another biopsy on a lymph node. That's kind of a painful procedure, and I was aware of that. I would have to submit to another bone marrow test, which is also painful to do. So I knew there were some extra procedures that I probably wouldn't have had to endure [otherwise]. However, if you have an illness like this, and you know it's incurable, you are, well, *I* am driven to the best pos-sible chance I have for remission, or hopefully cure. So those things were negligible for me. I mean I knew they were there, but the total package was attractive.

The woman stated that because the study offered her a medical treatment that she could not access otherwise, she decided to participate the moment her oncologist mentioned the possibility.

Thus, the process of informed consent does not have the same impor-tance to patient-subjects as it is meant to have according to bioethics and the federal regulation. In spite of sites' procedures for informed consent, coordi-nators related to me many stories about how challenging consent visits can be. For example, one told me,

> A lot of patients will say, "I don't care what the consent form says, I just want to do the study." They will read the informed consent while we sit there with them—and don't forget: when you read an informed con-sent, it gives you worse-case scenario, it gives you the *real* bad things that could possibly happen. And for example, I was in a research study myself, and I knew I wanted to participate in that particular study. When I read the informed consent, I knew that these bad things could possibly happen, but . . . at that point, that was what I wanted to do! So patients who are going through some type of disease . . . they don't care what the informed consent form says. No matter how bad it sounds, they are going to sign on the dotted line.

In other words, the details contained in consent forms become irrelevant to patient-subjects who know they want to participate regardless of any risks, benefits, or inconvenience.

Subjects' lack of interest in informed consent does not unequivocally mean that consent forms do not have any effect on their decision making about clinical trial participation. There are indeed patterns in what motivates people to turn to clinical trials and how much risk from studies patient-subjects are willing to tolerate as a result. One coordinator I interviewed had a very nuanced view of these dynamics, and her tone alternated between frustration and disbelief at what people will agree to according to their degree of desperation as they enter into clinical trials: "The importance of the informed consent just depends on the indication that we're studying and how important it is for them to get help for that problem." For example, in cases in which patient-subjects tend to be very desperate, informed consent is particularly insignificant. She explained,

> We're running an obesity trial now. Some of the people will just go, "Where do I sign?" They don't care if the drug may cause brain damage; they just say, "Well, I want to lose weight." So I guess their attention to informed consent forms just depends on their urgency as far as the indication that they are suffering from. Another example, I run a lot of the dermatology studies here. With psoriasis, I get a lot of that, where the people say, "I've tried everything!" They're desperate, they just want help, they say, "Show me where I sign!" . . . In those weight loss studies, we can have a drug that could cause coma, death!, death!, death! Number one problem. They don't care. They'll say, "I'm going to try it. I am going to try it." It's because they are so desperate to get rid of whatever is their problem.

In contrast, the coordinator conducts other studies in which patient-subjects take the consent forms, especially the description of the risks associated with the studies, much more seriously. She continued,

> I had an insomnia study once that listed the side effects, and it was so overwhelmingly scary, *nobody* was going to do this study, absolutely nobody. . . . There was some possibility of stroke, possibility of a heart attack. From an insomnia drug! They could be paralyzed on one side or the other! There was also the possibility of some nerve damage, liver function problems, *unbelievable!* . . . So I would give people the consent form, we'd be sitting there, they'd be reading it, and they'd just put it down and walk out and never say another word. You could see that the page was turned to those side effects, risks, discomforts, and so forth.

So, I don't think that everyone comes in with the foreknowledge that I'm *absolutely* going to do this, *period.* . . . [In cases] such as insomnia that these people have lived with their conditions for twenty, thirty, forty years, they're used to it! Yeah, it's a problem, but if it means possibly getting one of these side effects, it's not worth risking.

This shows that there is a critical threshold that some subjects will not cross. It does not negate, however, the governing force of structural constraints driving subjects' participation.

Another important way that the informed consent process affects patient-subjects' decisions about enrolling in studies is based on the logistics of the study. Oftentimes, patient-subjects are more disturbed by the level of activity that they have to consent to as part of the study than they are concerned about the risks of taking investigational products. For example, some studies require frequent, lengthy study visits. Many patient-subjects simply cannot make their schedules flexible enough to adapt to the protocols, or they live far enough away from the sites that they decide participation would be too burdensome. Another impediment to participation is that some studies have cumbersome data collection systems that patient-subjects must use as part of the study. The most common types are symptom diaries in which patient-subjects have to track at regular intervals any symptoms they might be experiencing. Symptom diaries can be paper-based or electronic, the latter using PDAs or automated telephone systems for data capture. Some patient-subjects simply do not want this level of participation. A coordinator related an example of recruiting for studies of this type:

I have a lot of people walk out because of the logistics of the study. . . . For example, I have one where a participant has to call every night between eight and midnight and talk to a machine; it's called a "voice activated response system," because that's how they're capturing their data. It asks: "How well did you sleep last night? Did you take your medication? What time did you go to bed? How long did it take you to fall asleep? How many times did you wake up?" There are thirteen questions that they have to answer. And if they don't call at least ten times out of fourteen days, we have to kick them out of the study because the pharmaceutical companies are losing their data. So there's a lot that we ask these participants to do too.

Another coordinator related similar examples of prospective patient-subjects' decisions not to participate in studies:

I think the biggest deterrent to their participation is the *time* involved. . . . Maybe it's just the study procedures, what's needed with each visit. When you tell people "You'll need to be here at least an hour," some people think it's going to be shorter than that. Also the length of the trial can be a deterrent because if it'll be a year trial, they might have to come in *monthly* for visits. So I would say the timing and the scheduling. As well as sometimes if they have to do *something* in the trial besides just take their pills. Like with the Palm Pilot studies [for recording symptoms], you know, somebody said, "I don't think I can handle using this Palm Pilot every day."

In other words, some patient-subjects may be put off by the logistics of the study when they find out that there is more to enrolling in clinical trials than receiving free medical appointments and investigational drugs.

The confluence of these factors in patient-subjects' reception of informed consent results in the mundane details or logistics of a study becoming what matters to potential patient-subjects more than study risks. When I asked patient-subjects which of the details about the study were important to them when they were deciding whether or not to enroll, I received very similar responses. For example, a white woman in her thirties said, "Well, how long the study would be, how much time it would entail, how far away the facility was. Definitely if it was too far, I wouldn't do it." The clinical trials industry has not overlooked this attitude, and it has shaped the way in which the industry views the informed consent process. If the majority of human subjects have already decided to participate in clinical trials by the time they appear at the clinic, informed consent can be used as a different type of tool by the clinical trials industry.

Mobilization of Informed Consent as an Enrollment Tool

Because informed consent was designed, in part, to empower human subjects to make decisions regarding their participation in studies, there was considerable unease about what effects it would have on the practice of scientific medicine. When informed consent as an official doctrine was first mandated by federal regulation in the early 1980s, many researchers in the scientific community worried that detailing the potential risks of participation would frighten away prospective human subjects.[15] A major concern was that informed consent might slow the pace of medical breakthroughs by making the enrollment of subjects impracticable.[16] Even within medicine more broadly, physicians initially perceived informed consent as an overly intrusive process that would diminish patients' trust in their doctors and negatively affect the provision of care.[17]

Today, in spite of evidence that informed consent does not significantly undercut physicians' authority or prove an obstacle to enrolling human subjects into clinical studies,[18] some anxiety remains in the scientific community regarding the content of consent forms. There is a strong tendency to frame study information as euphemistically as possible, especially details about risk to subjects and about investigators' conflicts of interest.[19] For example, rather than directly stating that investigators are paid for enrolling subjects in clinical trials, informed consent forms instead remark that investigators might have a "financial conflict of interest." In other words, the appropriate information is indeed included in consent forms, but the presentation of that information is not always as straightforward as it could or should be.[20] The use of euphemisms indicates a continued reticence, or at least discomfort, on the part of many researchers, as well as IRBs, to clearly state pertinent information about study protocols.

Within the clinical trials industry, however, informed consent is increasingly mobilized to *enable* the process of drug development. Over the past several years, the process of informed consent has been framed as an important strategy for subject recruitment and retention. For example, Kenneth Getz, a leading industry analyst,[21] delivered a lecture to representatives from investigative sites, CROs, and other clinical trials companies in 2002 called "Leveraging the Informed Consent Process as Strategic Recruitment and Retention Asset."[22] Getz argued that given the general public's lack of knowledge about clinical trials, informed consent must be used to shape potential subjects' perceptions of studies so that they can know what to expect of their participation. He emphasized that potential patient-subjects must understand the logistics of studies before they participate in order to fully comply with the protocols and be willing to complete the studies in their entirety. Because few patient-subjects fully understand their responsibilities as part of clinical development, many subjects are more interested in what they can personally gain from their participation and may drop out of the studies if they do not receive the benefits they had anticipated. The goal then is not to enroll *more* patient-subjects through informed consent but to orient those who do participate in studies to the goals and demands of clinical protocols. While this reframing of the informed consent form to meet the needs of sites and pharmaceutical companies may not be a surprise, it indicates that the communication of information is valued. The focus, however, is on the instrumental effects of this information for fashioning more responsible patient-subjects.

Given patient-subjects' general lack of interest in consent forms, the process of obtaining informed consent can be used by the clinical trials industry to emphasize subjects' responsibility to the pharmaceutical industry in delivering accurate and complete data. In this move, the focus of the informed consent process is transformed from the protection of human subjects to the augmentation of data.[23] The goal with this new construction of the consent process is to create engaged participants who actively contribute data to the study. This should not be confused with *empowered* subjects: their engagement with the studies has little personal benefit to them as individuals or as a group.

Informed Consent as Education

How do these industry logics manifest in the clinic? What are the ways in practice that informed consent takes on more instrumental meanings? Because so few patient-subjects are interested in the details of consent forms and because consent has to be a documented practice nonetheless, research staff are able to structure the interaction according to the goals of drug development. Specifically, coordinators understand the informed consent process as an effective mode of teaching patient-subjects the "responsibility" associated with clinical trials.

Informed consent procedures can be thought of as educational opportunities, and as such, most prospective patient-subjects' lack of interest in the subject is not sufficient to deter coordinators from their task. All students are not going to be equally interested in learning every subject in school, but teachers will nonetheless spend time on all relevant subjects. In a similar vein, coordinators feel that what it means to "do their job" is to explain studies by going page by page through the consent form, regardless of the level of interest of individual patient-subjects. By doing this, they are systematically ensuring that all potential patient-subjects receive the information they need. As one coordinator argued, "It doesn't matter if they're interested in the informed consent form. What matters is to have the time to *educate* the patient."

The emphasis in the clinic is that informed consent should be seen as a process. Most coordinators talk about consent as an ongoing educational procedure—as opposed to a simple form—and take their duty to inform the patient-subjects about the studies very seriously. One coordinator articulated how she operationalizes consent as a process:

Informed consent is an *ongoing* process. . . . It begins with the first phone call when I tell them about the study. They're scheduled to come to our office, most often specifically *just* to review the informed consent. I explain to them that it will describe in detail every step of the study, everything that's done, and that it is my intent that they know as much about the study, after they've read that and met me or another coordinator, as *I* do about it. And I also let them know that part of the consent process requires that they sign the document. They're not buying a car; it *simply* means they had the opportunity to read it, we offered to answer all of their questions, and that's simply just proof that that process has taken place.

The focus on process means that patient-subjects can continue to ask questions and learn about studies before they enroll and as they advance through the protocols. By making consent ongoing, coordinators can provide patient-subjects with a reminder of their rights (for example, to withdraw from the study) and their responsibilities (for example, to be compliant with the protocols).

Minimizing Subjects' Perceptions of Risk

The various pieces of information contained in consent forms does not receive equal attention in consent visits. Coordinators tend to emphasize the logistics of studies by carefully describing what subjects will be responsible for through their participation. Although patient-subjects are almost always given as much time to read consent forms as they would like, coordinators and others tend to downplay the section on risks. By federal law, they cannot skip it altogether, and I found no instance or indication that the risks of study participation were simply not covered during consent visits. However, coordinators have learned to reframe any risk information that might be construed as worrisome in consent forms.

A standard technique for mitigating patient-subjects' concerns about specific clinical trials involves the comparison of the relative risk of drug studies to substances that are already on the market which can be obtained over-the-counter or with a prescription. One coordinator described what she tells patient-subjects:

You always talk to them about the side effects that could happen. To explain it to them, we tell them: "Any time a pharmaceutical company has two people that have the same side effect, they have to publish it. So it doesn't necessarily mean that it will happen to you, but we have to inform you." And then we could also do a comparison: "Have you ever read the label for ibuprofen? You know if you read that, you probably wouldn't take it, but everybody else takes it, so you take it."

Another coordinator even compared the risks of clinical trials to the risks associated with food products:

> People are going to have these misconceptions about research. . . . I tell my friends it's just like anything else that you throw in your mouth, albeit peanuts, avocados, Skittles, anything, right down to the aspirin that you've been taking for twenty years. The next morning you could take it, you can have an adverse reaction to it; there are no real guarantees. Your body's changing, medications change, and it might not be compatible for you anymore, so you just kind of hold this in mind, Mr. Patient or Mrs. Patient.

Another mechanism that serves to minimize any concerns that potential patient-subjects might have about clinical trials is embedded in coordinators' pitches about phase III and IV studies. Many coordinators tell patient-subjects that in spite of the risks spelled out in consent forms, the products being tested in phase III studies must be safe enough and efficacious enough that they got through phase I and II trials successfully.[24] Coordinators frame phase IV studies as the safest clinical trials because they consist of comparisons of marketed drugs (so the FDA has already found those products to be safe and effective enough to be made available to the public).[25] One coordinator outlined her approach:

> I tell them that by the time the medication has gotten to us for a phase III trial, it's looking not only very effective, but also very safe. Otherwise the pharmaceutical company would not still be spending money on it to bring it to my office. Patients understand that these companies have business interests, so I take that business approach to have them look at it that way. And I think that's probably helpful for patients.

Another coordinator who was not so emphatic about the safety and efficacy of products being tested in phase III trials nonetheless used the financial interests of the pharmaceutical industry as indication that the studies are promising:

> We simply tell them, "We don't know if this product is going to work. We're hopeful that it will be better than what you currently have, and

you're going to help us find that out." So it's not coercive, but hopefully it's encouraging. You have to tell them that the *company* is encouraged because it wouldn't get to this point unless they thought the drug had something to offer, and I think you can always come back to that point. This company and this whole industry would not spend the time and the effort in financing a study unless they had the encouragement that the product is going to work.

In other words, the informed consent process can be used to minimize any concerns that patient-subjects might have about the risks associated with study participation.

Emphasizing Subjects' Responsibility

Coordinators also use the informed consent process to increase patient-subjects' understanding about their responsibility to pharmaceutical companies as they participate in studies. Coordinators understand not only that many patient-subjects are new to research but also that many do not understand the process of drug development and approval. They often feel that this "big picture" information is important for patient-subjects to know to be able to understand their role in studies. One coordinator commented, "I mean when you talk to people, how many of them are really aware of what clinical trials are and what they involve? I pride myself on the fact that we really discuss these things. For example, I tell them what an IRB is. . . . And they need to know about the sponsor too. For example, how many have heard of AstraZeneca? Well, most of them haven't." By educating patient-subjects about the "big picture" of drug development, coordinators are trying to show subjects that they are part of something bigger than themselves: the advancement of scientific knowledge and the progress of medicine.

Using informed consent to ensure that patient-subjects absorb the "responsibilities" that come with being part of a clinical trial is structured to indicate to subjects that they need to be active participants in studies. A coordinator articulated the role that she tries to motivate patient-subjects to assume:

> It's just important that people don't think that, "Okay, I'm going to volunteer for a clinical trial, and everything is out of my hands and I don't know anything." . . . You have to enroll patients who can understand *their* commitment toward the clinical trial that they're participating in. . . . "Let me tell you what we need from you. This is *your* responsibility in this clinical trial: being there for these visits, documenting your

diaries whether it's electronic or paper or whatever." I really impress upon them from the very beginning: "Your feedback, your documentation, your response is all that we have to give to the FDA for approval. . . . The information from you, *your* perception of all of this, whether it's pain level whatever, is *critically* important to whether or not a medication or device is approved."

Coordinators commonly draw upon the motif of patient-subjects' experiences of the investigational drug (or placebo) as critical information when explaining subjects' responsibilities.

Emphasized in coordinators' instructions about individuals' responsibility as patient-subjects is that subjects are committing not only to following a protocol by taking pills on schedule but also to being aware of the effects of those pills on their bodies and on their specific medical conditions. A coordinator said, "I like to teach the patients that it is *their* responsibility. They know their own bodies, so they need to know that if they're taking this drug and something strange feeling or strange thing happens, they need to write those things down. So educating patients about this is really an important part of the research process." Another coordinator explained her approach:

That's why I like for them to read consent forms here in our office. That way if it says you may have headaches or nausea or vomiting or this sort of thing, then we can remind them: "You begin taking a medication, and if your hair turns a different direction the next day, we want to know about it. And certainly if you take a medication and the next morning you're feeling nauseated and vomiting or having diarrhea, we want to know about it as soon as you do."

One implication of the individual responsibility approach to patient-subjects' participation in trials is that some coordinators are very uncomfortable enrolling patient-subjects who would need help from someone else to complete the details of the protocols.[26] For example, patient-subjects with memory loss might not be the best candidates for a study that is not directly targeting that illness because they might forget to take pills, fill out their symptom diaries, or have difficulty attending study visits. A coordinator said,

What really breaks my heart is that sometimes there are patients that are really very eligible for some of the studies that we are doing. It's just that they're not good candidates because they're not good historians. I really do hesitate to consent anyone that needs help with a study, like they are going to rely on their daughter. But you know, the daughter's not signing the consent form, the patient is. They should be able to report their symptoms themselves because everybody's interpretation is different, and that kind of presents a problem.

Although some patient-subjects might be put off by the level of commitment that coordinators demand from them, coordinators—and even physician-investigators—feel that this orientation is justified because it serves to weed out subjects who might not be well-suited for pharmaceutical research. In an echo of the industry view encapsulated in Getz's lecture, research staff feel that in order to get the data the pharmaceutical companies seek, patient-subjects need to follow the protocols well. If coordinators do not believe that potential patient-subjects are going to be able to do that, then it is better that those individuals do not enroll in the studies at all. The informed consent process can help determine who should or should not participate. One coordinator explained her view on this:

> Our job is really to educate our volunteers about their responsibility *to us*. If that means that they decline participation in a clinical trial, quite honestly it's better for us simply because we want a patient who's going to be compliant and who wants to give of themselves. *Because a clinical trial is giving of yourself.* [my emphasis] It's their time—collecting data from these patients—you're asking them to write in diaries, to do things that are perhaps many times outside of their normal schedule, to come in earlier, to stay longer for office visits, so we want the patients aware of all those things. But also we want a patient who's *inquisitive* and who wants to know more about the study, about the medication that they're going to be consuming, about the trials process, about what their responsibilities are. Ultimately, you want a person who's going to give you the kind of data that will either show that particular compound should never go on the market or that this compound will definitely make a positive impact upon people's lives.

Coordinators' emphasis on patient-subjects' responsibilities as part of the informed consent process often means that patient-subjects become very well informed about the logistics of the study protocols. As a result, the trend of potential patient-subjects deciding not to participate based on the logistics of the studies rather than on the risks or benefits can be traced to their interactions with coordinators and the tone of the consent process itself. It is not simply that patient-subjects are more interested in those details, but that those details are the ones that they are most likely to spend time discussing during informed consent visits.

Implications of Reframed Consent

The mobilization of informed consent by the clinical trials industry plays off of patient-subjects' minimal interest in details about drug studies printed in consent forms. On the surface, the claim that the clinical trials industry uses informed consent for its own ends may seem like an accusation of unethical misconduct in the industry. Although it may be true that the industry's instrumental framing of informed consent is not in the spirit of the federal regulation, it is *not* true that clinics that mobilize the process of informed consent in this way are necessarily engaging in unethical conduct.

Rather than focusing on ethics per se, my interest in the instrumental uses of informed consent for the clinical trials industry is to understand the operations of power. Specifically, I understand this practice to be another instantiation of neoliberalism in the organization of pharmaceutical drug development. Informed consent performs on multiple levels. It has the potential to empower patient-subjects, yet its potential to be manipulated by those in the industry is more salient. Because so many patient-subjects are disempowered by the health care or economic systems, the ideal of informed consent cannot be attained: those patient-subjects cannot afford to engage informed consent in the way the regulation intended as protection against research abuses. The industry capitalizes on and emphasizes human subjects' responsibility to the process of delivering study results, thereby solidifying participants' status as neoliberal subjects.

Conclusion

There are many obstacles to fulfilling the process of informed consent as it is conceptualized by bioethicists and required by U.S. regulation. What ethicists and regulators want human subjects to know about research is not necessarily what those human subjects want to know. Moreover, consent forms are valenced in such a way as to reduce the liability of research sponsors (whether pharmaceutical companies, government agencies, or universities) and investigative sites, to prevent the grossest forms of deception and coercion, and to act as symbols to human subjects that their rights are being protected.

Structural contingencies—from motivation to participate to lack of flex-ibility in how to participate—diminish the importance to patient-subjects of the information contained in what are oftentimes preposterously lengthy forms. Although getting patient-subjects to care about study details outlined in consent forms may appear to be the key challenge for informed consent, there is a conflict that emerges at the intersection of information about clinical trials and their contexts. The information contained in consent forms is supposed to empower potential patient-subjects to make the best decisions regarding their health, but the reality is that those who are seeking out clinical trials are already disenfranchised from the medical or economic systems and have few or no other choices that they can make. When there is little potential for decision making or for empowerment, it should be no surprise that patient-subjects often show little interest in the information contained in those forms.

The example of the Alzheimer's patient at the opening of this chapter illustrates the conflict between the regulatory assumption of "autonomous agents" who can make decisions about clinical trials based on information contained in consent forms and the structural conditions that influence people's decision making about their health care options. What is lost in the former model of potential patient-subjects' decision making are the power dynamics that shape the context of pharmaceutical clinical trials for those that participate. In sum, the informed consent process is always already undermined by the contingencies of individuals' social, political, and economic contexts: the reasons that draw many people to pharmaceutical clinical trials render informed consent less relevant. Structured by the broader goals of the clinical trials industry, however, patient-subjects' primary interaction with information about the studies can be used as a source of *post*-decision education. This information is used to emphasize to patient-subjects *their* responsibilities toward and commitment to the particular study, and is only rarely used by patient-subjects to decide *not* to participate at all.

What is absent from consent forms and therefore from U.S. regulation is an understanding of the structural conditions that limit subjects' autonomy. Because individuals do not make decisions in a vacuum, structural conditions can and do derail the ostensible mission of informed consent. Patient-subjects are not autonomous agents stripped of personal context as they are often rendered in philosophy; instead, they are neoliberal subjects motivated by their social and economic positions to benefit the best they can from the system of drug development. In particular, the people who are participating in healthy human subject studies—with the highest risk and therefore the highest compensation—are the people in our society who are most in need of material resources. Motivation for efficacy trials is based on access to health care and illness prognosis. In other words, obstacles to informed consent are rooted in contexts that diminish the possibility for true consent.

This is an important finding for understanding the role of medical neoliberalism in the domain of informed consent and enrollment of human subjects into clinical trials. It indicates that the current system of pharmaceutical research takes advantage of the conditions that draw human subjects to research and that obscure (or override) their understanding of clinical trials. Because of the current regulatory and political environments in the United States, the clinical trials industry benefits from neoliberal cutbacks to welfare, health care, and education programs. Within this context, the informed consent process is an impotent tool to counteract the new forms of exploitation embodied in the current system of conducting drug studies. In fact, informed consent is transformed into a tool to enhance the compliance and control of subjects for increased profit and decreased liability for the industry as a whole.

Chapter 8

Cultivating Pharmaceutical "Compliance"

Although the majority of my informants seemed to be people who really enjoyed their jobs in the clinical trials industry or who had positive experiences participating in drug studies, I occasionally interviewed someone who was dissatisfied with contract research. One such informant was Anne,[1] a veteran nurse turned disillusioned research coordinator. At the time of our interview, she had been working as a coordinator for eighteen months; she had been in her current position eight months, a personal record for her given that she was already on her third coordinator job. During the interview, it was obvious that she was frustrated and unhappy, not with her current position but with being a coordinator. It was no surprise a few months later when she contacted me to tell me that she had quit her job and was leaving the industry altogether.

Anne felt like she could not "cut it" as a coordinator, and she blamed herself for her "bad fit" in clinical research. Anne, like the majority of coordinators, experienced a role conflict as a nurse conducting clinical trials, yet attention to research ethics did not sufficiently mitigate that conflict. For her, ethics simply could not account for the larger structure of pharmaceutical drug development over which she had no control. Specifically, she could not "stomach" working for the benefit of large pharmaceutical companies instead of working to help individual patients. The conflict was greatest for her when patients who enrolled in studies were not doing particularly well, but she had to encourage them to remain in the studies and be compliant with the research protocols. Anne simply could not separate the aims of research from those of care. Not only could she not prioritize the retention of individual patient-subjects, she could not adapt herself to the industry.

While the recruitment and enrollment of subjects can be difficult because sites need to identify appropriate patient-subjects for clinical trials, study maintenance can be even more challenging, particularly when patient-subjects' conditions are worsening on the protocols. As long as patient-subjects' are not in danger, it is the duty of investigators and coordinators to encourage subjects to continue in the studies regardless of whether those subjects are benefiting from the clinical trial. To do so, coordinators and investigators must develop techniques that will motivate subjects to remain in studies for the sake of the data and drug development. These approaches often end up simultaneously motivating research staff to be more compliant with the goals of the pharmaceutical industry. Anne, too, became familiar with these various approaches, but she could not implement them effectively because she did not buy into the whole enterprise.

Indeed, the clinical trials industry mobilizes a discourse of medical progress to encourage the retention and compliance of patient-subjects in studies. This same discourse also serves to reinforce the commitment of research staff—coordinators, investigators, and site administrators—to the goals of drug development. Importantly, this process of cultivating the trust and loyalty both of patient-subjects and research staff succeeds in obscuring their role in pharmaceutical profit by underscoring instead their contributions to medical progress.

Political Economy of Pharmaceutical Trial Results

The retention of human subjects—and their compliance with study protocols—is inflected by the broader political economy. Like recruitment and informed consent practices, pharmaceutical companies' approaches to subject retention and compliance are structured to support financial gain. Profit is tied to retention and compliance at both the site and industry levels. The more compliant subjects retained in studies, the more revenue sites will generate. They are paid by pharmaceutical companies based on the number of subjects in studies, and they are more likely to receive future studies when they perform well. In addition, the pharmaceutical industry has the most potential for profit when patient-subjects are compliant because their data will be more robust. Even when drugs cannot be proven efficacious through clinical trials, the clinical data must nonetheless be accurate for companies to decide how to proceed with research and development in the therapeutic area under investigation.

Compliance is important to drug development because it can greatly influence the results of clinical trials. There are two primary ways of analyzing data from clinical trials: "per protocol" and "intent-to-treat" approaches.[2] The distinction between these modes of generating results lies in the treatment of data generated from patient-subjects who fail to complete the entire studies as written in the protocols. Depending on the type of analysis, those patient-subjects who withdraw from the studies may dilute the results from the clinical trial. If the results of a study are based on "per protocol" populations (that is, only those patient-subjects who are fully compliant and complete the study as it was designed), the results should show more difference between the experimental drug and placebo because the subjects would have taken both over a longer period of time or more consistently. By contrast, if the results of a clinical trial are based on the "intent-to-treat" population (all those patient-subjects who enrolled in a clinical trial including those who did not complete it), the pharmaceutical companies might have less persuasive evidence that their experimental drug worked better than a placebo.

Both data analyses must be submitted to the FDA as part of new drug applications. According to a pharmaceutical project manager, however, the FDA increasingly is basing approval decisions on the outcome of the "intent-to-treat" population analyses. The new focus on the "intent-to-treat" population is reflective of the FDA's interest in data that are more representative of the general population (in which people are generally not fully compliant with medical orders). The project manager explained what is at stake for her company's success in drug development given the FDA's priorities:

> There are two types of analysis [of clinical trial data]. The FDA is emphasizing more and more using the "intent-to-treat population" as the unit of analysis. What that means is if you have a clinical trial that's only supposed to last for six months and you get a dose of medication that you take for three months and then you move to India, you still get analyzed as if you'd completed the study. That's part of the intent-to-treat population. With the "per-protocol population" analysis, you wouldn't be analyzed because you didn't complete the study and you didn't follow along with the protocol. The FDA is now demanding that the intent-to-treat population be our analysis population, so our primary endpoint is only based on the intent-to-treat population. That means that if people aren't completing the studies, you're going to see a lot of failures of the products in the intent-to-treat population. So

you have to make sure that you have sites that understand *exactly* how important it is for subjects to complete the studies.

The pharmaceutical industry is placing the utmost importance on patient-subjects in both the placebo and experimental drug groups completing studies and being compliant with protocols. To underscore this point, pharmaceutical companies often stop making contracts with sites that "underperform" by having too much trouble retaining patient-subjects in studies.

The responsibility for compliance is passed down from the pharmaceutical companies developing the drugs to the investigative sites conducting the clinical trials to the patient-subjects enrolled in the studies. As is the case in health care more generally, patient-subjects are cast as neoliberal consumers who make choices about their health for which they are responsible for the outcomes. In the case of the clinical development of pharmaceutical products, however, patient-subjects' compliance is not simply a matter of responsibility to their own wellness but to the research enterprise itself. Sites, especially coordinators, impress upon patient-subjects their responsibilities to the success or failure of clinical research and medical progress.

Of course, patient-subjects' compliance cannot be empirically linked in such a simple way to either the success of the clinical trial in which they are participating or medical progress more generally. Nonetheless, the focus of the politics and economics of drug development place patient-subjects at the center of attention. Not unlike recruitment, where the enrollment of patient-subjects into clinical trials is said to "cost" the pharmaceutical industry millions of dollars in lost profits when subjects are not accrued rapidly enough, so too noncompliant patient-subjects are cast as costing the pharmaceutical industry its perfect data and the future success of its products. Instead of examining the different contingencies that enable or constrain patient-subjects' abilities to follow study protocols and complete studies (including tolerance of side effects or randomization to placebo groups), the pharmaceutical industry focuses on the ways in which patient-subjects jeopardize the profits that can be gained from future consumers.

Promoting Patient-Subjects' Compliance

The informed consent process has been appropriated by the clinical trials industry to communicate to potential patient-subjects the responsibilities that they are committing to by participating in clinical trials. The rationale behind this is that those patient-subjects enrolling in drug studies will then be better research participants because they are educated about their commitment to the research enterprise. Given that this discussion occurs *before* patient-subjects begin protocols, what are the mechanisms that reinforce these lessons about drug development and motivate patient-subjects to be compliant and remain in the studies?

Obstacles to Patient-Subject Compliance

Several factors affect the retention and compliance of patient-subjects: the context and/or structure of the studies, the age of patient-subjects, their motivation to participate in clinical trials, their symptoms during the course of the study, and their perceptions of placebos. First, the sites and the quality of interactions between patient-subjects and coordinators or investigators can have an important impact on retention and compliance rates. One coordinator commented on this dynamic:

> I think compliance and retention can sometimes depend on the coordinator. . . . If you respect the patient, you understand that they are taking an investigational medication, if you're flexible enough to work with their schedule, in a good mood, stuff like that, it really makes a difference to people. It's really, not only for compliance, but then also their retention of them. A lot of people just like to come in and talk, and if the office isn't clean and the staff is angry, just like anything else, I mean it shows, and then you see a drop.

Many sites, as a result, create welcoming spaces, minimize the amount of time subjects will have to wait for their appointments, and place a lot of emphasis on coordinators' social skills.

The design of the studies themselves can also pose a challenge to compliance and retention. If office visits are too lengthy or protocols come with too many restrictions on what subjects can do, patient-subjects are more likely to drop out or begin to comply only selectively with the study regimen. A coordinator complained,

> I think a lot of the studies don't respect the fact that these people have lives. A lot of patients have jobs that they just can't drop everything and come in and do a five-hour visit on these certain days. It's like one of the studies that we're doing right now: you have two-day visit windows and basically if you can't come into the office on one of those two days, we can't help you.

This coordinator found that he could not retain as many patient-subjects in the study because the pharmaceutical company dropped those patient-subjects who had difficulty with the time commitment and skipped the required study visits.

Clinical trials can be time-intensive, for tasks from lengthy office visits to logging symptoms in diaries. The time commitment can become a problem for patient-subjects if pharmaceutical companies cannot be flexible about obstacles that inevitably occur for patient-subjects, such as not being able to attend a scheduled office visit or forgetting to fill out entries in study diaries. In some cases, pharmaceutical companies can be reluctant to allow those patient-subjects to remain in the study because they are perceived as non-compliant. Pharmaceutical companies, however, are not insensitive to the fact that cumbersome studies might discourage patient-subjects from complying or being retained. A representative from a pharmaceutical company described the need to balance the data they would like to collect from patient-subjects during studies with what the average person taking a prescription will be willing to do:

> You need people that are going to be compliant, people that are willing to do what you *need* them to do. That goes back to why you don't put in a lot of really stupid restrictions in a phase III trial. You want phase III to mimic real life as much as possible, so you wouldn't want to say, "Okay, for the six months that you're on the study, you can't have any caffeine products or pop." That's unrealistic. It's not going to happen [people won't comply]. So you have to make sure that when you're designing the study that you take into account all of that stuff.

In other words, those making decisions about clinical trials at the pharmaceutical companies understand that too many conditions and restrictions can create problems for study participation. This acknowledgment may not always lead to perfectly designed studies from the perspective of those enrolled, but many pharmaceutical companies are willing to make individual exceptions when problems with patient-subjects' compliance do arise.

Compliance and retention are also affected by several characteristics of patient-subjects. Age tends to be a good predictor of how well they will follow study protocols and generally be compliant subjects over the entire length of clinical trials. Young adults are viewed as the least compliant group of potential patient-subjects because they have the busiest schedules, including all types of social activities that "distract" them from the responsibilities of the studies. As one coordinator explained,

> In the younger adults, from the ages of twenty to maybe twenty-eight, you see the same patterns and things: "It's Friday night, so I'd rather go dancing than go home and take my medicine and get in that Palm Pilot" [to track dose and symptoms]. Or "I don't want to have to go home after work. I want to meet my friends somewhere, so I'll just skip that dose of the medicine. It's no big deal." Then that night will be left blank. But most of the young ones get my drift when I start educating them [about compliance].

In pediatric studies, compliance often depends on the commitment of parents to make sure that their children are following the drug protocols appropriately. When parents are invested in this way, studies involving children have the best compliance and retention rates for clinical trials. A coordinator said,

> With kids' studies, you're usually dealing with a parent that by the time they come here they've probably tried a few things. This seems to be especially true in our ADHD studies or our bipolar studies. The parents, or guardian, would really like them to get some help, and they look at research as being an opportunity to do that, especially if there's a component of being able to have six months to a year of extension . . . [where they will receive] the study medication.

In contrast, if parents are expecting older children to follow the protocols on their own, compliance is usually diminished. As a coordinator said, "If they put the medication in the hands of the kid, because perhaps the parent is whatever, then we get *a lot* of problems."

Retirement-age or elderly patient-subjects can also be excellent study subjects based on their degree of compliance with the protocols. This group often has the time necessary for office visits and for filling out symptom diaries. Additionally, elderly patients are seen as volunteering for studies for more altruistic reasons and are, therefore, better able to understand the importance of compliance. A coordinator noted, "It often seems like the older people are doing [clinical trials] for the *real* reasons, like wanting a cure for [the potential illnesses of] their grandchildren." A potential difficulty for some older adults, however, is remembering to take pills or to track their symptoms; memory loss can pose an incredible problem to compliance. Many coordinators remarked on their surprise at how receptive older adults are to using PDAs, like Palm

Pilots, to track their symptoms. A coordinator said, "I thought the older people would not do well, having to put electronic data into a Palm Pilot, but they have surprised us, haven't they? We were so scared to give a sixty-nine-year-old a Palm Pilot and try to educate them on how to do it, but they're the ones that are on time for their appointments and use the Palm Pilots perfectly."

Coordinators find that patient-subjects' motivations for participating in clinical trials can have unexpected impacts upon compliance. A counterintuitive effect of motivation is that patient-subjects who are desperate for a cure for their illness are often not the ones that are the most compliant with the study protocols. One coordinator asserted that this variable matters more for compliance than do demographic differences: "We had anything from lawyers to people who never got out of the sixth grade in our studies. What I have seen is that the ones who came because they're sick and just wanted medicine, *any kind of medicine,* they were not compliant patients, and they did the worst" on the studies. Coordinators explained this group's noncompliance, in part, in terms of those patient-subjects having too much focus on themselves and their own medical conditions.

Compliance is also associated with subjects having a more altruistic orientation toward clinical trials rather than instrumental reasons. Likewise, the more motivated people are to participate in clinical trials for financial reasons, the less compliant they will be during the course of the study. A coordinator provided an example of this: "Studies for an anxiety or a depression drug, these people are *really* looking for, well, let's just say the compensation weighs heavy on them, and they ask about the money each visit. So in those studies, you get a lot of problems with compliance from people not showing up, not taking the meds, all kinds of stuff." Another coordinator described the connection she saw between financial motivations and compliance: "If money's their motivation and if it's a lot of money, they don't care. Then you'll find out later on where patients will take the medication home, they'll pop the pills through the casing every night and throw them out. They never really take them, and *you* don't know that."

Finally, the meanings that patient-subjects attribute to the study drugs, their symptoms, and their participation more generally are important indicators of how compliant they will be or how likely they are to complete studies. The best predictor of compliance, according to coordinators, is patient-subjects' perception of whether or not their illnesses, through their own assessment of their symptoms, are being ameliorated by the clinical trials. Studies that generate visible or marked improvements in patient-subjects' conditions prompt them to be compliant so that they sustain or augment those improvements to their illnesses. A coordinator explained,

> Compliance just depends on the indication. We have some protocols such as psoriasis where the participants actually see a difference. They'll say, "Oh, my psoriasis is clearing up! It's going away!" So in some studies, you can *see* the results. We have also other studies like with weight loss drugs too, they're seeing the results, and they're getting satisfaction, so those participants are pretty good about compliance.

On the other hand, this means that some studies are inherently harder to promote compliance because efficacy is less visible. Clinical studies for high cholesterol, high blood pressure, and osteoporosis tend to have more problems with compliance because patient-subjects can only assess whether the treatment is working through the mediation of diagnostic tests or procedures. According to one coordinator,

> We have studies such as osteoporosis where [the patient-subjects] felt fine when they came in and they're still feeling fine on the treatment. Whether they are randomized to the drug or to placebo, they're never going to *see* a difference, you know? So those are the types of clinical trials that are difficult [to get patients to comply with the protocols]. Really any illness where they're not getting the immediate satisfaction of seeing results.

Importantly, patient-subjects' suppositions (whether they are substantiated or not) that they have been randomized to the placebo group greatly diminish compliance because those subjects feel that they are not getting *any* medical treatment. One coordinator told me, "Usually the studies are blinded, so they don't know [if they are getting the drug]. But you know that if you're taking a medication and you're not getting any relief, you are going to suspect that you are getting a placebo. Of course, that may not be necessarily true." Because most patient-subjects are not motivated by altruism, they are disappointed if they do not experience any relief of their symptoms. A coordinator explained,

> If the study's not working for them, then yes, there's a problem with compliance. If it's working and they feel better and they think the drug is working wonderfully, then they're compliant and they continue with no problem. . . . Some illnesses just feel more urgent to patients

than other [illnesses do]. For example, we've done [studies on] rapid ejaculation, and if the guys are not seeing any results, then it's hard to keep them. We've seen even though there might be an open label for them at the end [the protocol gives everyone the experimental drug for a period of time], it's still hard to keep them motivated until that point [if they think they are on placebo] because it's such a major inconvenience for them *right now*.

The placebo is the foremost obstacle to compliance and retention in drug studies. Given that the vast majority of studies are placebo-controlled trials, individuals working in the clinical trials industry, from investigators and coordinators to study monitors and pharmaceutical company representatives, recognize that patient-subjects' perceptions of the placebo are a crucial part of making studies succeed or fail. In spite of the pharmaceutical industry's awareness that placebos can diminish retention and compliance, placebos are nevertheless still favored in trial design. This is because using drugs already available on the market as comparators to the investigational drugs is much more expensive and much less likely to show efficacy than placebo-controlled studies. Moreover, because most of the illnesses for which drugs are currently being developed are not immediately life-threatening, the use of placebos is considered both ethical and appropriate within the framework of current federal policy regulating clinical trials. In other words, regardless of the difficulties placebos might present in the clinic, the pharmaceutical industry has a better chance of successful clinical trials by comparing their investigational products to nothing (that is, the placebo) than to a product already proven to be effective.

Despite the advantages for the pharmaceutical industry, the placebo greatly diminishes the instrumental value patient-subjects place on clinical trials. Some patient-subjects participate in clinical trials because they do not have health insurance and seek access to medical treatments. Other patient-subjects are recruited by their personal physicians to participate in clinical trials as part of their regular medical care and, thus, expect the clinical trials to make their conditions better. Both types of patient-subjects are often concerned about being randomized into the placebo arm of drug studies and question whether they will receive the "real thing": the experimental drug instead of the placebo.

Although most patient-subjects understand the rationale behind the placebo, these explanations alone do not make them more receptive to the possibility of receiving it. During enrollment, coordinators report that what becomes important to potential patient-subjects are the odds of receiving the placebo. Part of the "education" patient-subjects receive during informed consent includes information about the different ratios governing randomization. Because individual studies have different ratios, patient-subjects have different odds of getting a placebo depending on the clinical trial. The communication of this information is one way in which to temper patient-subjects' concerns about the placebo, especially in cases in which more than half of the patients enrolled in a study will be randomized to the experimental drug. A coordinator explained,

> They don't want the placebo because they think, "I'm going to do all this work, a diary and office visits for a placebo?" In fact, when it's fifty-fifty, I think it's harder to recruit our private practice patients into a study versus if they've got a three out of five chance of getting the study drug or a four out of seven chance. In those cases, it's a lot easier to recruit patients. It makes a difference to them because you can say, "Listen now, you have three out of five chance of getting the study drug."

Despite explanations about scientific methods and the odds of randomization, the most palatable argument for why patients should enroll in studies in spite of the risk of receiving a placebo is that they can choose to withdraw from the study at any time. Although the role of the coordinator includes motivating people to complete studies, coordinators argue that it is much more important to emphasize the informed consent protection of discontinuing participation to encourage patient-subjects during recruitment than it is to let worries about the placebo prevent them from enrolling. After all, in order to get patient-subjects to complete studies, coordinators first need to enroll them in studies. As one coordinator said,

> I also will remind them, "There is a chance you get the study drug or you might get a comparator [a marketed drug] or you might even get a placebo. You know that if you get a placebo, you can drop out at any time." So if for some reason they just don't want to continue the study, they can always drop out because we can't make them stay in the study.

Once patient-subjects are enrolled in studies, some coordinators do not try to persuade patient-subjects to remain in those studies because they argue that it is the patient-subjects' right to withdraw. One coordinator explained,

They hope they don't get the placebo, but they also know that they can quit at any time and go back on their medicines. So if they're physically ill, they'll come to me and they say, "I just can't do it. I need to have my antihistamines. I need to have my Allegra®." I'm not going to get mad at them or anything; I'm going to go say okay. Then I simply put down in the case report form that the patient withdrew due to the fact that they just didn't feel they were getting the medication, and that [withdrawal] becomes that patient's data.

What goes unsaid, of course, is that the patient-subjects (or often the coordinators or investigators) do not know whether or not they are actually taking a placebo or the investigational drug. They can only guess based on their experience of their symptoms during the trial. When they find they have no relief of those symptoms, most patient-subjects (and many times coordinators and investigators) assume that they have been randomized to the placebo group.

When patient-subjects suspect that they are on placebo, they become noncompliant and often want to stop participating. A coordinator said, "If they think they're on the placebo—but maybe the drug's just not working, then those patients are hard to keep going." Many remember from the informed consent process that this is well within their rights. The challenge then is for coordinators to motivate patient-subjects to be compliant and to continue their participation in the studies *in spite of* their assumption that they are not receiving any personal benefit from them. This is especially true if they already had access to some treatment before enrolling in the clinical trial. A coordinator reflected about these cases: "I think, depending on the illness, if they're *asked* to give up a treatment that they're already on in order to participate in a clinical trial, and they give it their best shot, and it isn't helping them, then you're going to see drops."

Placebos, however, are not the sole reason patient-subjects decide to stop participating in efficacy clinical trials. Some patient-subjects are likely to drop out of a study when the experimental drugs have side effects that patient-subjects feel do not outweigh the benefit of that drug for their illness. This is surprisingly rare, however. A coordinator observed,

What I see in some studies is that problems with retention stem from side effects. Some people just cannot tolerate the side effects of whatever they're on. I don't want to overstate it though because with all the studies I have done, that's really a pretty low percentage. What is amazing is that most of the people just keep plugging away. They understand what they're doing, and why they're doing it, and they just keep coming back every six months for their visit. It's nice to see that people are able to do this.

In other words, most patient-subjects are more tolerant of negative side effects as part of a clinical trial than they are of receiving a placebo, or the impression of not receiving any treatment at all.

How big a problem are retention and compliance for pharmaceutical clinical trials? CenterWatch, the clinical trials industry's information clearinghouse, regularly conducts surveys of past patient-subjects to find out more about their experiences with study participation. In a recent report, they found that about 70 percent of people enrolled in phase III clinical trials (the large efficacy studies) completed them. This may not seem low, but in comparison to phase IV clinical trials (postmarketing studies in which participants almost always get an active drug) that have a retention rate of nearly 94 percent, many in the industry believe that retention could be greatly improved.[3]

Unfortunately, although there are data on retention, no similar data are available on compliance rates for drug trials. Within the clinical trials industry, there is considerable anecdotal evidence, if not hard data, that most patient-subjects are not fully compliant. In particular, patient-subjects who believe they have received a placebo are more likely than others to deviate from the protocols. Most people in the industry perceive compliance to be a bigger challenge than the retention of patient-subjects.[4] To be compliant, patient-subjects must follow study protocols faithfully, including ingesting the study medication, completing all data collection measures, and attending all study visits. Patient-subjects who skip pills, forget to fill out symptom diaries, or cancel appointments are all considered noncompliant. Of course, there are degrees of noncompliance, and in most cases, subjects can continue with studies even if sites or pharmaceutical companies discover deviations from the protocols.

A coordinator related an example of how noncompliance can be detected over the course of a clinical trial:

You'll come up with maybe an odd count of pills when they come in for their next visit, and when you question them, they'll come up with a decent excuse or something. But when it happens repeatedly . . . you pretty much get a feeling, and then you start questioning it a little further. . . ."Here you said you slept fine, and here you said you didn't sleep at all. Well, we're not changing the drug, are you really taking the drug?" So you can't accuse them, but you have to use your best judgment and just hope and pray that you selected the proper people for the study.

Whether the clinical trial is an insomnia study or a diabetes study, coordinators discuss the same pattern of noticing that patient-subjects have the wrong number of pills or their symptom diaries do not make sense. Even though coordinators are reluctant to accuse patient-subjects of noncompliance because they do not want to damage the rapport they have with subjects, they know that it is necessary to discuss the protocols again. A coordinator said when she suspects noncompliance, she knows that she has identified "the patients you want to spend a little more extra time with because you need to reeducate them about their responsibility as a patient that enters a clinical trial."

Reeducation of Patient-Subjects

The job of promoting patient-subject's compliance falls on coordinators. Because of the time they spend with patient-subjects, coordinators are expected to use the relationships that they have developed with subjects to emphasize the importance of compliance, particularly by "reeducating" them about the demands of study participation and subjects' responsibility to drug development. This education takes many forms, from discussing the organization of clinical trials to the operations of the FDA, but it usually focuses on the impact of subjects' participation on the future of medicine. In these discussions, coordinators often frame compliance as crucial for the data that are necessary for pharmaceutical products to be successfully developed and marketed.

To encourage patient-subjects to be compliant, coordinators rely on two discursive maneuvers in their interactions with (and reeducation of) patient-subjects. First, they stress the importance of patient-subjects' altruism and personal responsibility for providing the pharmaceutical companies with results from their participation in the research. Second, they emphasize to patient-subjects the visible, immediate study results that are occurring in the study. In both cases, coordinators' attention is focused on the types of results that are generated from clinical trials, but the two strategies achieve compliance in different ways. The first provides an orientation toward clinical trials that insists upon compliance more generally, whereas the second provides directed encouragement for subjects to comply with particular study protocols. Both techniques draw upon the same neoliberal logics structuring the conduct of clinical trials in the private sector.

The primary mode of coordinators' emphasis on patient-subject compliance can be seen in their mobilization of discourses of altruism and personal responsibility. The goal of this discursive move is to inspire patients as good neoliberal subjects to *choose* to remain in these studies for the "benefit of humanity" and the "progress of medicine." Even though most patient-subjects do not volunteer for clinical trials for altruistic reasons, coordinators report that patient-subjects can be educated so that they *stay* in studies for these reasons. As one coordinator remarked, "Most of them do try to stick it out because they *do* accept the responsibility that the data is important."

Gender plays an important role in patient-subjects' acceptance of coordinators' emphasis on compliance; women patient-subjects seem to be especially susceptible to coordinators' framing of the studies in terms that both emphasize personal responsibility and altruism. According to one coordinator,

> Most people are pretty good about [understanding why they need to stay in studies]. Of course, there are always a few that don't understand the importance of it, or they seem to be a little distracted. They're the ones just too busy with life, and this isn't really that important to them. But those patients are pretty rare. Most women, I've found, are very good about the responsibility that they've actually volunteered for. And they take it pretty seriously, even if they're not getting immediate results. I give them credit. They really do try to come when they're scheduled, and if they can't come, they'll call. They're pretty good about that for the most part. And luckily we get a lot more women participating, so our [retention] numbers are pretty good.

That women are more likely than men to accept that their participation in clinical trials is a responsibility and should be understood altruistically highlights the gendered nature of the discourse to make *all* patient-subjects more compliant. The goal of this neoliberal framing of personal responsibility and choice is for patient-subjects to internalize a new (learned) subjectivity toward clinical trials and to accept the goals of the research in spite of any instrumental motivations they may have to improve their own health or make money. The gendered acceptance of responsibility is critical for getting patient-subjects to complete studies, particularly when they think they are taking a placebo. Thus, coordinators reinforce the message at each study visit.

This helps to explain why sites often stress revisiting informed consent at each visit even when IRBs do not require it. Patient-subjects need to continuously re-consent not only to the study protocols themselves but also to their responsibilities in the system of pharmaceutical research.

According to coordinators, compliance can be thwarted by patient-subjects who are insincere about adopting an altruistic vision of clinical research. These patient-subjects are seen as willfully misrepresenting their intentions to sites. One coordinator argued that some patient-subjects pretend to be altruistic and act as though they accept the responsibility of being in a clinical trial. She felt that this type of patient-subject is reprehensible because they fool coordinators into believing that they are going to be compliant and complete studies:

> Most people can tolerate the placebo, and if they can't, then they're not a good research subject, okay? We do a lot to keep these people in our studies. What is different, I think, is that those very few that drop out have *snowed* us on the screening end. . . . We thought they were honest, they convinced us they really were going to do it and they were going to complete the study, they agreed that the data matters, and then they just flake out. That's a *waste* of time totally. You know, I think this happens most often with our bipolar studies because bipolar people are very crafty folks. . . . They're very manipulative, they're very sharp people, they're very intelligent, and if they want something, most of the times, they get it. Yeah, they can fool us, not always, but it happens.

This coordinator, one of the most vocal about the importance of teaching altruism to patient-subjects, made a distinction between those patient-subjects who are "honest" and those who are "crafty" about their commitment to clinical trials. From her perspective, being noncompliant is indicative of a character flaw, such as dishonesty or manipulation. The way this coordinator took patient-subjects' behavior personally illustrates the importance coordinators attach to their own compliance (about which more will be said below).

Because the majority of studies are done on an outpatient basis, coordinators have no control over patient-subjects' compliance. One way of trying to gain control is by selecting individuals whom they know personally or have experiences with as patient-subjects. As a coordinator stated,

> I always say that I like to deal with patients that I have known personally. Because when you go into the street population, patients aren't

always honest. In those cases, you really have to take your time in screening to find out little things. Like they tell you they don't smoke, but then you smell smoke, you know? They tell you that they're on no medication, but somewhere down the line, you find out they've been taking hypertension drugs. You have to be very, *very* careful in the screening when you don't know them.

In the case of private-practice patients, coordinators feel comfortable knowing that they have a longer perspective on the medical histories of those patient-subjects and that generally they—or at least the investigators—have already developed relationships with them. Moreover, private-practice patients can be counted on for higher rates of compliance because they often do not want to disappoint their own physicians.

In the case of serial participants, coordinators assert that those patient-subjects have already demonstrated their commitment to the studies by their compliance on prior clinical trials. This is not a trivial point for many coordinators, and it makes serial participants extremely valuable to coordinators for clinical trials of all phases of development. From a more practical point of view, coordinators insist that serial patient-subjects are more compliant. They claim that experienced subjects are better able to follow study protocols and can usually be counted on for completing the studies. A coordinator explained, "When we bring back patients that were research patients before, they are usually our best patients because they know how it works, they don't have a lot of questions, they're more compliant, and they finish the studies." This is seen as especially vital for sites that are not associated with a private practice and are therefore relying primarily on marketing to attract patient-subjects.

What appears to be the case from coordinators' experiences is that while emphasizing personal responsibility and altruism certainly encourages *retention* of patient-subjects, it does not always mean that they will be perfectly compliant with study protocols. Coordinators develop their own study "results" as an important means to mitigate patient-subjects' noncompliance. By framing a study in terms of what types of results are being generated, coordinators share with patient-subjects the news that the clinical trial is beneficial to other (read "compliant") subjects to explain why some patient-subjects (read "noncompliant") are not experiencing personal benefit from those studies. This manipulative explanation of why patient-subjects might be experiencing different results from their participation in clinical trials is meant to convince patient-subjects that following the protocol really is in their best interests.

As an example of this discursive tactic, one coordinator explained, "I have to let them know that Patient A—you don't name them, of course—has been compliant, and their viral count went down. And you are Patient B and because you don't seem to be taking your pills—and I know this because there are more here than there should be when I count them—your virus count, for instance, is getting higher." At the root of this discursive move to promote patient-subject compliance is the grounding of clinical trials in something much less abstract than personal responsibility and altruism. Instead, coordinators play it both ways, here flagging *tangible* benefits of the research to the patient-subjects themselves. This can be achieved in part by comparing one patient-subject's results from the clinical trial to another. Through the direct comparison of patients who have been randomized to the same arm of the study and are faring differently, coordinators try to motivate the ones who may be less compliant. Coordinators have found that this technique works so well that some admit to fabricating these types of results to deal with cases of noncompliant patient-subjects. According to one coordinator,

> Well, retention and compliance in any area of research is very, very crucial. [Pharmaceutical companies] need people to make it from the beginning to the end, not just drop out here and there. We [this site] have one of the highest retention rates in the country. . . . We even tell them, it's not lying exactly, but we talk about how well other people are doing on the studies even if we know that those people are not getting the same pill. If anything, we might be encouraging a placebo effect, so we think it's okay. The most important thing is compliance and keeping them in the study.

Here the coordinator rationalizes her dishonesty as an effective tactic that is acceptable for the good of her site (that is, their retention rates) and of drug development.

It is important to note a common theme within this rhetoric: the term "results" is used only to describe how the drug appears to be working to *improve* patient-subjects' conditions. Coordinators always classify any negative aspects of the study as "side effects" or "adverse events" in their conversations with patient-subjects; coordinators never label these negative aspects "results" of a study. For instance, one coordinator told me her response when patient-subjects complain about side effects: what was described "is an adverse event which may or may not be related to the study medication." This nonparallel way of mobilizing terms affects patient-subjects' perceptions of the studies. The language of "adverse event," the technical jargon of clinical trials, may be the correct words, but calling it that distances patient-subjects from their experience of side effects. In addition, results are framed as active and causal (that is, the drug is bringing about positive benefits), whereas negative outcomes of the studies are passive and incidental (that is, side effects are problems patient-subjects have).

On a more abstract plane, coordinators mobilize for patient-subjects an urgency to contribute to the pharmaceutical companies' data, so that the "results" of the products will speed them to market and contribute to "medical progress." Coordinators even tell patient-subjects that they need to be compliant so that they can say they personally contributed in a meaningful way to science. A coordinator said, "We always tell them that when *their* drug gets approved, they will be so proud because this is what they did, *they* made it happen." In this move, they transfer ownership of the product—"their drug"—and the rewards—pride that they made it happen—to patient-subjects.

This illustrates one way in which neoliberalism enters into what patient-subjects are told to perceive as results from the study. In this framing, it is not just the immediate visible results that patient-subjects may experience during the clinical trial that are relevant: they are asked to be compliant for the sake of the pharmaceutical products that will result from their participation in the studies, even if they themselves cannot benefit from the marketing of those products. This is different from coordinators' emphasis on altruism because in this instance, patient-subjects are asked to participate not just for the sake of general medical progress but for being part of the process of developing one particular product and owning it in some small way.

Some may argue that discursive efforts to instill within patient-subjects a particular orientation toward clinical trials may have limited utility in actually inducing compliance in individual patient-subjects. Given the absence of data, it is unclear how well most patient-subjects comply with study protocols given the possible difference between what they tell coordinators that they are doing and what their actual practices are within clinical trials. The framing of compliance and the discourse of results does, however, provide insight into the ways in which coordinators and other research staff construct compliance for their own work in the clinical trials industry.

Promoting Investigative Site Compliance

Given the ethic of care that coordinators have developed to govern their relations with patient-subjects and their conduct in clinical trials, what are the mechanisms encouraging *coordinators* to comply with their job descriptions? Likewise, how do *investigators* rationalize the limits to their professional authority that are imposed as part of conducting pharmaceutical studies? Research staff at investigative sites mobilize the same discourse about study "results" to transform their own participation in the clinical trials industry into what they see as concrete, positive outcomes for patient-subjects and for medicine. They do this by framing their work in terms of its contribution on two levels: the "little picture," or results for *individual patient-subjects*, and the "big picture," or results for *successful clinical trials*. In particular, coordinators, who experience the least financial benefit from their jobs at investigative sites, can be see as crafting these constructions of the positive outcomes of their labor to further assuage their role conflicts and thereby instill compliance or loyalty to the industry in spite of those conflicts. Importantly, this process occurs by discursively erasing the profit motive from the process of drug development and the profit motive of the individual sites at which they work. Broader narratives about medical progress supplant the reality of profit motives.

The "Little Picture" of Clinical Trials

The "little picture" of clinical trials, as described by research staff, consists of the benefits that individual patient-subjects experience as a direct result of their participation in drug studies. Coordinators especially are invested in the outcomes patient-subjects have from their enrollment in clinical trials. One coordinator said,

> A lot of times you'll see patients who have tried every drug that's on the market, or nearly every drug that's on the market, and they come in and they try a new drug, and it helps them. It's something that's just *remarkable* to suddenly *see* that people are being helped by a drug. People [that is, patient-subjects] get very excited about that, so that's a good reward to see. Our ability to help people out—because a lot of people do get a lot of benefit from doing clinical trials, drugs that normally they would not have any access to—is the main reward of working here.

These positive outcomes produce for coordinators and other site staff a reward that counterbalances the quotidian, oftentimes tedious activities that constitute jobs that are rife with ethical and role conflicts. In other words, the visible results produced in patient-subjects by clinical trials become the motivation for coordinators to continue on with their jobs. And then these results become the tangible proof of coordinators' altruism. A site manager remarked,

> I think the industry is very [emotionally] rewarding in general, which helps people to really enjoy research. What they get is the rewards of *seeing* the results: people, especially with certain indications that have not had good options for treatment, *see* positive options for treatment, have great progress, and have real turnaround [with experiences of their illnesses]. Especially in the last few years, it's been very reward-ing to work with people who have psoriasis and rheumatoid arthritis, the autoimmune diseases, because of the new biologics that have come out. It has been phenomenal for the patients. There really is a feeling in the industry that you can make a difference and help. And not just these people that come through our offices, we also know that if this product makes it to the market, it's going to affect millions of people. And that's very rewarding.

As part of the process of looking for results and one way to handle their role conflicts, particularly between research and care, coordinators treat the randomization of patient-subjects in placebo-controlled studies as a game. Although they understand the rationale for double-blind studies, most coor-dinators would prefer to think of these studies as a puzzle that they should try to solve. By adding a mystery to the conflict they experience in giving placebos to sick patient-subjects, coordinators create meaning and focus on the benefits of clinical research.

Coordinators understand that they need to be discrete about who they think is getting a placebo and who is getting the experimental drug, but look-ing for patterns in groups of patient-subjects to determine who seems to be doing better than the others is a way to get enjoyment out of the enterprise. As a coordinator explained,

> I guess [about which one is the placebo]. We all guess, and we even talk about it amongst ourselves. Because even we are blinded in a lot of the studies, we'll say, "I know that one's getting it, look at the increase in the pulmonary functions. And that other one that's just

kind of coming in and not making any progress, just kind of laying there after three or four weeks, most likely they're not getting the medication." Of course, you don't say any of that to them, but you try to figure out the puzzle yourself.

Adding to the mystery of identifying each substance is the possibility of a placebo effect occurring, so that it might seem as if both groups are getting the medication. In these cases, coordinators are even more intrigued, as it takes them longer to solve the puzzle of which group is which. A coordinator who works on psychiatric drug studies described how common placebo effects are in the studies that she manages:

> I would say probably 99 percent of all of our studies are placebo-control. Do you know the reason why in psychiatry, why you *have* to have placebo-control? You have a placebo *effect* is what happens. It happens all the time. They may think they're better, but they're really not. Like in an anxiety trial or something, they'll say, "Oh, I'm feeling much better." Really? Well, at first, we have *no* idea because we're double-blind. But the way these studies chew through a placebo effect is to make it such that it has a long-enough duration for whatever indication you're looking at. That's so you can determine if the study can bust through the placebo effect. For example, in a person who has anxiety disorder, we see that they can't maintain a placebo effect for more than two to three weeks, so you'll have a trial for six to eight weeks. That's really cool when you start to see the placebo effect dwindling in the group who thinks they're better when they're not because then we know who's on placebo.

Coordinators often look forward to finding out if their guesswork was on target when the pharmaceutical companies send information about which substance was the placebo. A coordinator told me, "After a study has been closed [that is, completed] for, I'm thinking, six to eight months, they will usually send us a letter unblinding the study so that we know which patients were actually on drug and which ones weren't, if the study was double-blind. So that's really exciting when they do that." They assert that these letters often validate their observations about how patient-subjects have fared in the clinical trial, but they also serve to solve the mystery in studies that are more difficult for them to crack which group was on placebo.

In spite of coordinators' desire to the contrary, many drugs in clinical development are not going to produce the visible results coordinators are expecting to see. Coordinators report that it is very difficult for them when they have a period of working on products that are not showing "results"— that do not seem to be making patient-subjects' conditions any better. When they have these studies, they describe that it is difficult to have positive morale with their work. A coordinator related,

> You know, it's a bit hard because I know in the last couple years, just as workers, we just haven't had anything that's just really exciting that has come through. We haven't had anything that we're just anxious for people to come in so we can see how well they're going to do. You know a lot of times you'll, I don't know, look forward to giving patients a medication so that you see a change in their quality of life. That's what is really exciting [about this job], especially if there isn't a medication on the market that can do the same thing. In those cases, you're really anxious just to see how well they do during the whole study. And then sometimes, like right now, it's just a bummer because of the products that we have to work with; they don't seem to be any good. I know it's just the chance that they take in being a volunteer, but it's a real bummer.

In order to combat their negative feelings about current studies that are not working as well as they would like to see, coordinators recall success stories of drugs having made it to market as a result of their own personal work on those clinical trials. A coordinator asserted,

> Sometimes we have to remind each other why we love research. I think the process is fascinating, especially when you look at what we've done. When we first started [doing clinical trials at this site], we did studies with Bextra® before it was approved by the FDA. We did studies on Levitra® before that was approved. And right now, I've been told that we have two or three studies that we worked on where the pharmaceutical company has just now submitted their application to the FDA for a new drug, which is really exciting for us. So even if we don't have any great studies *right now*, we are still hearing great results about ones we did.

The "Big Picture" of Clinical Trials

This mobilization of past results is generally effective and provides a rhetorical bridge between the little and big pictures of clinical trials. The "big picture" of results that research staff hope to see from their participation in clinical trials is the marketing of experimental drugs on which they worked. In other words, it is not enough to see individual patient-subjects benefit from clinical trials; coordinators, investigators, and even site administrators also want to see the clinical trials prove that experimental drugs should be made available on the market. A coordinator said, "It's interesting when you see either it published or you'll see somewhere where a drug is coming out, and you can go back and say, I worked on that drug, we had a study with that drug." Results of that scale are frequently mobilized in terms of making coordinating clinical trials worthwhile. For many research staff, it ensures that they remain in the industry in spite of whatever reservations they may have about their jobs and their interactions with patient-subjects.

Because they are so emphatic about the importance of the "big picture" for understanding their work, research staff often feel validated that their participation in clinical trials makes them part of the process of drug development. Whatever their role conflicts, they comfort themselves that they are insiders in an important industry. One way this part of their role identity manifests is in their framing of their knowledge about drug development as knowledge that only insiders would understand. For example, they assert that it was through their jobs as coordinators that they now understand the high cost of drugs. A coordinator told me that she feels that it is important to communicate this knowledge about pharmaceuticals to patient-subjects to have them become insiders as well:

> For me, it's just really very exciting, all the things that are being done.
> And it's been really interesting for me to see the flip side of this indus-
> try. When I was in family practice, I was just seeing a new drug coming
> out and would say, "Ooh, lookee here, a new drug!" But now I under-
> stand the process of how it gets to that point. And it's cool trying to be
> able to explain to patients why their prescriptions are so expensive.
> Not that it's a good news story, but what was the last statistic I heard?
> On the average $870 million to develop a drug from chemical to pre-
> scription, something like that. So I think that's interesting.[5]

As part of this focus on the big picture, research staff, particularly site administrators, often keep track of the FDA approved drugs for which their sites have collected data. Many use these statistics as a way of measuring their own success and the success of the site. A site director explained, "You can go online to the [pharmaceutical] company's Web sites, and you can track a product. Because we know the chemical formulations of these things, we can track them, and we do that. Of course, we do know a good product when we see it, typically after research. . . . We have a real good sense of where the products are in the [development] cycle." Investigators also mobilize those products that are approved by the FDA as successes and results that belong to their sites. For example, a physician remarked,

> This is our tenth anniversary [of doing clinical trials] this year. We were just talking about, gosh, the things that we have done over ten years and the hundreds of people that have been in studies. We look at all the drugs that are available now [in our therapeutic area] and really, the bulk of the ones that have been approved since we started doing this work, we did the pivotal studies [for those products] here. . . . We'll see somebody on a drug that we were really instrumental in helping it get approved, and you stop and think, "Oh my gosh, we were 50 percent of the data for this!" So I have absolutely no regrets [about doing clinical trials full-time]. It's been so satisfying because of the results we've had.

The problem, however, from the point of view of most sites, is that pharmaceutical companies do not effectively communicate the progress of a product through drug development. The focus on the "big picture" does not originate from the pharmaceutical companies; research staff actively seek the information themselves. That pharmaceutical companies do not automatically share the data can be discouraging, but the excitement in hearing about a successful product, even if indirect, still motivates sites. For example, a site manager said,

> More often than not, [you find out the results of the clinical trials because] you see a commercial on TV and say, "Oh, that sounds like the drug we tested!" We don't know the name oftentimes when we're doing the research. Actually, it doesn't have a name yet, it's usually going by a chemical name, and then the marketing people get a hold of it and give it a name. So we say, "Oh, we did that study" because they'll say what the generic name is. But we may not know [about the products] until they get to market, and we just happen to find out either through physicians or advertising or that type of thing. . . . I really do wish that there was more feedback from the sponsors to the sites that did the research on where they are with the process. I know all of us are very interested in where those drugs are going.

In other words, the lack of communication about the results of drug studies can be frustrating to sites, especially given how important the products become to them. According to a coordinator, "I think it's a fascinating area of work, and everything goes on behind the scenes is a little bit, it's not *secret,* but there's so much that goes on once the data leaves here, that we don't really understand. . . . I wish we knew more about all of that."

By way of an explanation, a project manager at a pharmaceutical company commented on this problem during an interview. She acknowledged that it is a problem that sites are not given the information because she understood how important it is to their morale. She added that the problem could not be easily resolved because it was not simply an oversight on the part of pharmaceutical companies:

> That's kind of sad too because what happens is they work so hard on all these studies and stuff, and they may never hear a word, they may never know the results, they may never know what happened. . . . I mean it's amazing how much and how often that happens. . . . [We don't share the information because what the] pharmaceutical companies have to guard against is if the results are sent to a doctor, the doctor might write a paper and publish. That can't happen until you're completely through your NDA [New Drug Application with the FDA]. So that may have something to with why it's so hard [for sites] to get results from a sponsor.

According to this representative, the data need to be protected and that limits the amount of communication pharmaceutical companies can have with investigative sites about their products.[6] Her comments have an underlying assumption in common with that of the coordinators: the investigative drugs *will* make it successfully through clinical trials. What she did not comment on is that pharmaceutical companies are not communicating their *failed* clinical trials with sites, either. Although pharmaceutical companies may be missing an opportunity to motivate coordinators and others at sites with positive news about their products, they are also sparing sites any discouraging news resulting from studies in which drugs did not meet the development expectations.

Regardless of the success or failure of the clinical trials, the claim of proprietary information as justification for the limited dissemination of results from drug studies is important because it makes the profit motive of pharmaceutical companies visible. While those at sites, particularly coordinators, seek to frame their work in terms of altruism and progress, the industry itself is not organized around those goals. Instead, pharmaceutical companies contribute to coordinators' experience of role conflict by prioritizing their proprietary rights over information that would support the meanings coordinators create about their work. Thus, the mobilization of a discourse of results—both at the level of the little and big pictures—can be seen as an attempt by investigative sites to make meaning out of an industry that does not fulfill the progressive mission it sets for itself—and that others attribute to it—as it pursues profit.

Conclusion

The meanings that investigative sites attach to the results of clinical trials are both tangible and abstract. On the tangible side, coordinators are keen to find visible improvements in the conditions of patient-subjects who have enrolled in drug studies. On the abstract side, coordinators, investigators, and site administrators are interested in making a contribution through their work to medical progress and the buffet of pharmaceutical treatments available. They engage in the discursive construction of "results" to help inspire patient-subjects to be compliant and complete studies. Moreover, their framing of results justifies their own compliance to the study protocols that they are asked to put before the individual needs of patient-subjects.

Importantly, the types of conflicts occurring among participants in the clinical trials arena are due in large measure to the logics embedded in the political economy of drug development and the culture of medical neoliberalism. Because the potential for profit is the underlying basis for the proliferation of the clinical trials industry, the economic rationalities of drug development permeate the relations between and within organizations. Conflict erupts, however, due to the discomfort sites, particularly coordinators, experience from understanding their participation in clinical trials in economic terms. Profit within the standard practice of medicine can be justified in terms of the ethic of care and the individual attention patients receive for fees collected by clinics. With the delivery of clinical trials to patient populations, however, the profits generated are more difficult to rationalize because benefits to patient-subjects are often spurious.

Coordinators would instead prefer to approach their work and their own positions by framing them in terms of altruism in spite of the obvious profit motive underlying the clinical trials industry as a whole and the sites at which they work in particular. For them, the work cannot *just* be about the financial benefits of conducting clinical trials for the sites or the potential profit pharmaceutical companies will gain from their next blockbuster drug.

Instead, these profit motives must be discursively suppressed by overlaying the broader, liberatory purpose of medical progress.

Although investigative sites' mobilization of results is not a complete fabrication, it is nonetheless problematic because it frames the activities of the clinical trials industry in an uncritical light. Rather than dealing directly with the potential pitfalls of profit motives, the focus on results obscures those hazards by celebrating the process of drug development as a de facto instantiation of progress: within this discursive sphere, the types of studies that are being done and why they are being done cannot be critically engaged. The possibility that medical progress should not be equated with the approval of another cholesterol-lowering drug or another antidepressant remains unexamined, even when research staff recognize that those drugs do not make a difference or sometimes even have a negative impact upon the lives of patient-subjects.

The rhetorical attempt to translate patient-subjects' and sites' participation in clinical trials into tangible and beneficial results is not antithetical to medical neoliberalism. Although it is primarily a reaction to the logics embedded in the structures of for-profit drug research, it simultaneously reifies the logic of the system. If medical neoliberalism is engendered in an industry that insists that its products are what is needed to address the health concerns of the world, the "results" discourse that sites disseminate furthers the claim that medical progress is based on pharmaceutical products. The "big picture" of clinical trials, advanced by investigative sites in the clinical trials industry, is dangerous because it artificially occludes the profit motive and the instrumental use of human subjects in its portrait of progress. This discourse can be seen as a means to construct the compliant neoliberal subjects needed for drug development. In the case of Anne, the coordinator quoted at the beginning of this chapter, the "education" of subjects and staff was simply not enough, indicating the fallibility of the neoliberal curriculum.

Chapter 9

Changing Markets in
Pharmaceutical Research

The broader context of health care in the United States shapes the organization of pharmaceutical clinical trials. Physician-investigators who conduct studies for pharmaceutical companies and patient-subjects who participate in them do so largely in response to limitations in the structure of health care delivery. The majority of private-sector physicians become interested in drug studies in order to increase their income. Many patient-subjects enroll in clinical trials as their only means to access any medical attention for their illnesses, and others see drug studies as an extension of care from their own physicians. Meanwhile, healthy-subject clinical trials enroll impoverished, largely minority populations who leverage their good health for a source of income. Physicians use the market for contract research to their advantage, but what about patient-subjects who sign on to drug studies?

Individuals who participate in clinical trials can and do have good experiences as human subjects; they may even receive health benefits as a result of access to experimental drugs. Yet the larger social, political, and economic trends that motivate many people to enroll in studies are troubling. The constraints of managed care, insufficient federal and state programs to subsidize health care, and inadequate benefit-bearing employment all converge in the interests of drug development. For example, the number of investigative sites in the Midwest has been growing since 2000 because of this region's loss of manufacturing jobs that have historically provided good wages and health insurance to workers.[1] Those working in the clinical trials industry are quick to point out the problems with U.S. health care system as well as the role of the pharmaceutical industry in "assisting" those in need. In the words of a clinical trials monitor, "People are just not getting *care* anymore. I don't know what we're going to do with things going the way they're going. . . . *Research* is the only care people will get. It could be because that's the only place that they're willing to pay. Pharmaceutical companies are willing to pay, so patient-subjects get the care." These issues of who is willing to pay, what kind of care is available, and who has access to which types of care are characteristics of medical neoliberalism.

Within the frame of neoliberal economic policies, inequality is both an inevitable outcome of market-driven, commodified health care and an opportunity to supply the market with research subjects. Mobilizing the inequalities of the health care system to its advantage, the pharmaceutical industry cultivates two customer bases in the United States: those who will buy prescription drugs and those who will test their safety and efficacy. In spite of claims about the "care" that clinical trials provide for study participants, it remains the case that patient-subjects are not getting individualized care or *treatment* for their illnesses, but are instead receiving an investigational product to measure what effects—positive or negative—it will have on the body. Within this model of pharmaceutical medicine, everyone is a consumer, but not all consumption is equal.

Role conflicts in the clinic are indicative of the effects of neoliberalism on the ground. Some conflicts, such as those of investigators, coordinators, and monitors, are born through the process of professional identity formation, in negotiating the demands of the research position with their commitments to the health care system. Physician-investigators fashion themselves as entrepreneurs forging new clinical practices while simultaneously being constrained within an emissarial role of obeying pharmaceutical companies' study protocols and promoting their products. Coordinators experience a conflict between research and care that has led to the construction of their own ethical codes of conduct, dictating that the needs of patient-subjects should come before those of the pharmaceutical industry. Monitors mediating the relations between pharmaceutical companies and investigative sites are put in a position of power, yet their authority is frequently undermined because of restrictions on their decision making set by their employers. In contrast to those working in the clinical trials industry, patient-subjects are placed in a conflict between their rights and their needs. Given the structural reasons propelling patient-subjects into clinical trials (for example, lack of health insurance, poverty, illness), there are limits to the extent to which federal regulations like informed consent can protect them or influence the decisions they make about their participation in drug studies.

Thus, problems with the U.S. health care system position this country as an ideal location for pharmaceutical research and development. In spite of recent debates about the future of health care, there is little evidence that the system will soon be overhauled in such a way to make the United States a less appealing location for testing pharmaceutical products. At the same time, the clinical trials industry has become increasingly global. This points to difficult questions about the future of clinical research: To what extent will those changes affect the organization of clinical trials in the United States? And what is the pharmaceutical industry seeking in other nations that the U.S. context does not or cannot provide?

The Future of Clinical Trials in the United States and Globally

In addition to the expansion of the clinical trials industry in the United States, drug development has rapidly become a global enterprise. Patterns of outsourcing globally have been shifting since the 1990s. In the mid-1990s, Eastern Europe, particularly the Russian Federation, became the hot place to conduct clinical trials. In 2000, the pharmaceutical industry began eyeing Latin American for drug development. Most recently, India and China are being hailed as the ideal countries for clinical studies. As the market shifts to new regions, the clinical trials industry does not disappear in well-established places, but the growth of the markets in those regions slows or stalls.

While some fear that the United States will eventually lose its own clinical trials industry, an inspection of the pharmaceutical industry's investment in research and development (R&D) indicates a different pattern. Since 1980, the amount of R&D investment in the United States compared to the rest of the world has been remarkably steady with approximately 80 percent of the contracts going to the U.S. market and 20 percent to the rest of the world.[2] What has changed dramatically, however, is the total amount of money that pharmaceutical companies are investing in R&D: $1.98 billion in 1980, $8.42 billion in 1990, $26.03 billion in 2000, and $38.79 billion in 2004.[3] In other words, the expansion of the clinical trials industry throughout the world is enabled by the more general expansion of the pharmaceutical industry's investment in R&D. Current markets do not necessarily have to fear losing contracts to conduct studies because industry investments are increasing even faster than is outsourcing to new markets.

Although it is certainly cheaper to conduct clinical trials in the developing world, outsourcing drug studies to those countries has limitations that cannot be justified by the cost of studies alone.[4] As a clinical testing ground, the United States provides legitimacy—both scientific and ethical—as well as markets for the pharmaceutical industry. Just as the pharmaceutical industry continues to outsource to academic medical centers because the participation of those physicians (identified as "thought leaders") increases the legitimacy of the results of clinical studies, so too does the outsourcing of studies to American physicians and patient-subjects increase the legitimacy of the products themselves. Because the United States has an extensive infrastructure for oversight that is mandated by the federal government, there is the assumption that what goes on within the borders of the United States is ethical. Many of the clinical trials in the developing world are the focus of critiques about coercion and exploitation of study volunteers because of lax policies regarding and oversight of human subjects research in those countries.[5] Thus, clinical trials conducted in the United States are perceived as more legitimate from an ethical perspective as well. Additionally, it is not inconsequential that the United States is the primary market for drugs after their approval by regulatory agencies. By outsourcing clinical trials within the United States, physicians conducting the studies as well as patient-subjects participating in them are exposed to products before they are available for sale. Clinical trials are a way to premarket pharmaceutical products and generate interest in new drugs; after they are approved for use, there are already physicians ready to prescribe them and patients ready to consume them. This is less the case in developing countries.

Recent attention on the expansion of pharmaceutical clinical trials to the developing world, however, has focused on the suitability of the U.S. population for certain types of drug studies.[6] The pharmaceutical industry has claimed that it is seeking "treatment-naïve" human subjects in the developing world.[7] According to this position, human subjects who have never received treatment for their illnesses are especially valuable test populations because they provide a more accurate assessment of investigational products. Those analyzing the ethics or organization of clinical trials using "treatment-naïve" subjects must be cautious not to buy wholesale the pharmaceutical industry's rhetoric. Given that this clinical framing originates from the pharmaceutical industry and is laden with the values of drug development and profit, it is likely that the industry is employing this discourse to justify its exploitation of the most abject of the world's populations.

Pharmaceutical companies may indeed have difficulty recruiting treatment-naïve subjects for studies in the United States and other industrialized nations. Clinical trials for HIV, diabetes, asthma, and schizophrenia are just a few of the disease groups for which pharmaceutical companies seek treatment-naïve populations, both in the developing world *and* the United States. The decision to enroll only treatment-naïve human subjects is rooted in pharmaceutical companies' maneuver to prove the efficacy of their products. Specifically, pharmaceutical companies anticipate that the *initial* treatment for an illness will have more dramatic effects on curbing symptoms or the development of the disease than would the same treatment introduced in people who have already been managing the disease. Thus, treatment-naïve populations could be better understood as *treatment-bereft* populations that have no access to many of the effective medications that the majority of Americans take for granted. The use of these populations is not in the name of pure, objective science but rather expediency in "proving" the utility of new products.

While the business world has focused on the economic forecast for the clinical trials industry, there have been many other problems reported. The media, for example, have covered the exploitation of human subjects worldwide, including the deaths and injuries of healthy human subjects.[8] During the past five years, there have been many examples—both high and low profile—of clinical research going awry. For example, in February 2004, nineteen-year-old Traci Johnson volunteered as a healthy human subject for a clinical trial on an antidepressant at an Eli Lilly testing facility in Indianapolis. After being administered the drug and then taken off it as part of the trial, she committed suicide at the study center.[9] Other media coverage has focused on phase I healthy subject testing centers, including an exposé in November 2005 about the recruitment of undocumented immigrants in a Miami facility.[10] That story was followed in December 2005 by coverage of an outbreak of tuberculosis after an infected subject enrolled in a healthy human study conducted in Montréal.[11] In a TeGenero study run by Parexel (a major CRO) in their London facility in March 2006, the six men in the study experienced multiple organ failure and nearly died.[12] More remarkable than the sensational stories about phase I studies is that in spite of the negative media coverage, that sector of the industry is one of the fastest growing, with more CROs offering phase I services to the pharmaceutical industry than ever before.[13] In other words, the negative media coverage has not changed the profitability of the clinical development market, and growth of the clinical trials industry within the United States and worldwide has continued apace.

Although the economics of drug development dramatically shape the operations of the clinical trials industry and the conduct of studies at investigative sites, the pharmaceutical industry frames its work instead in terms of philanthropic or humanitarian priorities. For example, the Pharmaceutical Research and Manufacturers of America (PhRMA), the industry's major lobbying group, currently uses the slogan "Disease is our enemy. Working to save lives is our job."[14] Pfizer similarly declares that it is "Working for a Healthier World.™"[15] A tour of major pharmaceutical companies' Web sites provides iterations of similar taglines on the theme of social responsibility.[16] Part of what is ignored in this rhetoric is the industry's overcommitment to the development of "me-too" drugs that are designed not to treat illnesses in novel ways but to capture some of the market share of products from which companies' competitors are profiting.

The ancillary companies in the clinical trials industry, such as CROs, are also characterized by a strong discourse about the importance of pharmaceutical products for health and the need for individuals to embrace product-driven health care.[17] Where one might expect that those working in the clinical trials industry were cynical about the profit-centered nature of the business, what one finds instead is that recognition of profit is erased by rhetoric about the expense of developing new products. Many people who work in the clinical trials industry are *more likely* to believe that the high cost of drugs is justified by pharmaceutical companies' investments in R&D. Furthermore, many working in the clinical trials industry feel *less* critical of the pharmaceutical industry because of their experiences with drug studies, and they are more likely to endorse altruistic pictures of the industry and their role within it. For example, many clinical trials professionals believe that the development of new pharmaceutical products is synonymous with medical progress. New drugs are automatically taken to be better than old ones in spite of the fact that many of the newest drugs are in fact less effective and have more serious side effects than previous generations of pharmacological treatments.[18] This is an extraordinary cultural construction of a for-profit industry, and it should be understood as characteristic of U.S. capitalism and neoliberal politics wherein being critical of profit is portrayed as un-American.

The profit versus philanthropy debate sets a false dichotomy, however, within the industry. Or put another way, the problem is not simply that the pharmaceutical and clinical trial industries pursue profitable ventures. Instead, the problem is that when it comes to clinical development of new pharmaceutical products, the industry is structurally situated to exploit those without access to health care and those who are economically disadvantaged. Regardless of intentionality, the system is set up in such a way that it preys upon vulnerable populations. The point of federal regulation should not be just to protect *individual* human subjects but also to create a system of clinical development that is not so extractive.

Human Subjects Research Ethics and Regulation

The current system of research ethics, institutionalized through U.S. federal regulation, is disconnected from the political and economic context of clinical trials. Current discussions by bioethicists and policymakers tend to focus on the moment of participation—both for potential human subjects as well as physicians and others involved in the research enterprise—rather than the conditions that make pharmaceutical studies appealing to individuals and groups. For example, the process of informed consent is intended to prevent deception of subjects by researchers and to provide information that subjects can use in decision making. Yet most human subjects decide to participate long before reading informed consent forms, and those forms have little impact on subjects' participation. Likewise, discussions about physicians' ethics primarily concentrate on the effects of financial conflicts of interests on physicians' clinical decision making or judgment about subjects' appropriateness for research studies. These debates around conflicts of interest ignore the fact that financial incentives draw physicians to clinical trials in the first place. Thus, the approach of examining the ethics of clinical trials at the moment of study participation does not attend to the problems and conditions that make clinical trials an attractive option for human subjects and investigators.

What would it mean for bioethicists and policymakers to take the political and economic contexts of pharmaceutical clinical trials seriously? Policies regarding the government's responsibility to its citizens in the provision and distribution of health care may seem incidental to the protection of human subjects, but these policies establish significant incentives or disincentives to participate in clinical research. By recognizing the ways in which neoliberal policies have created differential access to health care and exacerbated inequality in contemporary American society, new questions about the ethics of human subjects research emerge. Is it ethical to rely on poor and uninsured populations as test subjects for the development of new pharmaceutical products? What is required to make the inclusion of economically disenfranchised and uninsured individuals in clinical trials as ethical as possible? How can we ensure that the distribution of risks and benefits of pharmaceutical research is fairer, given the problems of access to new products for the poor and uninsured? Oftentimes, bioethicists are concerned about reducing the coercion of prospective human subjects, but there is also a danger in exploiting individuals if they are not sufficiently rewarded for their investment of time and exposure to risk.

By expanding the view of ethics to include contextual factors in clinical trial participation, the regulatory approach to protecting human subjects from harm could be redirected to challenge the status quo of health care in the United States. Although health care and clinical trials have historically been seen as separate issues, they have been and continue to be intimately connected. An ethics of human subjects research that does not account for the general lack of access to health care is dangerously limited. Pharmaceutical clinical trials in the United States—and globally as well—cannot be ethical until social inequalities are recognized and mitigated through more expansive measures to protect human subjects. Universal health care may be the best defense in creating an ethical system of research and development. Yet even without such a radical change in the provision of health care in the United States, it is clear that it is time for the bioethics debates occurring in scholarship, the mainstream media, and public policy to contend with the impact of political and economic constraints upon ethical research practice and the provision of care.

Appendix: On Methods

My research on the clinical trials industry consisted of twelve months of fieldwork in the southwestern United States. I conducted interviews and observation at more than twenty for-profit research organizations in two major cities. I clustered the semi-structured interviews to get the perspective of multiple employees at individual investigative sites, including physicians, research staff, site administrators, and human subjects. The investigative sites included represent a diverse sample of organizational forms: private practices, dedicated research sites, SMOs, CROs, large (nonacademic) hospitals, as well as two not-for-profit investigative sites. At least one individual at 75 percent of sites in one city and 50 percent of sites in the other agreed to an interview. Additionally, I attended clinical trials conferences and joined professional organizations in order to tap into broader trends in the industry.

I primarily gained access to research organizations and their employees through cold calls to investigative sites. I relied on CenterWatch, the clinical trials industry's information clearinghouse, for its online listing of companies, organized by geographic region, to find specific organizations and also contact names of individuals to request in my calls. As the research progressed, many informants supplied names of other contacts that I then contacted directly. In general, I found that the technique of cold-calling companies was much more effective when the contact information for the organization was a research coordinator or an administrator. These contacts were much more willing to chat over the phone about my project and were very likely to schedule some time with me for a formal interview. Physicians, on the other hand, were difficult to get on the phone, and it was rare for physicians to return my phone calls. As a result, interviews with physicians were generally obtained when I was finished interviewing coordinators or administrators, whereupon those informants asked the physicians if they had time for an interview. In only two cases (out of ten physicians) did my interview with the physician precede interviews with other staff members. In part, coordinators and administrators were easier to interview because they were more likely to answer their telephones and to return calls left on their voicemail. Additionally, coordinators in particular were often excited to find out that I valued their expertise. As a result, coordinators were happy to take the time to be interviewed, and the majority talked with me much longer than did physicians.

I made contact with all pharmaceutical representatives and CRO staff through the recommendation of individuals at investigative sites. Interviews in this group were more difficult to acquire, with most individuals I contacted never returning my phone calls. In addition, these informants were much more guarded in their interviews than were those at the investigative site level of the clinical trials industry. In part, I attribute this to my request for phone interviews, rather than face-to-face interactions, with those individuals. It was much more difficult to develop rapport with informants over the phone than it was in person. Also, representatives from pharmaceutical companies were much more concerned about proprietary information about their products despite my assurances that my interest was not in particular drugs under development.

The most difficult interviews to conduct, however, were those with human subject volunteers. In part, the issue was identifying who was actually participating in pharmaceutical studies. With the enactment of patient privacy provisions outlined in the Health Insurance Portability and Accountability Act (HIPAA) in 2003, just months before I entered the field, it became impossible for investigative sites to provide any information to me about any of the subjects participating in their studies. Due to uncertainties about HIPAA, many sites additionally felt unsure about whether they could ask subjects' permission for their names to be released to me. Four interviews with human subjects were conducted during participant observation at one site. Another organization allowed me to post a flyer in their offices, and this was useful in providing contact with two human subjects for interviews. The other interviews with human subjects were obtained by advertising in a free weekly newspaper and posting messages on various health-related Internet forums.

In total, I conducted sixty-three semi-structured interviews with ten physician-investigators, eighteen research coordinators, three recruiters, nine investigative site administrators, nine pharmaceutical and CRO representatives and monitors, and fourteen human subject volunteers. Efforts were made to create a sample of demographically diverse informants in spite of the overall racial and gender homogeneity of the organizational positions within the industry. The clinical trials industry is made up of predominantly white, non-Hispanic individuals. Investigators tend to be men; coordinators and other research staff, site administrators, and monitors tend to be women.

In my sample, nine physicians were men and one was a woman (nine white, one Hispanic); fifteen coordinators were women and three were men (sixteen white, two Hispanic); all three recruiters were women (two white, one black); five site administrators were women and four were men (eight white, one Hispanic); five monitors were women and one was a man (five white, one Hispanic); and eight human subject volunteers were women and six were men (ten white, four Hispanic).

Interviews lasted an average of forty minutes, ranging from ten minutes to ninety minutes. As part of my research methods, I personally transcribed all interviews in their entirety. As mandated by my IRB, interview transcripts were sent either electronically or by mail to all informants who had requested copies of their transcripts to review. All transcripts received back from informants were labeled as "approved" transcripts and were then the only transcripts used for quotes. Additionally, in the case that informants did not send back modified transcripts, I requested their permission to quote from the transcripts I had sent them and transferred these documents to the "approved" transcript category. All transcripts that were not requested by informants were automatically placed into the "approved" category after being stripped of all identifying information. Unless otherwise indicated, all italicized portions of quotes in the book reflect the original stresses informants placed on those words.

The benefit of the arduous process of transcribing the interviews was that it became part of the first stage of coding and analyzing my data. It enabled me to find themes and issues about the clinical trials industry that I had not originally hypothesized. As a result of transcribing each interview while continuing to conduct new ones, I was also able to hone questions and identify areas in which to ask questions other than those originally planned. After completing the interviews, I mapped the major themes to code as part of my analysis, and I combed through each transcript for insights from informants on those themes.

The most important influence that the process of transcribing and coding had on the organization of this book was in its representation of the clinical trials industry. Throughout chapters 3 through 8, I adopt an ethnographic mode of writing that relies on what my informants had to say about organizational cultures within which they operate every day.[1] I use extensive quotes to highlight how my informants speak about and understand the world of pharmaceutical clinical trials and the types of role and ethical conflicts they experience as part of that world.

The statistics in this book are drawn heavily from CenterWatch's publications because CenterWatch is one of the only organizations systematically collecting data on the industry and publishing its findings. Ken Getz, the highly visible president and CEO of CenterWatch, wrote the following: "Through the primary and secondary research that we routinely conduct, to our investigative reporting and interviewing, CenterWatch has had a unique and unprecedented opportunity to serve as a watchdog, messenger, and curator."[2] This does not mean that I always agree with the findings and analysis generated by CenterWatch, but they nonetheless provide empirical information on the larger context of pharmaceutical clinical development.

Notes

Chapter 1 — Clinical Trials: Coming Soon to a Physician Near You

1. CenterWatch, *2005 State of the Clinical Trials Industry* (Boston: Thomson Center-Watch, 2005).
2. CenterWatch, *An Industry in Evolution* (Boston: Thomson CenterWatch, 2003).
3. CenterWatch, *2005 State.*
4. Contract research is often contrasted with "investigator-initiated" research. The latter implies that investigators conceive of all elements of the research and conduct (or directly supervise) the protocols themselves. Investigator-initiated research continues to be more typical of academic physicians who are often rewarded more by their universities for successful grant proposals to government agencies such as the National Institutes of Health than they are for their contracts with the pharmaceutical industry.
5. Gina Kolata and Kurt Eichenwald, "Stopgap Medicine: For the Uninsured, Experiments May Provide the Only Treatment," *New York Times,* 22 June 1999; Christine Pace, Franklin G. Miller, and Marion Danis, "Enrolling the Uninsured in Clinical Trials: An Ethical Perspective," *Critical Care Medicine* 31, no. 3 (2003): S121–25.
6. Larry Gorkin et al., "Clinical Trial Enrollers vs. Nonenrollers: The Cardiac Arrhythmia Suppression Trial (CAST) Recruitment and Enrollment Assessment in Clinical Trials (REACT) Project," *Controlled Clinical Trials* 17, no. 1 (1996): 46–59.
7. Vanessa B. Sheppard et al., "If You Build It, They Will Come: Methods for Recruiting Latinos into Cancer Research," *Journal of General Internal Medicine* 20, no. 5 (2005): 444–47.
8. G. Marie Swanson and Amy J. Ward, "Recruiting Minorities into Clinical Trials: Toward a Participant-Friendly System," *Journal of the National Cancer Institute* 87, no. 23 (1995): 1747–59.
9. This research is part of the growing social science literature engaging the field of bioethics. The earliest examples of this approach to medical ethics can be traced to the following works: Renée C. Fox, *Experiment Perilous: Physicians and Patients Facing the Unknown* (New Brunswick, NJ: Transaction Publishers, 1959); Renée C. Fox, "Advanced Medical Technology—Social and Ethical Implications," *Annual Review of Sociology* 2 (1976): 231–68; Bernard Barber et al., *Research on Human Subjects: Problems of Social Control in Medical Experimentation* (New York: Russell Sage Foundation, 1973); Bernard Barber, *Informed Consent in Medical Therapy and Research* (New Brunswick: Rutgers University Press, 1980); Bradford H. Gray, *Human Subjects in Medical Experimentation: A Sociological Study of the Conduct and Regulation of Clinical Research* (Huntington, NY: R. E. Krieger, 1975); and Charles Bosk, *Forgive and Remember: Managing Medical Failure* (Chicago: University of Chicago Press, 1979).

   More recent examples include Charles Bosk, *All God's Mistakes: Genetic Counseling in a Pediatric Hospital* (Chicago: University of Chicago Press, 1995); Oonagh P. Corrigan, "Empty Ethics: The Problem with Informed Consent," *Sociology of Health* and *Illness* 25 (2003): 768–92; Raymond G. DeVries, "How Can We Help? From 'Sociology in' to 'Sociology of' Bioethics," *Journal of Law, Medicine, and Ethics* 32 (2004): 279–92; Sydney A. Halpern, *Lesser Harms: The Morality of Risk in Medical Research* (Chicago: University of Chicago Press, 2004); Adam Hedgecoe, *The Politics of Personalized Medicine: Pharmacogenetics in the Clinic* (New York: Cambridge University Press, 2004); Sergio Sismondo, "Pharmaceutical Maneuvers," *Social Studies of Science* 34, no. 3 (2004): 149–59; and Robert Zussman, *Intensive Care: Medical Ethics and the Medical Profession* (Chicago: University of Chicago Press, 1992).

10. See the appendix for more detailed information about my methods and about the organizations included and informants interviewed.

11. CenterWatch, *2006 State of the Clinical Trials Industry* (Boston: Thomson CenterWatch, 2006); Thomas Bodenheimer, "Uneasy Alliance: Clinical Investigators and the Pharmaceutical Industry," *New England Journal of Medicine* 342, no. 20 (2000): 1539–44.

12. Pharmaceutical Research and Manufacturers of America, "Biopharmaceutical Industry Research and Development Tops $49 Billion in 2004," in Pharmaceutical Industry Profile 2005 (Washington, DC: PhRMA, March 2005).

13. CenterWatch, *An Industry.*

14. "Trials and Tribulations: More Effective Clinical Trials May Be Just Around the Corner," *Economist*, Feb. 21, 1998, 13–15.

15. CenterWatch, *An Industry.*

16. B. Rainville, "Strategic Outsourcing with Contract Research Organizations: Targeting Corporate Goals," *Drug Information Journal* 36, no. 1 (2002): 77–81.

17. For a more nuanced analysis of the framing of populations as "ready-to-recruit," see Jill A. Fisher, "'Ready-to-Recruit' or 'Ready-to-Consent' Populations?: Informed Consent and the Limits of Subject Autonomy," *Qualitative Inquiry* 13, no. 6 (2007): 875–94.

18. CenterWatch, *An Industry.*

19. ACRO (Association of Clinical Research Organizations), "Clinical Research Participation: Today's Challenges, Tomorrow's Possibilities" (paper read at ACRO Webcast, 2004).

20. There is considerable (long-standing) debate about how much it costs to bring a drug to market. According to the pharmaceutical industry, the average cost is an estimated $802 million (see Joseph A. DiMasi et al., "The Price of Innovation: New Estimates of Drug Development Cost," *Journal of Health Economics* 22 [2003]: 151–85). Industry critics, however, claim that the actual cost is closer to $100 million (Marcia Angell, *The Truth about the Drug Companies: How They Deceive Us and What to Do About It* [New York: Random House, 2004]; Public Citizen, *Rx R&D Myths: The Case against the Drug Industry's R&D "Scare Card"* (2001), http://www.citizen.org/documents/rdmyths.pdf, accessed 24 March 2008.

21. CenterWatch, *2006 State.*

22. Ibid.

23. CenterWatch, *An Industry.*

24. CenterWatch, *2006 State.*

25. CenterWatch, *An Industry.*

26. Kelly Scientific, "Issues and Trends: Management of Clinical Trials in an Era of Outsourcing," http://www.kellyscientific.com/ksrwhitepapers, accessed 24 March 2008.

27. CenterWatch, *2005 State.*

28. This book uses the term "physician-investigator" to refer to physicians working as contract researchers to differentiate their role from the traditional meaning of "PI" in the academic research setting. In academia, a PI is generally understood to be the individual crafting investigator-initiated projects and overseeing funded research. In contract research, however, physicians have no part in designing the studies or analyzing the data. They simply execute the protocols in their clinics and send the data to the pharmaceutical companies that have hired them.

29. CenterWatch, *An Industry.*

30. Ibid.

31. *Parexel's Pharmaceutical R&D Statistical Sourcebook 2005/2006* (Waltham, MA: Parexel International Corporation, 2005).

32. CenterWatch, *2006 State.*

33. CenterWatch, *An Industry.*

34. Ibid.

35. Ibid.

36. *Parexel's Pharmaceutical R&D.*

37. U.S. Food and Drug Administration, *Prescription Drug User Fee Rates for Fiscal Year 2008,* http://www.fda.gov/cber/pdufa/userfees08.htm, accessed 24 March 2008.

38. Arthur W. Frank has developed the term "medical neoliberalism" in his writing. This book adds to his conceptualization of the ways in which neoliberalism infuses health and medicine. Frank, "What's Wrong with Medical Consumerism?" in *Consuming Health: The Commodification of Health Care,* edited by S. Henderson and A. Petersen (New York: Routledge, 2002); and "Emily's Scars: Surgical Shapings, Technoluxe, and Bioethics," *Hastings Center Report* 34, no. 2 (2004): 18–29.

39. "Neoliberalism" refers to a variation on liberalism as a political philosophy. It should not be confused with popular uses of the term "liberal" in the United States. In fact, neoliberalism is generally associated with the political and economic agendas of conservatives, particularly those who are considered "neocons." See David Harvey, *A Brief History of Neoliberalism* (New York: Oxford University Press, 2005).

40. Jean Comaroff and John L. Comaroff, "Millennial Capitalism: First Thoughts on a Second Coming," *Public Culture* 12, no. 2 (2000): 291–343; Nikolas Rose, *Powers of Freedom: Reframing Political Thought* (New York: Cambridge University Press, 1999).

41. On welfare, see Sanford F. Schram, *Welfare Discipline: Discourse, Governance, and Globalization* (Philadelphia: Temple University Press, 2006); Virginia Eubanks, "Technologies of Citizenship: Surveillance and Political Learning in the Welfare System," in *Surveillance and Security: Technological Politics and Power in Everyday Life,* edited by T. Monahan (New York: Routledge, 2006); John Gilliom, *Overseers of the Poor: Surveillance, Resistance, and the Limits of Privacy* (Chicago: University of Chicago Press, 2001). On health care, see Frank, "What's Wrong" and "Emily's Scars." On education, see Torin Monahan, *Globalization, Technological Change, and Public Education* (New York: Routledge, 2005); Henry A. Giroux, *The Terror of Neoliberalism: Authoritarianism and the Eclipse of Democracy*

(Boulder, CO: Paradigm Publishers, 2004). On social security, see Christopher Niggle, "Globalization, Neoliberalism, and the Attack on Social Security," *Review of Social Economy* 61, no. 1 (2003): 51–71.

42. Lisa Duggan, *The Twilight of Equality?: Neoliberalism, Cultural Politics, and the Attack on Democracy* (Boston: Beacon Press, 2003).

43. Ellen Shaffer and Joseph Brenner, "Trade and Health Care: Corporatizing Vital Human Services," in *Sickness and Wealth: The Corporate Assault on Global Health,* edited by M. Fort, M. A. Mercer, and O. Gish (Cambridge, MA: South End Press, 2004); Deborah A. Boehm, "The Safety Net of the Safety Net: How Federally Qualified Health Centers 'Subsidize' Medicaid Managed Care," *Medical Anthropology Quarterly* 19, no. 1 (2005): 47–63.

44. Torin Monahan and Tyler Wall, "Somatic Surveillance: Corporeal Control through Information Networks," *Surveillance and Society* 4, no. 3/4 (2007): 154–73.

45. Saras Henderson and Alan R. Petersen. *Consuming Health: The Commodification of Health Care* (New York: Routledge, 2002).

46. Stefan Timmermans and Marc Berg, *The Gold Standard: The Challenge of Evidence-Based Medicine and Standardization in Health Care* (Philadelphia: Temple University Press, 2003).

47. Frank, "What's Wrong."

48. "Technoluxe" discussed in Frank, "Emily's Scars." Gregor Wolbring, "The Unenhanced Underclass," in *Building Everyday Democracy,* edited by P. Miller and J. Wilsdon (London: Demos, 2006); Carl Elliott, *Better than Well: American Medicine Meets the American Dream* (New York: W. W. Norton, 2003).

49. W. Richard Scott et al., *Institutional Change and Healthcare Organizations: From Professional Dominance to Managed Care* (Chicago: University of Chicago Press, 2000).

50. Ezekiel J. Emanuel and Nancy Neveloff Dubler, "Preserving the Physician-Patient Relationship in the Era of Managed Care," in *The Social Medicine Reader,* edited by G. E. Henderson et al. (Durham: Duke University Press, 1997).

51. As a response to managed care dipping into their incomes, physicians began to invest in for-profit ancillary-care ventures to spread the reach of the products and services they could offer to patients. (Bradford H. Gray, *The Profit Motive and Patient Care: The Changing Accountability of Doctors and Hospitals* [Cambridge, MA: Harvard University Press, 1993]).

52. Lorna Ronald, "Empowered to Consume: Direct-to-Consumer Advertising and Pharmaceutical Governance," PhD diss., Science and Technology Studies, Rensselaer Polytechnic Institute, Troy, NY, 2006. It should be noted that direct-to-consumer advertising proponents have clearly appropriated language regarding empowerment from the women's health movement and HIV/AIDS activism. Leanna Darvall, *Medicine, Law, and Social Change: The Impact of Bioethics, Feminism, and Rights Movements on Medical Decision-Making* (Brookfield: Dartmouth Publishing Group, 1993); Sandra Morgen, *Into Our Own Hands: The Women's Health Movement in the United States, 1969–1990* (New Brunswick: Rutgers University Press, 2002); Steven Epstein, *Impure Science: AIDS, Activism, and the Politics of Knowledge* (Berkeley: University of California Press, 1996).

53. Dennis John Mazur, *The New Medical Conversation: Media, Patients, Doctors, and the Ethics of Scientific Communication* (Lanham, MD: Rowman and Littlefield, 2002).

54. John S. Hoff, *Medicare Private Contracting: Paternalism or Autonomy* (Washington, DC: American Enterprise Institute Press, 1998).

55. Joy V. Fuqua, "'Ask Your Doctor About . . . ': Direct-to-Consumer Prescription Drug Advertising and the HIV/AIDS Medical Marketplace," *Cultural Studies* 16, no. 5 (2002): 650–72; Jonathan Metzl, *Prozac on the Couch: Prescribing Gender in the Era of Wonder Drugs* (Durham, NC: Duke University Press, 2003).

56. David Healy, *Let Them Eat Prozac: The Unhealthy Relationship between the Pharmaceutical Industry and Depression* (New York: New York University Press, 2004); Nikolas Rose, "Neurochemical Selves," *Society* 41, no. 1 (2003): 46–59.

57. Sjaak van der Geest, Susan Reynolds Whyte, and Anita Hardon, "The Anthropology of Pharmaceuticals: A Biographical Approach," *Annual Review of Anthropology* 25 (1996): 153–78; M. Nichter and M. Nichter, *Anthropology and International Health: Asian Case Studies* (Amsterdam: Gordon and Breach, 1996); Adriana Petryna, Andrew Lakoff, and Arthur Kleinman, eds., *Global Pharmaceuticals: Ethics, Markets, Practices* (Durham, NC: Duke University Press, 2006); Elliott, *Better than Well*; Rose Weitz, *Sociology of Health, Illness, and Health Care: A Critical Approach*, 4th ed. (Belmont: Wadsworth, 2007).

58. Pace, Miller, and Danis, "Enrolling the Uninsured."

Chapter 2 — Governing Human Subjects Research

1. One exception is the U.S. Department of Health and Human Services (HHS) Office of the Inspector General report issued in June 2000. Specifically, the OIG identified practices associated with the recruitment of subjects in private-sector pharmaceutical research as a "fundamental concern" because "the consent process may be undermined when, under pressure to recruit quickly . . . investigators misrepresent the true nature of the research or when patients are influenced to participate in research due to their trust in their doctor" (Office of the Inspector General, *Recruiting Human Subjects: Pressures in Industry-Sponsored Clinical Research* [Washington, DC: Department of Health and Human Services, 2002], 2).

2. George J. Annas and Michael A. Grodin, eds., *The Nazi Doctors and the Nuremberg Code: Human Rights in Human Experimentation* (New York: Oxford University Press, 1992).

3. Ruth R. Faden and Tom L. Beauchamp, *A History and Theory of Informed Consent* (New York: Oxford University Press, 1986).

4. Barbara Mishkin, "Law and Public Policy in Human Studies Research," *Perspectives in Biology and Medicine* 43, no. 3 (2000): 362–72.

5. Harriet A. Washington, *Medical Apartheid: The Dark History of Medical Experimentation on Black Americans from Colonial Times to the Present* (New York: Doubleday, 2007).

6. Patricia A. King, "The Dangers of Difference," in *Tuskegee's Truths: Rethinking the Tuskegee Syphilis Study*, edited by S. Reverby (Chapel Hill: University of North Carolina Press, 2000).

7. Sarah E. Chinn, *Technology and the Logic of American Racism: A Cultural History of the Body as Evidence* (New York: Continuum, 2000).

8. Todd L. Savitt, "The Use of Blacks for Medical Experimentation and Demonstration in the Old South," *Journal of Southern History* 48 (1982): 331–48.

9. V. N. Gamble, "Under the Shadow of Tuskegee: African Americans and Health Care," in *Tuskegee's Truths*.

10. Savitt, "The Use of Blacks," 341.

11. James H. Jones, *Bad Blood: The Tuskegee Syphilis Experiment* (New York: Free Press, 1981); Susan Reverby, ed., *Tuskegee's Truths: Rethinking the Tuskegee Syphilis Study* (Chapel Hill: University of North Carolina Press, 2000).

12. Allan M. Brandt, "Racism and Research: The Case of the Tuskegee Syphilis Experiment," in *Tuskegee's Truths*.

13. Benjamin Roy, "The Tuskegee Syphilis Experiment: Biotechnology and the Administrative State," *Journal of the National Medical Association* 87 (1995): 56–67.

14. Jonathan D. Moreno, *Undue Risk: Secret State Experiments on Humans* (New York: Routledge, 2001); Andrea Smith, *Conquest: Sexual Violence and American Indian Genocide* (Cambridge, MA: South End Press, 2005).

15. Peter H. Eichstaedt, *If You Poison Us: Uranium and Native Americans* (Santa Fe: Red Crane Books, 1994).

16. Elizabeth Siegel Watkins, *On the Pill: A Social History of Oral Contraceptives, 1950–1970* (Baltimore: Johns Hopkins University Press, 2001).

17. Laura Briggs, *Reproducing Empire: Race, Sex, Science, and U.S. Imperialism in Puerto Rico* (Berkeley: University of California Press, 2002).

18. Maurice H. Pappworth, *Human Guinea Pigs: Experimentation on Man* (Boston: Beacon Press, 1967).

19. An important implication of this position is that the mentally institutionalized had no other value to society than as bodies or vessels to be used by others for the good of "humanity" in scientific studies.

20. David J. Rothman and Sheila M. Rothman, *The Willowbrook Wars* (New York: HarperCollins, 1984).

21. Ibid.

22. Jon H. Harkness, "Research behind Bars: A History of Nontherapeutic Research on American Prisoners," PhD diss., University of Wisconsin, Madison, 1996; *Experiments and Research with Humans: Values in Conflict* (Washington, DC: National Academy of Sciences, 1975).

23. Allen M. Hornblum, *Acres of Skin: Human Experiments at Holmesburg Prison* (New York: Routledge, 1998).

24. The exposé was Jessica Mitford's 1971 book, *Kind and Usual Punishment: The Prison Business* (New York: Knopf, 1971).

25. Jones, *Bad Blood*; Faden and Beauchamp, *A History*.

26. Vivien Spitz, *Doctors from Hell: The Horrific Account of Nazi Experiments on Humans* (Boulder, CO: Sentient Publications, 2005).

27. On codes of conduct for researchers, see Anita Guerrini, *Experimenting with Humans and Animals: From Galen to Animal Rights* (Baltimore: Johns Hopkins University Press, 2003); Susan E. Lederer, *Subjected to Science: Human Experimentation in American before the Second World War* (Baltimore: Johns Hopkins University Press, 1995). On following codes, see Halpern, *Lesser Harms*.

28. In addition to the researchers themselves, students have also played a large role as human subjects in many fields from medicine to psychology. Not only a convenient population, students have been thought to make good study subjects because of their level of education and presumed familiarity with the areas under investigation. See Heather Munro Prescott, "Using the Student Body: College and University Students as Research Subjects in the United States during the

Twentieth Century," *Journal of the History of Medicine* 57 (2002): 3–38. Lederer, *Subjected to Science;* Halpern, *Lesser Harms.*

29. P. Dalla-Vorgia, J. Lascaratos, and P. Skiadas, "Is Consent in Medicine a Concept Only of Modern Times?" *Journal of Medical Ethics* 27 (2001): 59–61.

30. Lederer, *Subjected to Science.*

31. See Robert K. Merton, "Science and the Social Order," in *The Sociology of Science* (1938; rpt. Chicago: University of Chicago Press, 1973).

32. Today, the preservation of the autonomy of American science has been argued based on a model of exceptionalism (Daniel Kleinman, *Politics on the Endless Frontier: Postwar Research Policy in the United States* [Durham: Duke University Press, 1995]). In this view, science is outside of the realm of public policy and democratic participation because it is (and should be) an elite institution. Because science is rooted in the search for "truth," is conducted by trained experts, and offers the promise of economic gain in return for its investment, it is seen as uniquely able to self-regulate and, moreover, too complex for popular control. See Bruce Bimber and David H Guston, "Politics by the Same Means: Government and Science in the United States," in *Handbook of Science and Technology Studies*, edited by S. Jasanoff et al. (Thousand Oaks, CA: Sage, 1995). Although much scholarship within the sociology of scientific knowledge has challenged this construction of science (e.g., Sal Restivo, *Science, Society, and Values: Toward a Sociology of Objectivity* [Allentown, PA: Lehigh University Press, 1994]; Karin Knorr-Cetina, *Epistemic Cultures: How the Sciences Make Knowledge* [Cambridge, MA: Harvard University Press, 1999]; Bruno Latour and Steve Woolgar, *Laboratory Life: The Construction of Scientific Facts* [Princeton, NJ: Princeton University Press, 1986]), science policy continues to be viewed at the national level as different from other policy domains and as such requiring less intervention.

33. Nancy D. Campbell, *Discovering Addiction: The Science and Politics of Substance Abuse Research* (Ann Arbor: University of Michigan Press, 2007); David J. Rothman, *Strangers at the Bedside: A History of How Law and Bioethics Transformed Medical Decision Making* (New York: Basic Books, 1991).

34. Faden and Beauchamp, *A History.*

35. Gerald Kutcher, "Risk to Medicine or the Autonomy Rights of Subjects? Governing American Medical Research" (paper read at Vital Politics, London, 2003).

36. Mishkin, "Law and Public Policy."

37. Faden and Beauchamp, *A History.*

38. Annas and Grodin, *The Nazi Doctors.*

39. In spite of the intellectual and symbolic value of the Nuremberg Code, it has proven disappointing in its influence on legal and legislative systems around the world (Faden and Beauchamp, *A History*). In large part, this is because the Nuremberg Code was designed to assess scientific practice retrospectively. Because its concern was judging the conduct of completed research, the tribunal gave little guidance for practicing ethical research into the future (James F. Childress, "Nuremberg's Legacy: Some Ethical Reflections," *Perspectives in Biology and Medicine* 43, no. 3 [2000]: 347–61).

40. The WMA has amended the Declaration of Helsinki several times, most recently in 2000. Although the declaration has been an admirable and interesting document from its inception, it has no particular legal status. As a set of ethical principles alone, it serves as a model for "Good Clinical Practices" (GCP), rather than

a mandate to govern and oversee research enterprises. See Ezekiel J. Emanuel et al., eds., *Ethical and Regulatory Aspects of Clinical Research: Readings and Commentary* (Baltimore: Johns Hopkins University Press, 2003).

41. George J. Annas, "The Changing Landscape of Human Experimentation: Nuremberg, Helsinki, and Beyond," *Health Matrix Journal of Law and Medicine* 2 (1992): 119–40.

42. Paul M. McNeill, *The Ethics and Politics of Human Experimentation* (New York: Cambridge University Press, 1993).

43. Faden and Beauchamp, *A History.*

44. Emanuel et al., *Ethical and Regulatory Aspects.*

45. There are two problems with how the risk/benefit analysis is operationalized in the Belmont Report. First, risk is assessed as a function of both probability and magnitude, while benefit is assessed only in terms of magnitude (see Tom L. Beauchamp and James F. Childress, *Principles of Biomedical Ethics* [New York: Oxford University Press, 1983]). This is to say that a potential huge benefit that has a very small probability of materializing can be legitimately performed in the United States even if there is a moderate risk (in terms of both magnitude and probability) to the people used in the research studies. This indicates that beneficence itself is not the key element in evaluating studies (see Susan M. Wolf, ed., *Feminism and Bioethics: Beyond Reproduction* [New York: Oxford University Press, 1996]). A second problem with the risk/benefit analysis as defined by the Belmont Report is that risk is defined almost exclusively for the research subject while benefit is defined to a large extent for society (see Susan Sherwin, "Feminism and Bioethics," in *Feminism and Bioethics*). Although benefits to the individuals participating in research studies are generally described when there are some (i.e., it is often a general lack of benefit that excludes this portion of the analysis), no critical evaluation of risk to society needs to be performed (see Nancy M. P. King, Gail E. Henderson, and Jane Stein, eds., *Beyond Regulations: Ethics in Human Subjects Research* [Chapel Hill: University of North Carolina Press, 1999]).

46. The principle of justice in the Belmont Report has been mobilized since to advocate for the explicit inclusion of women and minorities in clinical trials. See Steven Epstein, *Inclusion: The Politics of Difference in Medical Research* (Chicago: University of Chicago Press, 2007); Nancy E. Kass, "Gender and Research," in *Beyond Consent: Seeking Justice in Research*, edited by J. P. Kahn, A. C. Mastroianni, and J. Sugarman (New York: Oxford University Press, 1998); Patricia A. King, "Race, Justice, and Research," in *Beyond Consent*; Matthew Weinstein, "A Public Culture for Guinea Pigs: U.S. Human Research Subjects after the Tuskegee Study," *Science as Culture* 10, no. 2 (2001): 195–223.

47. The Belmont Report does not ignore the ethical abuses that occurred in the United States. In fact, it reads:

> Against this historical background, it can be seen how conceptions of justice are relevant to research involving human subjects. For example, the selection of research subjects needs to be scrutinized in order to determine whether some classes (e.g., welfare patients, particular racial and ethnic minorities, or persons confined to institutions) are being systematically selected simply because of their easy availability, their compromised

position, or their manipulability, rather than for reasons directly related to the problem being studied.

The Belmont report even mentions the Tuskegee syphilis study explicitly. However, the report gives no concrete indication how to prevent these types of abuses from continuing to occur or how "respect for persons" and informed consent could provide solutions (Belmont Report, http://ohsr.od.nih.gov/guidelines/belmont.html, accessed 24 March 2008).

48. Faden and Beauchamp, *A History*.
49. Emanuel et al., *Ethical and Regulatory Aspects*.
50. Recently, however, there is increasing interest in relaxing the regulation on use of prisoners in research. In addition, there are now federal incentives, such as extensions of patent protections, for companies to conduct pediatric clinical trials.
51. Laura A. Siminoff, Marie Caputo, and Christopher Burant, "The Promise of Empirical Research in the Study of Informed Consent Theory and Practice," *HEC Forum* 16, no. 1 (2004): 53–71; Jill A. Fisher, "Procedural Misconceptions and Informed Consent: Insights from Empirical Research on the Clinical Trials Industry," *Kennedy Institute of Ethics Journal* 16, no. 3 (2006): 251–68.
52. Now Department of Health and Human Services (HHS).
53. Charles R. McCarthy, "The Evolving Story of Justice in Federal Research Policy," in *Beyond Consent*.
54. Ruth Macklin, "Justice in International Research," in *Beyond Consent*.
55. Philip J. Hilts, *Protecting America's Health: The FDA, Business, and One Hundred Years of Regulation* (New York: Knopf, 2003).
56. Kutcher, "Risk to Medicine."
57. King, Henderson, and Stein, *Beyond Regulations*.
58. Kutcher, "Risk to Medicine"; McCarthy, "The Evolving Story of Justice"; David N. Weisstub, *Research on Human Subjects: Ethics, Law, and Social Policy* (Oxford: Pergamon, 1998).
59. Weisstub, *Research on Human Subjects*.
60. Faden and Beauchamp, *A History*.
61. John C. Fletcher and Franklin G. Miller, "The Promise and Perils of Public Bioethics," in *The Ethics of Research Involving Human Subjects: Facing the Twenty-first Century*, edited by H. Y. Vanderpool (Frederick, MD: University Publishing Group, 1996); Wolf, *Feminism and Bioethics*.
62. Rothman, *Strangers at the Bedside*.
63. U.S. 45-CFR-46.
64. Nancy M. P. King, "The Line between Clinical Innovation and Human Experimentation," *Seton Hall Law Review* 32 (2003): 573–82.
65. McCarthy, "The Evolving Story of Justice."
66. Within the regulatory system, bureaucratic requirements related to liability concerns often eclipse the proactive protection of human subjects (see Kutcher, "Risk to Medicine"). For example, paperwork and time delays, not critical thinking about ethics, are the norm when dealing with IRBs (see Lisa Eckenwiler, "Moral Reasoning and the Review of Research Involving Human Subjects," *Kennedy Institute of Ethics Journal* 11 [2001]: 37–69).
67. Conference presentation, American Society of Law, Medicine, and Ethics, 9 November 2001.

68. Bernard Lo and M. Groman, "NBAC Recommendations on Oversight of Human Subject Research," *Seton Hall Law Review* 32, no. 3 (2003): 493–512.
69. Norman Howard-Jones, "Human Experimentation in Historical and Ethical Perspectives," *Social Science and Medicine* 16, no. 15 (1982): 1429–48.
70. Dean Cocking and Justin Oakley, "Medical Experimentation, Informed Consent, and Using People," *Bioethics* 8, no. 4 (1994): 293–311.
71. Oonagh P. Corrigan, "Empty Ethics: The Problem with Informed Consent," *Sociology of Health and Illness* 25 (2003): 768–92; Fisher, "Procedural Misconceptions."
72. Sherwin, "Feminism and Bioethics"; Hilde Lindemann Nelson and James Lindemann Nelson, "Justice in the Allocation of Health Care Resources: A Feminist Account," in *Feminism and Bioethics*.
73. Mary B. Mahowald, "On Treatment of Myopia: Feminist Standpoint Theory and Bioethics," in *Feminism and Bioethics*.
74. Campbell, *Discovering Addiction*; Harkness, "Research behind Bars."
75. Trudo Lemmens and Paul B. Miller, "The Human Subjects Trade: Ethical and Legal Issues Surrounding Recruitment Incentives," *Journal of Law, Medicine, and Ethics* 31 (2003): 398–418.
76. Vanessa Merton, "Ethical Obstacles to the Participation of Women in Biomedical Research," in *Feminism and Bioethics*; Deborah Narrigan, Jane Sprague Zones, Nancy Worcester, and Maxine Jo Grad, "Research to Improve Women's Health: An Agenda for Equity," in *Women's Health: Complexities and Differences*, edited by S. B. Ruzek, V. L. Olesen, and A. Clarke (Columbus: Ohio State University Press, 1997); Epstein, *Inclusion*.
77. Epstein, *Inclusion*.
78. D. Evans, M. Smith, and L. Willen, "Big Pharma's Shameful Secret," *Bloomberg Markets* Special Report, December 2005, http://www.bloomberg.com/specialreport/pharma.pdf, accessed 24 March 2008.
79. Donald Light, "Ironies of Success: A New History of the American Health Care 'System,'" *Journal of Health and Social Behavior* 45 (extra issue) (2004): 1–24; Jill Quadagno, *One Nation, Uninsured: Why the U.S. Has No National Health Insurance* (New York: Oxford University Press, 2005).
80. Beauchamp and Childress, *Principles of Biomedical Ethics*. One exception is the inclusion of women and minorities in clinical trials.
81. Carol Mason Spicer, "Federal Oversight and Regulation of Human Subjects Research: An Update," *Kennedy Institute of Ethics Journal* 10, no. 3 (2000): 261–64.
82. Cocking and Oakley, "Medical Experimentation"; Sherwin, "Feminism and Bioethics"; Nelson and Nelson, "Justice in the Allocation."

Chapter 3 — Pursuing Contract Research

1. A pseudonym.
2. For a detailed examination of the ways in which physicians forge paid relationships with the pharmaceutical industry in addition to conducting clinical trials, see Jerome P. Kassirer, *On the Take: How America's Complicity with Big Business Can Endanger Your Health* (New York: Oxford University Press, 2005). See also Bimal H. Ashar et al., "Prevalence and Determinants of Physician Participation in Conducting Pharmaceutical-Sponsored Clinical Trials and Lectures," *Journal of General Internal Medicine* 19 (2004): 1140–45.

3. Interestingly, Richard did not speak nostalgically about the experience doing studies he gained during his residency. In fact, he referred to this exposure to academic clinical trials as "forced indoctrination."

4. There is evidence that the number of phantom investigators is quite high. For instance, the FDA reported that 37 percent of investigators audited by the federal agency in 2001 received warnings—or the more serious and official Notice of Initiation of Disqualification Proceedings and Opportunity to Explain (NIDPOE)—for their failure to supervise adequately the clinical trials for which they were responsible (Valerie Gamache, "Chasing Away Phantom Investigators," *Center-Watch Monthly* 8, no. 11 [2001]: 1–5).

5. Ed Cray, *In Failing Health: The Medical Crisis and the AMA* (New York: Bobbs-Merrill, 1970); Edward M. Kennedy, *In Critical Condition: The Crisis in America's Health Care* (New York: Simon and Schuster, 1972); Paul Starr, *The Social Transformation of American Medicine: The Rise of a Sovereign Profession and the Making of a Vast Industry* (New York: Basic Books, 1982).

6. W. Richard Scott et al., *Institutional Change and Healthcare Organizations: From Professional Dominance to Managed Care* (Chicago: University of Chicago Press, 2000).

7. Quadagno, *One Nation, Uninsured.*

8. Kassirer, *On the Take.*

9. Ivan Illich, *Medical Nemesis: The Medical Expropriation of Health* (New York: Pantheon Books, 1976).

10. Howard Waitzkin and Jennifer Fishman, "Inside the System: The Patient-Physician Relationship in the Era of Managed Care," in *Competitive Managed Care: The Emerging Health Care System,* edited by J. D. Wilkerson, K. J. Devers, and R. S. Given (San Francisco: Jossey-Bass, 1997).

11. Ezekiel J. Emanuel and Nancy Neveloff Dubler, "Preserving the Physician-Patient Relationship in the Era of Managed Care," in *The Social Medicine Reader.*

12. Cindy A. Stearns, "Physicians in Restraints: HMO Gatekeepers and Their Perceptions of Demanding Patients," *Qualitative Health Research* 1 (1991): 326–48.

13. David Mechanic, "Changing Medical Organization and the Erosion of Trust," *Milbank Quarterly* 74 (1996): 171–89; Audiey C. Kao et al., "The Relationship between Method of Physician Payment and Patient Trust," *Journal of the American Medical Association* 280, no. 19 (1998): 1708–14.

14. Hoangmai H. Pham et al., "Financial Pressures Spur Physician Entrepreneurialism," *Health Affairs* 23, no. 2 (2004): 70–81.

15. Ha T. Tu and Paul B. Ginsburg, "Losing Ground: Physician Income, 1995–2003," Washington, DC: Center for Studying Health System Change, 2006.

16. Ibid.

17. These data were reported by adjusting to constant 2000 dollars in Marc A. Rodwin, Hak J. Chang, and Jeffrey Clausen, "Malpractice Premiums and Physicians' Income: Perceptions of a Crisis Conflict with Empirical Evidence," *Health Affairs* 25, no. 3 (2006): 750–58.

18. Tyler Chin, "Doctors' Costs Going Up Faster than Revenues," *American Medical News,* 21 November 2005.

19. HIPAA was enacted in 1996 to protect workers' access to insurance when they change or lose their jobs. It is better known for the health care privacy provisions that were written into the bill and went into effect in 2003.

20. Rodwin et al., "Malpractice Premiums."
21. Ann Mech, "Medical Malpractice Reform," *Policy, Politics, and Nursing Practice* 4 (2003): 227–29.
22. Rodwin et al., "Malpractice Premiums."
23. James C. Robinson, *The Corporate Practice of Medicine: Competition and Innovation in Health Care* (Berkeley: University of California Press, 1999).
24. Bradford H. Gray, *The Profit Motive and Patient Care: The Changing Accountability of Doctors and Hospitals* (Cambridge, MA: Harvard University Press, 1993).
25. Pham et al., "Financial Pressures."
26. Deborah Borfitz, "Make Your Practice More Profitable," *Medical Economics* 78 (2001): 106; Deborah A. Sullivan, *Cosmetic Surgery: The Cutting Edge of Commercial Medicine in America* (New Brunswick: Rutgers University Press, 2001).
27. Pham et al., "Financial Pressures."
28. Ibid.
29. Ellis W. Lader et al., "The Clinician as Investigator: Participating in Clinical Trials in the Practice Setting," *Circulation* 109 (2004): 2672–79.
30. Jason E. Klein and Alan R. Fleischman, "The Private Practicing Physician-Investigator: Ethical Implications of Clinical Research in the Office Setting," *Hastings Center Report* 32, no. 4 (2002): 22–26.
31. CenterWatch, *An Industry in Evolution* (Boston: Thomson CenterWatch, 2003).
32. Data indicate that the number would be higher if charting the growth in the number of new investigators. From 1986 to 1990, the period preceding outsourcing to the private sector, there were 4,067 new investigators. During 1996–2000, 6,669 physician-investigators were new investigators. Preliminary data on the next period charts 8,616 new investigators from 2001 to 2004. The number of new studies also increased dramatically: from 10,701 between 1985 and 1990 to 36,839 between 2001 and 2004. See CenterWatch, *2006 State*.
33. A study found that 26 percent of all private-practice physicians who graduated from one medical school were involved with pharmaceutical clinical trials (Tom Lloyd, Brenda R. Phillips, and Robert C. Aber, "Factors that Influence Doctors' Participation in Clinical Research," *Medical Education* 38 [2004]: 848–51).
34. Harris Interactive, "Most Physicians Do Not Participate in Clinical Trials Because of Lack of Opportunity, Time, Personnel Support, and Resources" (2004), http://www.harrisinteractive.com/news/allnewsbydate.asp?NewsID=811, accessed 24 March 2008.
35. Tim Gray, "Getting the Most Out of Community-Based Research," *ACP Observer* (2004), http://www.acponline.org/journals/news/apr04/cbr.htm, accessed 24 March 2008.
36. CenterWatch, *2006 State*.
37. My sample of physicians mapped well demographically onto national trends of physicians who become clinical trial investigators. Physicians tend to be later-career white men with an average age of fifty-one. A female informant attributed the low percentage of women physicians (18 percent) in the industry to the difficulty women have balancing the competing demands of their medical practices and their families, therefore they are generally reticent to seek out more (or different) work. See CenterWatch, *An Industry*. See the appendix for more detailed information.
38. Similarly, an easier route for many physicians into clinical trials is to first become "subinvestigators" on a study. What this means is that they merely refer their

patients to specific clinical trials—rather than conduct studies themselves—and are paid per patient who successfully enrolls in the study.

39. The motive of those working at SMOs is to identify successful private practices with large patient populations and sizeable staffs that would be attractive to pharmaceutical companies. Because SMOs obtain the business, negotiate the details of contracts, provide basic training for physicians and their staff, and manage much of the regulatory aspects of clinical trials, the SMO approach is very attractive to many neophyte physician-investigators. The downside of working with an SMO is that the investigators must share the profits from all contracts with the SMO.

40. CenterWatch, *An Industry.*

41. An industry how-to book on becoming a clinical investigator provides a budget worksheet for calculating revenue. See David Ginsberg, *Becoming a Successful Clinical Research Investigator* (Boston: Thomson CenterWatch, 2005). There are now software applications to help physicians or administrators better calculate budgets.

42. CenterWatch, *An Industry.*

43. While these arguments for the private sector seem convincing, the extent of the differences between the sectors may be inflated. According to a pharmaceutical company project manager, there is little difference beyond IRB review between how well private-sector physicians run studies as compared to those in academia, especially given the prevalence of the phantom investigator problem in the private sector.

44. This split between scientists and contract researchers is interesting because it parallels traditional discourse about differences between doctors and nurses. Physicians have historically been seen as the health care providers with highly specialized knowledge and valued for this type of expertise whereas nurses have been seen as the providers with techniques of caring for patients and valued for their execution of preassigned tasks. Here in the context of clinical trials, it is the pharmaceutical companies with the scientific expertise dictating tasks to physicians.

45. Although in most cases physician-investigators have no input into the study protocols, there are rare exceptions to the rule. Physicians are occasionally invited to participate in "Distinguished Investigator Meetings." These meetings generally include a handful of investigators, most from academia, who have worked on phase II clinical trials for a specific product. They are asked to provide information on what elements they think are important to be included in the design of phase III studies (which are considerably more expensive than phase II studies). Investigators make suggestions about the inclusion-exclusion criteria, the types of procedures that should be performed, and the number of visits that patient volunteers can tolerate. Although physician-investigators admit that being invited to these meetings is indeed flattering, most do not think this level of involvement is a benefit to them and their work. Instead, because of the time and travel they see it as too much of a commitment to be something to seek out.

46. Lader et al., "Clinician as Investigator."

47. Generally speaking, the only legal case that can be made against an investigator is that proper informed consent was not obtained. Given the amount of bureaucracy surrounding informed consent, however, it is increasingly difficult to bring a successful case against an investigator on these charges. Most plaintiffs who

have been injured in clinical trials will likely have a stronger case against the pharmaceutical company that sponsored the study.

48. One possible exception to the protection investigators feel that clinical trials provide is in psychiatry studies because the inclusion-exclusion criteria are based on less-objective symptoms or diagnoses. In these cases, physician-investigators are asked to come to a clinical diagnosis as part of the screening and enrollment process.

49. A similar trend of delegating responsibility has been described as a neoliberal strategy of "fragmented centralization" (Torin Monahan, *Globalization, Technological Change, and Public Education* [New York: Routledge, 2005]).

50. CenterWatch, *2005 State.*

51. CenterWatch, *An Industry.*

52. Aside from complaints, the FDA also initiates audits of investigators when studies are deemed of pivotal importance, sites have higher-than-average enrollment of human subjects, and sites submitted data that are inconsistent with other investigative sites.

53. CenterWatch, *2006 State.* Interestingly, the only country that had significantly more actions resulting from FDA audits than the United States (61 percent) in the period between 2000 and 2005 was China (75 percent). In comparison, Brazil (62.5 percent), Canada (61 percent), Russia (59 percent), and the EU (66.7 percent) were in the same range as the United States, and Australia (50 percent) and South Africa (43 percent) did significantly better than the United States.

54. In 2004, there were 239 FDA inspections of investigators. The most common findings from these audits included "inadequate and incorrect records" (60 percent); "failure to adhere to protocol" (42 percent); "failure to notify IRB of changes" (8 percent); "inadequate drug accountability" (7.5 percent); "failure to report adverse events" (4 percent); "failure to obtain consent (6 percent); "inadequate patient consent forms" (4 percent). Ibid.

55. Ginsberg, *Becoming.* Also see chapter 5 for an example of an investigator who was fined and imprisoned as a result of study fraud.

56. Other scholars have written about the conflict between research and care that is experienced by physicians as they work in these dual roles. Most notable is Renée Fox's ethnography of a metabolic ward in which "treatment" was often limited to experimental medicine. Renée C. Fox, *Experiment Perilous: Physicians and Patients Facing the Unknown* (New Brunswick, NJ: Transaction Publishers, 1959). More recently, Sydney Halpern's sociological examination of the history of vaccine development also delves into the ways in which researchers have made decisions about the ethics of inoculation research (Halpern, *Lesser Harms*).

57. "Naïve" here means that the study protocol requires that subjects enrolled in the studies have never received prior treatment of any kind for their condition.

Chapter 4 — Coordinating Clinical Trials

1. A pseudonym.

2. Margarete Sandelowski, *Devices and Desires: Gender, Technology, and American Nursing* (Chapel Hill: University of North Carolina Press, 2000).

3. Arlene M. Davis et al., "The Invisible Hand in Clinical Research: The Study Coordinator's Critical Role in Human Subjects Protection," *Journal of Law, Medicine, and Ethics* 30 (2002): 411–19; Mary-Rose Mueller and Laura Mamo, "The Nurse

Clinical Trial Coordinator: Benefits and Drawbacks of the Role," *Research and Theory for Nursing Practice* 16 (2002): 33–42.

4. Susan Reverby, *Ordered to Care: The Dilemma of American Nursing, 1850–1945* (New York: Cambridge University Press, 1987); Sue Fisher, *Nursing Wounds: Nurse Practitioners, Doctors, Women Patients, and the Negotiation of Meaning* (New Brunswick: Rutgers University Press, 1995).

5. Mary-Rose Mueller, "From Delegation to Specialization: Nurses and Clinical Trial Co-ordination," *Nursing Inquiry* 8 (2001): 182–90.

6. C. Fedor and P. Cola, "Preliminary Results of the 'Clinical Researcher' Coordinators' Survey," *Clinical Researcher* 3 (2003): 18–22.

7. Mueller and Mamo, "The Nurse"; Helga Kuhse, *Caring: Nurses, Women and Ethics* (Cambridge: Blackwell, 1997).

8. Daniel F. Chambliss, *Beyond Caring: Hospitals, Nurses, and the Social Organization of Ethics* (Chicago: University of Chicago Press, 1996), 63.

9. Mary-Rose Mueller, "Science versus Care: Physicians, Nurses, and the Dilemma of Clinical Research," in *The Sociology of Medical Science and Technology*, edited by M. A. Elston (Oxford: Blackwell, 1997).

10. The primary guide to learning how to be a coordinator states that no background in medical care is needed for the job but that it is useful to coordinators who possess it. It highlights instead the skills that are necessary for the job: "CRCs [clinical research coordinators] must possess many skills. CRCs must have extremely good organizational skills, including the ability to handle a number of different tasks simultaneously. They must be detail-oriented (being picky and a perfectionist is helpful) in order to handle the paperwork aspects of the job well. CRCs must also be people-oriented, as they must interact with patients, sponsor companies and others on a regular basis. CRCs must be self-confident, flexible, and adaptable to change. They must also be focused, manage time well and follow through on problems and commitments. And perhaps most of all, CRCs need to have a high energy level—they are usually very busy people" (K. E. Woodin, *CRC's Guide to Coordinating Clinical Research* [Boston: CenterWatch, 2004], 3). In addition to being gendered, this passage has overtones of postindustrial values in labor, mainly flexibility and high energy, that are reminiscent of Emily Martin's work (*Flexible Bodies: The Role of Immunity in American Culture from the Days of Polio to the Age of AIDS* [Boston: Beacon Press, 1994]).

11. Jill A. Fisher, "Re-inscribing Gender within New Modes of Medical Expertise: The Investigator-Coordinator Relationship in the Clinical Trials Industry," *Gender, Work, and Organization* (forthcoming).

12. According to CenterWatch, more than 70 percent of coordinators make less than $49,000 per year. Only 2 percent make more than $80,000 (CenterWatch, *2006 State*). In a 2005 survey of the clinical trials industry, the median income of coordinators was $45,000, with a reported range of $10,000 to $170,000 (Jill A. Fisher, "Report on the Preliminary Results from the 2005 Survey of Clinical Trials Industry Personnel" [2007], http://www.jillfisher.net/papers/report.pdf, accessed 24 March 2008).

13. According to a survey of the industry, less than 15 percent of coordinators are men (Fisher, "Report").

14. Mueller, "From Delegation"; Karen Spilsbury et al. "The Role and Potential Contribution of Clinical Research Nurses to Clinical Trials," *Journal of Clinical Nursing* (forthcoming).

15. For example, these educational opportunities are available from the Association for Clinical Research Professionals (ACRP), Drug Information Association, and local community colleges. The ACRP builds their courses into the certification process. Coordinators who are already members (at $120 per year membership) pay $399 for the review course. Nonmembers who would like to join the organization pay $519 for the course, and nonmembers who do not want to join pay $549. For those coordinators who go on to take the certification exam, the fee is $369 for members and $489 for nonmembers (whether they want to join or not). Individuals taking the exam must be physically present at one of the hundreds of exam locations throughout the country, and some coordinators may incur travel and lodging costs. As an example of a community college course, Gateway in Maricopa County, Arizona, holds several clinical research courses each year at roughly $260 per course (the rate for residents of the county). All fees were posted on the organizations' Web sites.

16. Most private-sector physicians must pay for their own continuing medical education courses, and they seem to perceive coordinator training in the same way. When coordinators are certified by professional organizations, they need to keep up their certification by doing twenty-four hours of continuing education credit every two years. Most coordinators pay out-of-pocket for the cost of obtaining and maintaining their certification status.

17. Davis, "The Invisible Hand."

18. Referral in this context generally means that the physician tells patients that they might qualify for a clinical trial and then asks them if they would like to speak to a coordinator for more information. If the patient answers in the affirmative, a coordinator will usher that patient to her office at the conclusion of the patient's regular appointment.

19. In other words, formal ethics regarding human subjects research is generally framed in terms of universal principles that dictate how subjects should or should not be treated. Coordinators depart from a universalistic ethics by applying instead particularistic ethics that are dependent on the subjects themselves and the studies that coordinators are conducting. Scholarship in the sociology of science has shown that it is very common in the practice of science that researchers rely upon particularistic criteria, instead of universal values and norms, in their actions and decisions regarding their research and the organization of their work. Generally, however, analyses in the sociology of science have shown how departure from universal principles in science creates bias or prejudice. In contrast, coordinators seem to be mobilizing a particularistic approach to research ethics in order to provide better protection of patient-subjects. For a more detailed discussion on universalism and particularism in science, see David Hess, *Science Studies: An Advanced Introduction* (New York: New York University Press, 1997).

20. Jill A. Fisher, "Practicing Research Ethics: Private-Sector Physicians and Pharmaceutical Clinical Trials," *Social Science and Medicine* 66 (2008): 2495–2505.

21. Association on Clinical Research Professionals, "A Celebration of the First Thirty Years," *Monitor* special anniversary issue (2006): 9–51.

22. Kurt Eichenwald and Gina Kolata, "A Doctor's Drug Trials Turn into Fraud," *New York Times*, 17 May 1999, 1. The next chapter will discuss clinical trial fraud in more detail.

23. Nicholas Wade, "Patient Dies in Trial of Gene Treatment; Patient Dies during a Trial of Therapy Using Genes," *New York Times*, 29 September 1999, A1; Gina Kolata, "Johns Hopkins Admits Fault in Fatal Experiment," *New York Times*, 17 July 2001, A16.
24. See discussion in chapter 2 about the history of human subjects research on African Americans and Native Americans.
25. It is telling that this recruiter raises the specter of Tuskegee in talking about conducting research on minorities, but it should not be assumed the current regulation governing research places these abuses of human subjects in the distant past. It should also be noted that "culture" here becomes the reason to participate in research when differential values placed upon culture and race were the reasons that excused the Tuskegee practices for so long.
26. See chapter 2 for description of Tuskegee study.
27. For more detailed treatment of Eunice Rivers, see Susan Reverby, ed., *Tuskegee's Truths*.
28. Fisher, "Re-inscribing Gender."

Chapter 5 — Monitoring the Clinical Trials Industry

1. A pseudonym.
2. The FDA crafted this guidance by adopting the principles of "Good Clinical Practices" (GCP) from the International Conference on Harmonization (ICH). For more information, see http://www.fda.gov/oc/gcp/.
3. For more on audit culture, see Marilyn Strathern, ed., *Audit Cultures: Anthropological Studies in Accountability, Ethics, and the Academy* (New York: Routledge, 2000).
4. Quoted from Tamar Nordenberg, "Physician Sentenced for Doctoring Drug Data," *FDA Consumer* (May–June 1999).
5. Food and Drug Administration, "Letter to Dr. Robert A. Fiddes" (2002), http://www.fda.gov/ohrms/dockets/dailys/02/May02/051302/80045981.pdf, accessed 24 March 2008.
6. Eichenwald and Kolata, "A Doctor's Drug Trials."
7. Karen E. Woodin and John C. Schneider, *The CRA's Guide to Monitoring Clinical Research* (Boston: Thomson CenterWatch, 2003), 16.
8. There are no statistics on the ratio of women to men who are monitors. In speaking with people in the industry, I heard a fairly wide range of answers regarding the percentage of women monitors (i.e., 65–95 percent).
9. For analysis on nurses' subtle everyday manipulations of physicians, see Robert Zussman, *Intensive Care: Medical Ethics and the Medical Profession* (Chicago: University of Chicago Press, 1992).
10. Woodin and Schneider, *The CRA's Guide*, 15.
11. Ibid, 16.
12. CenterWatch, *State of the Clinical Trials Industry* (Boston: Thomson CenterWatch, 2006).
13. Susanna Space, "Monitoring Change among CRAs," *CenterWatch Monthly* 10, no. 7 (2003): 1–5.
14. Steve Zisson, "Clinical Research Jobs in the New Economy," *CenterWatch Monthly* 8, no. 9 (2001): 1–6.
15. Space, "Monitoring Change."

16. In general, the derogatory view of CRO monitors that coordinators and investigators hold is widely acknowledged in the industry. Interestingly, these perceptions are even echoed in statements made by pharmaceutical monitors about their CRO counterpoints. As one pharmaceutical company monitor who had never worked at a CRO said,

> From my opinion, it's better to work directly for the pharmaceutical company. It's better for the physicians because you get direct answers. The monitors who work for pharmaceutical companies are generally more knowledgeable about the pharmaceutical [company] in general: like how they operate, who to contact, you just get answers a lot quicker. And they're just really more knowledgeable about the protocol, just because they work directly for the company and have specific training. The physicians seem to like it better when you're a pharmaceutical monitor. From the feedback I've gotten from the doctors, we're trained a little better and have more experience usually.

Because coordinators and physicians frequently repeat the views about CRO monitors, they become truths within the industry.

17. Monitors, like physicians, experience the trend of increased responsibility and decreased authority within organizations. Monahan described this managerial strategy as "fragmented centralization" (Torin Monahan, "The School System as a Post-Fordist Organization: Fragmented Centralization and the Emergence of IT Specialists," *Critical Sociology* 3, no. 4 [2005]: 583–615).

Chapter 6 — Recruiting Human Subjects

1. My intention to enroll in a phase I study with this company as part of my project did not involve deception of any kind. I contacted an informant to ask permission, and she took the issue up with the company's legal department. Within a week of my request, they gave me permission to conduct my research there, provided my presence would not interfere with the normal functioning of their studies.

2. This quote comes from the informed consent form for the study.

3. It was, however, probably fortunate for my health that I did not qualify for the study. According to the consent form, results from one previous study in humans showed that this particular drug in multiple doses produced nausea (~60 percent of subjects), headache (~70 percent of subjects), upset stomach (~40 percent of subjects), vomiting (~30 percent of subjects), dizziness (~30 percent of subjects), decreased appetite (~20 percent of subjects), and loose stools (~20 percent of subjects).

4. Bernadette D. Protor and Joseph Dalaker, *Poverty in the United States: 2002* (Washington, DC: U.S. Department of Commerce, Economics, and Statistics Administration, U.S. Census Bureau, 2003).

5. Carmen DeNavas-Walt, Bernadette D. Proctor, and Cheryl Hill Lee, *Income, Poverty, and Health Insurance Coverage in the United States: 2005* (Washington, DC: U.S. Department of Commerce, Economics, and Statistics Administration, U.S. Census Bureau, 2006).

6. Steven Epstein, *Inclusion: The Politics of Difference in Medical Research* (Chicago: University of Chicago Press, 2007).

7. Fisher, "Ready-to-Recruit."

8. For example, it took me weeks of calling the phase I clinic's hotline to prequalify for any study because of my sex and age.

9. A 2006 case involving six healthy men who experienced multiple organ failure and nearly died following the administration of one dose of an experimental drug is a frightening example of why constant monitoring of subjects is necessary in early clinical studies (See Alastair J. J. Wood and Janet Darbyshire, "Injury to Research Volunteers: The Clinical Research Nightmare," *New England Journal of Medicine* 354, no. 18 [2006]: 1869–71).

10. The risks associated with phase I clinical trials are often compared to everyday risks such as accidental injuries or motor vehicle accidents. CenterWatch lists the risk of dying from an accidental injury as one in 3,000, from a motor vehicle accident as one in 6,000, and from clinical trial participation as one in 10,000. CenterWatch, *An Industry in Evolution* (Boston: Thomson CenterWatch, 2003).

11. It should also be noted that although cancer and HIV/AIDS treatments are important diseases within the pharmaceutical industry's R&D portfolio, the pharmaceutical industry's contribution to these areas of research are dwarfed by noncommercial sectors. Specifically, the pharmaceutical industry is developing only 33 percent and 24 percent of the active investigational new drugs in cancer and HIV/AIDS research respectively. In other words, the public sector, particularly NIH-funded projects, is the largest contributor to R&D in those areas of medicine. This pattern no doubt has important implications for which human subjects enroll in cancer and HIV/AIDS clinical trials (CenterWatch, *2006 State*).

12. G. Marie Swanson and Amy J. Ward, "Recruiting Minorities into Clinical Trials: Toward a Participant-Friendly System," *Journal of the National Cancer Institute* 87, no. 23 (1995): 1747–59.

13. Steven Epstein, *Impure Science: AIDS, Activism, and the Politics of Knowledge* (Berkeley: University of California Press, 1996).

14. These tests were ordered to determine whether the study medication could have caused the patient-subjects' anemia. When "adverse events" like this occur during studies, the research staff have to make their best determination about the extent to which it is related to the investigational drug.

15. The issue of providing money to human subject volunteers is a much-debated topic among ethicists and within the clinical trials industry. One of the manifestations of these debates surrounds how money should be referred to so that it is not framed as a form of coercion: "reimbursement" or "compensation." See "Paid in Full?" *American Journal of Bioethics* 1, no. 2 (2001): 40–69.

16. According to U.S. census reports, the percentages of Asians and non-Hispanic whites without health insurance are very similar (DeNavas-Walt et al., *Income*).

17. This framing was also applied to Native Americans by one recruiter I interviewed. It was very rare, however, for those in the clinical trials industry to explicitly refer to Native Americans as a group when talking about the ethnic and racial differences affecting recruitment and enrollment of clinical trials.

18. In 2006, a first-in-human study received worldwide media attention when the six healthy men who were participating at a CRO in London nearly died (see Wood, *Injury to Research Volunteers*).

19. See Jordan Goodman, Anthony McElligott, and Lara Marks, *Useful Bodies: Humans in the Service of Medical Science in the Twentieth Century* (Baltimore: Johns Hopkins University Press, 2003).

20. These policies were crafted after the thalidomide tragedy in the 1960s and contin-
    ued until the 1991 U.S. federal mandate to include women in clinical trials. See
    Epstein, *Inclusion.*

Chapter 7 — Mobilizing Informed Consent

1. Because of the perceived complexity of the study, the investigator was conducting the informed consent visit himself rather than leaving it to a coordinator as is
   customary in these settings.
2. Belief in a therapeutic benefit to clinical studies when there is none is referred to
   as a "therapeutic misconception." For an important review of the literature and
   recommendations for minimizing these beliefs in human subjects, see Paul S.
   Appelbaum and Charles W. Lidz, "The Therapeutic Misconception," in *The Oxford
   Textbook of Clinical Research Ethics,* edited by E. J. Emanuel et al. (New York:
   Oxford University Press, 2008). Elsewhere, I develop the concept of "procedural
   misconceptions" to highlight the ways in which clinical contexts can create false
   expectations about research (Fisher, "Procedural Misconceptions").
3. While my inclination is to problematize the paternalism that I witnessed in the
   relationship between the mother and son, it was impossible for me to determine
   the degree to which the woman had already been affected by Alzheimer's disease.
   What is probably more worthy of discussion is the physician's acceptance of the
   son's role as decision maker without evaluating the competency of the woman to
   make decisions for herself.
4. Ruth R. Faden and Tom L. Beauchamp, *A History and Theory of Informed Consent*
   (New York: Oxford University Press, 1986).
5. Arthur Caplan, *Due Consideration: Controversy in the Age of Medical Miracles*
   (New York: John Wiley and Sons, 1998).
6. Guy A. M. Widdershoven and Frank W.S.M. Verheggen, "Improving Informed
   Consent by Implementing Shared Decisionmaking in Health Care," *IRB: Ethics and Human Research* 21, no. 4 (1999): 1–5; Greg A. Sachs et al., "Conducting
   Empirical Research on Informed Consent: Challenges and Questions," *IRB: Ethics
   and Human Research* 25, no. 5 (2003): S4-S10.
7. For a discussion about the role of the concept of autonomy in bioethics, see Paul
   R. Wolpe, "The Triumph of Autonomy in American Bioethics: A Sociological Perspective," in *Bioethics and Society: Constructing the Ethical Enterprise,* edited
   by Raymond G. DeVries and Janardan Subedi (Upper Saddle River, NJ: Prentice-
   Hall, 1998).
8. Paul S. Appelbaum, Charles W. Lidz, and Alan Meisel, *Informed Consent: Legal
   Theory and Clinical Practice* (New York: Oxford University Press, 1987); Oon-
   agh P. Corrigan, "Empty Ethics: The Problem with Informed Consent," *Sociology
   of Health and Illness* 25 (2003): 768–92; Rebecca Dresser, *When Science Offers
   Salvation: Patient Advocacy and Research Ethics* (New York: Oxford University
   Press, 2001); Nancy M. P. King, Gail E. Henderson, and Jane Stein, eds., *Beyond
   Regulations: Ethics in Human Subjects Research* (Chapel Hill: University of
   North Carolina Press, 1999); Robert Zussman, "Sociological Perspectives on
   Medical Ethics and Decision-Making," *Annual Review of Sociology* 23 (1997):
   171–89.
9. In 2003, 3.62 million Americans participated in clinical trials (CenterWatch, *2005
   State*).

10. The randomized controlled trial may be considered the gold standard in clinical development, but this does not mean that the design of this type of study is static or exempt from economic and political pressures. See Harry M. Marks, *The Progress of Experiment: Science and Therapeutic Reform in the United States, 1900–1990* (New York: Cambridge University Press, 1997); Stefan Timmermans and Marc Berg, *The Gold Standard: The Challenge of Evidence-Based Medicine and Standardization in Health Care* (Philadelphia: Temple University Press, 2003); David J. Hess, *Can Bacteria Cause Cancer?: Alternative Medicine Confronts Big Science* (New York: New York University Press, 2000).

11. This procedure is usually discussed as "consenting" patient-subjects. Although it is shorthand for coordinators to refer to the process, it is nonetheless interesting that the active role in the consent process is given to coordinators, not to patient-subjects. There are examples of this turn of phrase in the quotes in this and other chapters in this book.

12. Zussman, "Sociological Perspectives."

13. Scott D. Halpern, "Towards Evidence Based Bioethics," *British Medical Journal* 331 (2005): 901–3; Laura A. Siminoff, Marie Caputo, and Christopher Burant, "The Promise of Empirical Research in the Study of Informed Consent Theory and Practice," *HEC Forum* 16, no. 1 (2004): 53–71.

14. Gerry Kent, "Shared Understandings for Informed Consent: The Relevance of Psychological Research on the Provision of Information," *Social Science and Medicine* 43, no. 10 (1996): 1517–23.

15. Recall that the norm within medicine was already in place that researchers should obtain consent from subjects (Lederer, *Subjected to Science*). The regulation caused some discomfort, however, because of how the information would be presented to potential subjects and the external oversight of IRBs (David J. Rothman, *Strangers at the Bedside: A History of How Law and Bioethics Transformed Medical Decision Making* [New York: Basic Books, 1991]).

16. Bernard Lo and Michelle Groman. "NBAC Recommendations on Oversight of Human Subject Research," *Seton Hall Law Review* 32, no. 3 (2003): 493–512; David N. Weisstub, *Research on Human Subjects: Ethics, Law, and Social Policy* (Oxford: Pergamon, 1998).

17. Kathryn M. Taylor and Merrijoy Kelner, "Informed Consent: The Physicians' Perspective," *Social Science and Medicine* 24, no. 2 (1987): 135–43.

18. Karen Cox, "Informed Consent and Decision-Making: Patients' Experiences of the Process of Recruitment to Phases I and II Anti-Cancer Drug Trials," *Patient Education and Counseling* 46 (2002): 31–38; Sarah J. L. Edwards et al., "Informed Consent for Clinical Trials: In Search of the 'Best' Method," *Social Science and Medicine* 47, no. 11 (1998): 1825–40; Frank Verheggen, "Myth and Reality of Informed Consent in Clinical Trials," *Medicine and Law* 16, no. 1 (1997): 53–71.

19. Richard R. Sharp and Mark Yarborough, "Informed Trust and the Financing of Biomedical Research," *Journal of Law, Medicine, and Ethics* 34, no. 2 (2006): 460–64.

20. Sheldon Zink has advocated for more direct information about studies in consent forms. She faults researchers for being afraid to say it like it is when it comes to risk and financial conflicts of interest in research. She asks, until we stop trying to present information about studies in euphemisms, how can we expect participants to have a truly informed sense of the research enterprise? Sheldon Zink,

"How Do We Properly Inform Research Subjects?" *U.S. Office of Human Research Protections Conference on Quality Improvement for Research Subject Protection,* Philadelphia, Pennsylvania, 6 May 2004. See also Leslie Cannold, "'There Is No Evidence to Suggest . . . ': Changing the Way We Judge Information for Disclosure in the Informed Consent Process," *Hypatia* 12, no. 2 (1997): 165–84.

21. Getz is president and CEO of CenterWatch and cofounder and board chair of the Center for Information and Study on Clinical Research Participation (CISCRP).

22. Ken Getz, "Leveraging the Informed Consent Process as Strategic Recruitment and Retention Asset," in *Patient Recruitment Strategies for Clinical Trials,* Philadelphia, 17 October 2002.

23. This does not mean, however, that human subjects' rights are jeopardized by the industry's appropriation of the consent process. In fact, the refocus on consent forms probably ensures that prospective subjects will be given more information during initial site visits, even if the information is being mobilized for the industry rather than for subjects' protection.

24. Coordinators' perceptions are not entirely off base. About 80 percent of all drugs that go into phase III testing do eventually get FDA approval for marketing (CenterWatch, *An Industry*).

25. While it is rare for products to be found unsafe after FDA approval, it can and does happen. The 2004 Vioxx scandal provides recent evidence that not all marketed pharmaceutical products are without serious risks (Justin Biddle, "Lessons from the Vioxx Debacle: What the Privatization of Science Can Teach Us about Social Epistemology," *Social Epistemology* 21, no. 1 [2007]: 21–39). According to PhRMA, the pharmaceutical industry's lobbying group, about 3 percent of approved drugs had to be removed from the market during the last twenty years (Shankar Vedantam, "FDA Told U.S. Drug System Is Broken," *Washington Post,* 23 September 2006, A1).

26. Pediatric studies are an exception to this rule because in those studies parents or guardians are asked to give informed consent, the child is asked to assent, and the implication is that the adults will be responsible for ensuring the child's compliance. See Robert M. Nelson, "Children as Research Subjects," in *Beyond Consent: Seeking Justice in Research,* edited by J. P. Kahn, A. C. Mastroianni, and J. Sugarman (New York: Oxford University Press, 1998).

Chapter 8 — Cultivating Pharmaceutical "Compliance"

1. A pseudonym.

2. Jonas H. Ellenberg, "Intent-to-Treat Analysis versus As-Treated Analysis," *Drug Information Journal* 30 (1996): 535–44.

3. This report was generated from an analysis of data collected from 25,855 study volunteers in 2003 (CenterWatch, *2006 State*).

4. For a discussion of patient-subjects' compliance with study diaries, see "Editorial, 2006 in Review: Industry Adapts and Adopts," *CenterWatch Monthly* 14, no. 1 (2007): 1, 10–12. The article reports on a recent study that found that although 94 percent of patient-subjects claimed they were filling out paper-based study diaries on schedule and completely, only 11 percent actually were doing so.

5. This is very much an insider's view on the industry. For a critical view on the cost of development, see Marcia Angell, *The Truth about the Drug Companies: How They Deceive Us and What to Do about It* (New York: Random House, 2004).

6. For more discussion of the pharmaceutical companies' (mis)trust in physician-investigators and research staff, see Jill A. Fisher, "Institutional Mistrust in the Organization of Pharmaceutical Clinical Trials," *Medicine, Health Care, and Philosophy* (forthcoming).

Chapter 9 — Changing Markets in Pharmaceutical Research

1. Karyn Korieth and Sara Gambrill, "The New Frontier: Tapping into Rural U.S.," *CenterWatch Monthly* 12, no. 7 (2005): 1–7.
2. The biggest change in the distribution of R&D investment occurred during the 1970s. In 1970, 91.5 percent of all R&D dollars were spent in the U.S., but by 1980, this percentage dropped to 78.4 percent. (*Parexel's Pharmaceutical R&D*).
3. These figures are for total R&D investment, which includes clinical trials (ibid.).
4. The median cost of clinical trials per patient in 2002 was $6,621 in the United States and $4,631 in western Europe. The cost of trials in developing countries or emergent markets is considerably less. For example, the cost per patient of doing a trial in Poland, Hungary, or the Czech Republic is 58 percent, 57 percent, and 43 percent, respectively, of the cost per patient in the U.K. (*Parexel's Pharmaceutical R&D*).
5. For example, Solomon R. Benatar, "Avoiding Exploitation in Clinical Research," *Cambridge Quarterly of Healthcare Ethics* 9 (2000): 562–65; Kristin Peterson, "Global HIV Clinical Trials," in *Experimental Systems, States, and Speculations: Anthropology at the Intersection of Life, Science, and Capital* (conference at the University of California–Irvine, 2007); Sonia Shah, *The Body Hunters: How the Drug Industry Tests Its Products on the World's Poorest Patients* (New York: New Press, 2006); Melinda Cooper, "Clinical Capital: Neo-Liberalism and the Will to Experiment (US and China)," in *Experimental Systems, States, and Speculations.*
6. For example, Joseph Dumit and Kaushik Sunder Rajan, "Biocapital, Surplus Health, and Clinical Trials: Toward a Health Theory of Value," in *Experimental Systems, States, and Speculations*; Adriana Petryna, "Globalizing Human Subjects Research," in *Global Pharmaceuticals: Ethics, Markets, Practices,* edited by A. Petryna, A. Lakoff, and A. Kleinman (Durham, NC: Duke University Press, 2006).
7. Patrick McGee, "Clinical Trials on the Move," *Drug Discovery and Development* 9, no. 6 (2006): 16–22.
8. Shah, *The Body Hunters.*
9. G. Harris, "Student, 19, in Trial of New Antidepressant Commits Suicide," *New York Times,* 12 February 2004, A30.
10. Evans, Smith, and Willen, "Big Pharma's Shameful Secret."
11. David Evans, "SFBC Employees in Montreal Found to Have Latent Tuberculosis," *Bloomberg Report,* 8 March 2006.
12. Raymond G. DeVries and Carl Elliott, "Why Disclosure?" *Journal of General Internal Medicine* 21, no. 9 (2006): 1003–4; Wood and Darbyshire, "Injury to Research Volunteers."
13. According to industry sources, CROs are particularly keen on running phase I studies for pharmaceutical company sponsors because they hope to continue to work with those companies throughout the entire process of clinical development for a particular product. Currently, at least 50 percent of all phase I studies and as much as 95 percent of bioequivalency studies for the generic market are

being outsourced to CROs (Karyn Korieth and Steve Zisson, "Phase I Market Consolidates," *CenterWatch Monthly* 14, no. 1 [2007]: 1, 6–9).

14. Pharmaceutical Research and Manufacturers of America (PhRMA), http://www.phrma.org, accessed on May 10, 2007.

15. Pfizer, http://www.pfizer.com, accessed on May 10, 2007.

16. Nick King has discussed the pharmaceutical industry's promotion of themselves, especially in advertisements appearing in the media, as a means to justify the medicalization of everyday life and the profits these companies make from their products (Nicholas B. King, "Pharma Porn: Making the Case for Medicalization," paper presented at the Society for Social Studies of Science Conference, Pasadena, CA, 22 October 2005).

17. Companies within the clinical trials industry, however, do not follow the pharmaceutical companies' embedding of the rhetoric of philanthropy in the corporate framing of their work. These companies' slogans are aimed not at the general public but at the pharmaceutical companies from whom they are seeking contracts. The following are examples of major CROs' current taglines: "Expertise that makes the difference" (Parexel), "No one gets medicine into the system faster" (PPD), and "Trust is based on facts" (SGS Life Science Service).

18. The most notable example of this is Vioxx®. This overprescribed arthritis treatment has been shown to be less effective for treating symptoms of the disease than aspirin and has much more dangerous side effects. Due to mounting evidence of the drug's link to severe cardiovascular problems, Merck decided it could no longer afford to continue to ignore the clinical data about the drug's effects and removed it from the market in October 2004. For an excellent piece on the scandal surrounding Vioxx®, see Biddle, "Lessons from the Vioxx Debacle."

Appendix: On Methods

1. George Marcus, *Ethnography through Thick and Thin* (Princeton, NJ: Princeton University Press, 1998); Dorothy E. Smith, *Institutional Ethnography: A Sociology for People* (New York: AltaMira, 2005).

2. Foreword to CenterWatch, *An Industry*, xi.

Index

About the Author

Jill A. Fisher holds a Ph.D. in science and technology studies and is an assistant professor in the Center for Biomedical Ethics and Society at Vanderbilt University.